Empire and subject peoples

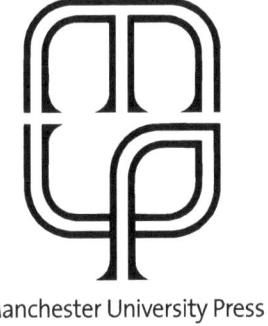

Manchester University Press

THEORY FOR A GLOBAL AGE

Series Editor: Gurminder K. Bhambra, Professor of Historical Sociology in the School of Global Studies, University of Sussex

Globalisation is widely viewed as a current condition of the world, but there is little engagement with how this changes the way we understand it. The Theory for a Global Age series addresses the impact of globalisation on the social sciences and humanities. Each title will focus on a particular theoretical issue or topic of empirical controversy and debate, addressing theory in a more global and interconnected manner. With contributions from scholars across the globe, the series will explore different perspectives to examine globalisation from a global viewpoint. True to its global character, the Theory for a Global Age series will be available for online access worldwide via Creative Commons licensing, aiming to stimulate wide debate within academia and beyond.

To buy or to find out more about the books currently available in this series, please go to: https://manchesteruniversitypress.co.uk/series/theory-for-a-global-age/

Empire and subject peoples

Herbert Adolphus Miller and the political sociology of domination

Jan Balon and John Holmwood

MANCHESTER UNIVERSITY PRESS

Copyright © Jan Balon and John Holmwood 2025

The right of Jan Balon and John Holmwood to be identified as the author of this work has been asserted in accordance with the Copyright, Designs and Patents Act 1988.

Published by Manchester University Press
Oxford Road, Manchester, M13 9PL
www.manchesteruniversitypress.co.uk

This book was written as part of the research project 'Rethinking Domination' (grant no. GA20–28212S), funded by the Czech Science Foundation (GAČR) and resolved at the Institute of Philosophy of the CAS, v.v.i.

British Library Cataloguing-in-Publication Data

A catalogue record for this book is available from the British Library

ISBN 978 1 5261 6860 3 hardback

First published 2025

The publisher has no responsibility for the persistence or accuracy of URLs for any external or third-party internet websites referred to in this book, and does not guarantee that any content on such websites is, or will remain, accurate or appropriate.

Typeset
by Cheshire Typesetting Ltd, Cuddington, Cheshire

Contents

Illustrations	vi
Series foreword	vii
Preface	ix
Acknowledgements	xi
Introduction: 'One who knows'	1
1 Forgotten sociologists and roads not taken	15
2 The 'old pedagogue'	35
3 Race relations and immigration	65
4 Americanisation, assimilation or pluralism?	80
5 Empire and international relations	108
6 From Fisk to dismissal	132
7 A political sociology of domination	156
Conclusion	176
Bibliography	180
Index	196

Illustrations

2.1 Extract from Oberlin Catalogue   51
4.1 Map: The bulwark of freedom   98

Series foreword

From his contributions to the Mid-European Union and Czechoslovakian independence in the early twentieth century to his involvement in movements for Korean and Indian independence in the inter-war period, combined with his lifelong commitment to racial equality in the US and beyond, Herbert Adolphus Miller immediately stands out as an unusual figure. His pragmatist sociology may have been informed by his early engagements with the Chicago school, but he departed from many of their positions to carve out a distinctive position that, as Jan Balon and John Holmwood note, truly make him a theorist of a global age.

In *Empire and subject peoples: Herbert Adolphus Miller and the political sociology of domination*, Balon and Holmwood not only recover the life and work of a forgotten figure within US sociology, but mobilise his sociological insights to illuminate ongoing issues of social and political domination both within nations and globally. In relation to the nation – and here the focus is on the US, although the arguments would apply beyond that – Miller's critique of assimilationist policies and advocacy for a multicultural pluralism continue to resonate profoundly for our times. Globally, his perspective on domination placed minority rights at its heart. Even as he supported anti-colonial movements against colonial domination, Miller was conscious of how new minorities could emerge and remain politically precarious within those new nations if their position was not, for example, explicitly addressed through modes of plural sovereignty.

Balon and Holmwood provide us with a comprehensive account of Miller as sociologist and of his academic and political commitments. They set out the ways in which Miller came to be a public sociologist of his time – for example, conducting empirical research on race relations and writing about his findings for wider publics – and indicate how he continues to be relevant for our times. While Miller may have been located within the hegemonic sphere of US sociology, his erasure from it was likely in no small part to his explicit concern with global others and, perhaps more importantly, in thinking through what could be learnt through that engagement. By drawing on Miller's reflections on global events and considering how his participation in them shaped his own thinking, Balon and Holmwood superbly fulfil one of the key aims of the Theory for a Global Age series: to provide resources for the rethinking of issues of global concern through an engagement with the global.

Gurminder K. Bhambra
University of Sussex

Preface

This book had a serendipitous origin in a chance footnote in a PhD thesis on the history of sociology. The author of the thesis had searched titles of sociology books and articles written in the first half of the twentieth century and found just one item which included the word 'domination' – Herbert Adolphus Miller's *Races, Nations and Classes: The Psychology of Domination and Freedom*, published in 1924. The book was not available in any library to which we had access, but it was available cheaply online from a second-hand bookseller (it is now available via print-on-demand from a reprint service). Intrigued as to what it could be arguing, we purchased it and discovered that it was about 'subject minorities' and 'nationalism' and that Miller seemed to be very familiar with the situation of Czechoslovakia. Digging further, we discovered that Miller had been involved in drafting the Czechoslovakian Declaration of Independence and, together with Tomáš Garrigue Masaryk, presented it to US President Woodrow Wilson in November 1918, securing the latter's endorsement.

There was very little published about Miller, but it was clear that he was both an advocate of racial equality and of anti-colonial movements against European (and other) empires. Not only had he written extensively about these topics, but he was also very active in political associations directed towards these ends. These concerns seemed to us to be very contemporary. Our 'discovery' of Miller coincided with the rise of populism and hostility towards migrants in Europe, including in the Czech Republic. In the years after the First World War, in 1939, newly independent Czechoslovakia was invaded by Germany and divided into separate republics, following Slovakia's appeasement of Hitler. It was reunited in 1945, fell under Soviet domination in 1948, became an independent post-communist republic in 1990, and was divided again shortly afterwards. We thought it significant that a major figure advocating Czechoslovakian nationhood had posted warnings – grounded in novel sociological concepts – about the dangers of nationalism while also advocating for the self-determination of subject groups, whether races, nations or classes.

Our project is bookended by the Russian invasion of Crimea in 2014 (followed by its more comprehensive invasion of Ukraine in 2022) and by the Hamas massacre in Israel and Israeli razing of Gaza after 7 October 2023. These were events whose origins were formed in the political crisis that emerged during and after the First World War, a crisis that was at the centre of Miller's concerns. His analysis was sharply relevant then and appears prescient now.

Our timetable and plans were severely disrupted by the COVID-19 epidemic when libraries and archives were closed to visitors. Here is another echo of the past. Miller's efforts in support of Czechoslovakian independence and other subject minorities took place during the global influenza epidemic which had become a major public health concern in Chicago, New York and Philadelphia by the autumn of 1918. Indeed, a young aide-de-camp at the US State department, who had been seconded to support Miller, contracted the illness and died. Miller delivered a eulogy at his interment in Arlington Cemetery in the morning and returned to Washington to work through the night on drafting the Czechoslovakian Declaration of Independence. The events that were organised to promote it, including a launch and rally at Independence Hall in Philadelphia, did not meet health guidelines.

Acknowledgements

We would like to thank the following colleagues for their support in providing material, suggestions and reading drafts: Gurminder K. Bhambra, Michael Burri, Plummer 'Al' Jones, Christian Karner, Desmond S. King, Lawrence C. Nicholls and Stephen P. Turner.

Some of the material in this book has been published in different versions as following:

'Immigration, Domination, and "Proportional Patriotism": Recovering the Sociology of Herbert Adolphus Miller', *American Sociologist* 53(3), 314–340 (2022).

'Race, Nation and Empire: The Forgotten Sociology of Herbert Adolphus Miller', *Journal of Classical Sociology* 24(2), 130–51 (2024).

This book was written as part of the research project 'Rethinking Domination' (grant no. GA20–28212S), funded by the Czech Science Foundation (GAČR) and carried out at the Institute of Philosophy of the Czech Academy of Sciences, v.v.i. We are grateful for their support.

We are grateful to the archivists and librarians who were willing to retrieve and copy material for us. In particular, we thank Leah Richardson, Special Collections Librarian, George Washington University; Louisa Hoffman, Oberlin College Archive; Phillip Cunningham, Head of Research Services, Amistad Research Center, Tulane University; Robert Spinelli and Brynna Farris, John Hope and Aurelia E. Franklin Library, Fisk University, John Hope and Aurelia E. Franklin Library, Special Collections; Margery E. Sly

Temple University; Vanessa Lee, Rare Book & Manuscript Library, Columbia University in the City of New York; Dagmar Hájková, Lucie Merhautová and Soňa Martinovská, Masaryk Institute and Archives of the Czech Academy of Sciences.

Introduction: '*One who knows*'

This is a book about a largely forgotten figure in North American sociology, Herbert Adolphus Miller (1875–1951), but it is also a book about the different contexts in which sociology was pursued and how those contexts structured the way in which sociology developed. Miller was a pragmatist in his science, a progressive in his politics and an early advocate of a 'global consciousness' for sociology. This consciousness was grounded in a strong commitment to racial equality, both within the US and more widely. He was a firm critic of European imperialism, as well as that of Japan, and an advocate of pluralism locally and internationally.

Our attempt to bring him to the attention of current readers carries some risks of anachronism and of judging past sociologies by the standards of the present. This has been a common response to those seeking to question the established canon, especially concerning issues of gender and race, as they became the focus of attention of later generations of sociologists. More recently, interest has turned to issues of colonialism and 'decolonising the university' and the charge of anachronism has been repeated against those expressing such concerns. Yet there were voices in the past that fell outside the mainstream, while believing themselves to be part of it and contributing to the future development of the discipline. Miller was one of the few sociologists within the White academy – universities in the US were formally segregated in the Southern states until the 1960s, and *de facto* segregated elsewhere[1] – to address issues of colonialism and empire, drawing out the interconnections between domestic race relations, immigration and international relations.

In that context, Miller reminds us that there was a sociological and moral standard in the past that has a direct alignment with concerns in the present. Another sociology was possible then, just as it is now. Miller was writing about events – and providing a sociological scheme to explain them – that is directly relevant to our present. The protests associated with Black Lives Matter, for example, have a direct connection with the period after the First World War in the US when the Ku Klux Klan enjoyed a resurgence, including within universities. Scientific racism in the form of eugenics had a significant role in public policy, especially concerning immigration and the creation of racialised hierarchies among groups. Not until the late 1920s did mainstream sociology in the US eschew eugenics (Hinkle 1952). Miller was one of the first to do so in his PhD thesis, written in 1905.

The First World War represented a conflict among imperial powers. These included empires on the European continent such as the Russian, German, Austro-Hungarian and Ottoman, as well as European overseas empires, such as the British, Dutch, Belgian and French. One phenomenon was the rise of nationalism within Europe, but also anti-colonial movements outside Europe. It is in this context that Miller raised the issue of subject minorities, connecting the oppression of African Americans and indigenous people in the US to other forms of oppression. He addressed pan-Slavic nationalism and issues of self-determination in the Baltic through eastern and central Europe down to the Adriatic, and was

---

1 As Christi Smith (2016) argues, many colleges and universities began as integrated in the nineteenth century, but began to resile from that commitment at the turn of the twentieth century (see also Wilder 2013). Universities founded in the latter period tended to be segregated on a *de facto* basis. Black students were admitted to PhD programmes, but were rarely able to continue their academic careers in the same universities. The University of Chicago, for example, was founded in 1890, but did not make its first permanent Black faculty appointment – Abram L. Harris – until 1945, and then only to teach in the undergraduate division (Wilson 2006).

witness to the collapse of the Russian empire and the creation of the new 'un-national', federal Soviet state that purported to support minority rights.[2]

Although Miller was conscious of social injustices associated with class exploitation, these were not the primary focus of his interest in the Soviet Union. He connected racial justice to class justice and advocated inclusive reform within what he envisaged as an ideal of a pluralistic and federal political system. Immigrants were not understood by him to be a threat to the integrity of the nation state, but to provide different religious and ethical traditions as part of a national conversation informed by wider human values. Patriotism, Miller wrote, should be 'proportionate', where only 10–25 per cent is made up of national values, with the rest being international (Miller, 1924a: 186). He opposed the dominant perspective on assimilation advocated by other sociologists associated with the Chicago school.

In our terms, Miller was a public sociologist in a period when the discipline was professionalising. But, for him, as a pragmatist, politics did not precede his science, but followed from it. It would be a mistake, then, to see him as a throwback to a progressivism in US politics that was already in retreat after the First World War. In our view, what is distinctive about Miller is his conceptual innovation and the rigour and scope of his analyses. The fact that he combined science, teaching and advocacy makes amnesia about him something of a puzzle. Addressing that puzzle will reveal an illustrious career, but also the social and political structures integral to the development of sociology in the US, and further afield, which would become barriers to his recognition.

Where Miller is acknowledged at all, it is as a minor figure within the milieu of Chicago sociology. This is evident in his status as co-author with Robert E. Park of a book derived from a Carnegie Corporation-funded research project carried out between 1918 and 1919 on 'Methods of Americanization'. This book, *Old World Traits Transplanted* (1921), would become part

---

2 The term 'un-national state' is taken from Carlyle Macartney (1934), a near-contemporary of Miller and a historian of the League of Nations.

of the canon of what became known as the first Chicago school (Fine, 1995). Yet Miller barely figures in any account of Chicago sociology, however comprehensive. He features neither in Robert Faris's (1967) account of Chicago sociology between 1920 and 1932, nor in Andrew Abbott's (1999) more recent 100-year history of the department.

Even his role as co-author with Park has been undercut. By 1936, Floyd House (who had been a graduate student in the Chicago department in the early 1920s) could write in his *Development of Sociology*, 'it is an open secret that *Old World Traits Transplanted*, published over the signatures of Robert E. Park and H. A. Miller, was the product, chiefly, of the work of Thomas' (House, 1936: 284). William I. Thomas, it seems, had been embroiled in a sex scandal. This had already led to his dismissal from the University of Chicago and their withdrawal from the publication of his and Florian Znaniecki's five-volume *The Polish Peasant in Europe and America* (published by another press between 1918 and 1920). A puzzle, perhaps, is why *Old World Traits* appears under the joint names of Park and Miller. Why not one, or the other?

Winifred Raushenbush (1979), Park's research assistant on another strand of the Carnegie project, recalled in her later years that Thomas was employed as Park's assistant (following his dismissal from the University of Chicago as a consequence of the scandal). This is incorrect. As we shall see, when we examine the episode in detail, Thomas was the director of the strand, taking over from Miller who had left the project halfway through the period allotted to the research. Miller left to take up a position as director of the Mid-European Union, a body advocating for subject minorities in central and eastern Europe. Nonetheless, his citation as co-author reflected an equal role in the prosecution of the research, even if Thomas, as we shall see in a later chapter, did not use any material gathered by Miller and separately published in articles during his period with the Carnegie project. Miller would himself publish a book based on this material, *Races, Nations and Classes: The Psychology of Domination and Freedom* (Miller, 1924a).

It was in his role as director of the Mid-European Union that we first became interested in Miller, initially to understand how a pragmatist sociologist from the US became involved in the struggle for

Czechoslovakian independence and the drafting of its Declaration of Independence. In pursuing these events, a more profound life in sociology and politics emerged. However, it was something that had to be pieced together from a mosaic of sources. Miller, it would transpire, was a footnote in many stories. As we discovered by digging deeper, his role in each of these narratives was seriously misrepresented. In each of them, Miller seems to have had a brief moment on a stage where the light fell on the performances of others before returning to what was assumed to be a modest obscurity – the life of a provincial Midwestern professor of sociology – worthy, but in no way salutary. Indeed, in the only article-length study of the Mid-European Union, Arthur May concludes with the comment, 'In mid-summer of 1919, Miller wound up the affairs of the organization and returned to the tranquility of Oberlin' (May, 1957: 488).

Once we had pieced together the different fragments, our conclusions were the opposite. Miller's life in sociology was remarkable and, indeed, salutary for understanding the development of sociology in the inter-war period, too. For example, after 1919, he became involved in the movement for Korean independence from Japanese imperial rule and the movement for Indian independence from British rule. He was also called in to chair a committee at Fisk University convened in 1924–25 to resolve an inflamed student dispute. Miller's diplomatic skills engineered a resolution that favoured the student protesters and set Fisk on course to be one of the centres for Black sociology. It would go on to employ graduates from Chicago, including Charles S. Johnson, and set the ground for Park's relocation there after his retirement from Chicago. Miller's role in facilitating that outcome, which subsequently burnished the reputation of the Chicago approach to race relations in the years before Gunnar Myrdal's *An American Dilemma* (1944), is left out of that history.

In fact, as we shall see, Miller's relation to Fisk was continuous throughout his career. He was appointed as its first lecturer in sociology in 1899 (Wright II, 2010). He left after three years to undertake a PhD at Harvard, which he completed in 1905, but he retained contact and frequently returned to give lecture courses. He was close to W. E. B. Du Bois, a famous alumnus of

Fisk, who was also involved in the student protests that began following a commencement address he made in 1924. Indeed, as we have commented, Miller's PhD at Harvard was one of the first to criticise eugenics in defence of racial equality, and he was the only White scholar to be published in a volume on the topic by Du Bois in 1906 (a volume that had a foreword by Franz Boas). Miller was also interested in immigration to the US and the treatment of migrants from outside northern Europe, especially those from Czechoslovakia and central Europe. Unlike others, including Park and Thomas, he did not adopt an assimilationist stance, and he was a sharp critic of programmes of 'Americanization'.

His interest in racial domination in the US and the subjection of religious and ethnic minorities under the Austro-Hungarian empire brought him to a wider concern with problems of empire. Yet no sooner does he enter view than he disappears and frequently with an erroneous epitaph, as in the case of Arthur May cited above. Fred Wacker, for example, in his 1983 study of the Chicago approach to race relations, correctly places Miller in the Chicago milieu of Thomas and Park and their common interests in immigrants from central Europe and the role of nationalist sentiments among them. He argues they shared a common approach to the gradual assimilation of immigrants and comments that, 'although I do not have any direct proof, I believe that they shared the nationalistic sentiments of immigrant nationalists' (Wacker, 1983: 25). But, as we will set out, Miller was always a critic of nationalism, believing that it potentially created new subject minorities and could embody pathological forms (indeed, he was early to warn that this was the case in Germany with the rise of the Nazi party). According to Wacker, Miller retreated to a more conservative position, one that was transcended by Park. In effect, for Wacker, Miller's marginality derived from his more provincial outlook.

The direction of Miller's thought, however, was the opposite. His criticisms of nationalism were made in the context of also endorsing revolution against imperial orders of rule, whether of those within Europe, those embodied by Europe externally, such as the British in India, or of Japan in its relations with Korea and China. Indeed, his involvement with such revolutionary movements led to him being dismissed by Ohio State University in 1932.

There is evidence – or, at least, Miller believed there was – that his dismissal was lobbied for by the Ku Klux Klan. He was not unsympathetic to the Bolshevik revolution in Russia, as Wacker supposes, but expressed his concern that it would experience a crisis of legitimacy and potentially become authoritarian and impose a police regime. His political sympathies, when directly expressed, lay with the Socialist Party of America.

We do not doubt the accuracy of a description of Miller as modest. The archives are sparse and scattered. Miller is present as part of wider stories and frequently working behind the scenes. He kept a regular log of his activities as a sociologist, and of his extensive travels – much in the manner of C. Wright Mills's later protocols for 'intellectual craftsmanship' set out in *The Sociological Imagination* (Mills, 1959). He seems to have sent many of these 'logs' – especially those from his travels – to colleagues, and they turn up in other archives (for example, the Masaryk archive in Prague), but there is little material collected by him. There is a small archive relating to Miller at Oberlin College (where he was employed between 1914 and 1924) and at other places where he was employed. It seems that his son Maurice inherited his papers and made them available both to May (writing on the Mid-European Union) and to a former PhD student of Miller's at Ohio State around the time of his dismissal, the criminologist Negley Teeters. The latter wrote a short obituary in the *American Journal of Sociology* (Teeters, 1951) and seemed to have been planning something longer which did not come to fruition, apart from a short article on the Mid-European Union which repeats much of what May had written earlier (Teeters, 1966). Teeters deposited some of the material in an archive at Temple University. Luther Bernard, for his part, elicited a lengthy manuscript from Miller as part of his project on the lives of US sociologists. There is a letter thanking Miller and commenting on the length and richness of the document, but the document itself is missing.

Nonetheless, there is a rich archive of published work. Miller wrote extensively. These included academic articles and books, but also articles in popular literary and social science magazines associated with the survey movement (*The Survey*), Christian socialism (*The World Tomorrow*), the Ba'hai ecumenical movement (*World

Unity) and *The Crisis* (the magazine of the National Association for the Advancement of Colored People). Together these magazines represented Miller's interests in progressive social reform, racial equality, pacificism, and a developing global consciousness outside the hegemony of Western thought (edited versions of his travel logs, for example, appeared in *World Unity* between 1927 and 1932).

Finally, if Miller's recognition within sociology appears scant, he was nonetheless active within the American Sociological Society (ASS) and chairman of its sub-committee on international relations. His name appears as an elected member of the Executive Committee on the society's headed notepaper at the time of his dismissal from Ohio State University in 1931. The society did not maintain an archive until after it became the American Sociological Association in 1959 and so the record of Miller's role is lost.[3] He received other forms of public recognition. He was a founding member of the Foreign Policy Association, Chair of the Columbus (Ohio) branch of the Urban League, and President of the Association for International Students. The latter was not an insignificant and ceremonial role – international students were understood by Miller as one of the conduits for a global consciousness, and it was through them that he had direct contact with revolutionary anti-colonial movements in Korea, India and China. Finally, Miller was recognised by the award of the highest civilian honours by the Czechoslovak government in December 1938 and the independent government of Korea in 1950.[4] Perhaps most significant to him was

---

3 Some early material from the ASS was transferred to the Library of Congress and then to the archive at Penn State. The early material was mainly gathered by Matilda White Riley, who was executive officer of the ASS from 1949 to 1960 (and President of the ASA in 1986). There is some material from the 1940s, but none covering Miller's period of active involvement in the ASS.
4 Miller was unwell and his wife, Bessy Cravath Miller, accepted the award on his behalf. There is some confusion about the nature of the medal, whether the Order of National Foundation, or the Order of Taeguk (Third Class). A website dedicated to Korean medals proposes that the Order of Taeguk was not available in the Republic of Korea. Nonetheless, the ambassador officiating in the ceremony in Washington described the award as the Order of Taeguk, and declared that the award of first class was available only

his election two weeks before his Czechoslovakian honour as chief of the Eel Clan of the Onondaga people, one of the five original nations of the Haudenosaunee (Iroquois) Confederacy. His given name was *Ra hyah na ree*, or 'One who knows'.

Miller's optimism about a growing global consciousness had to be sustained in the face of deep disappointments, albeit disappointments determined by 'pathologies' that he had diagnosed. During his lifetime, Czechoslovakian independence was lost following the Nazi invasion in 1939, the descent of the Soviet Union into a police state had become more evident, 'warlordism' had taken over in China, Korea was divided and fought over by external powers, and the prospect of Indian pluralism had been set back by a partition that unleashed horrific violence. Many of these issues continue through into the present, with the collapse of the Soviet Union creating new nationalisms. Perhaps most significant, in the light of Miller's own interests, is the resurgence of an irredentist Russia and its invasion of Crimea in 2014 and Ukraine more widely in 1922.

Miller experienced straitened circumstances following his dismissal from Ohio State University. His last years were spent in sessional teaching and a poorly paid position (with accommodation) at Black Mountain College in North Carolina. Among the last archival entries for him are those showing him organizing between 1941 and 1944 an annual Seminar for Refugee Scholars at a number of locations, including at Wolfeboro, New Hampshire where he had attended the local school. He also worked on a project to provide work and opportunities in rural North Carolina for demobilised troops at the end of the Second World War. His was a spirit undimmed.

Our research into Herbert Adolphus Miller has been a journey of discovery, both about Miller as citizen and as sociologist, and of the contexts, national and global, in which US sociology developed. Miller's entanglements were complex, but his character and convictions remained constant. His was a sociology learned and developed

---

to a President of the Republic deemed worthy, and the second class only to a Vice-President, leaving the third class the highest honour available to citizens and foreign nationals alike. See https://koreanmedals.com/one-mystery-solved/#easy-footnote-1-1618.

in practical engagements and applied to those engagements, many of which are at some distance from us now despite remaining highly relevant in the issues they addressed. This has made writing the book rather difficult. The whole of Miller's life in sociology is greater than the sum of its parts, but each of its parts is distinctive and requires separate elucidation. It may sometimes appear that we are 'circling' our subject, keeping back some of the material that might provide the interpretive key. It also means that we will track back over earlier episodes in his career to recontextualise them in later articulations of his arguments. Miller does connect race relations in the US to global issues of empire from his earliest writings through to his last. His attention moves from the local to the global, but the former is always in his mind. However, the significance of what he argued from the outset of his career comes into focus only when his later engagement with global social movements is to the fore.

We begin in Chapter 1 with a discussion of *Forgotten sociologists and roads not taken*. Here we consider the institutionalisation and professionalisation of sociology in the US. The chapter sets out the transition from individual patronage to the centralisation of research funding through philanthropic initiatives, particularly the role played by the Social Science Research Council. Within this context, US sociologists, Miller among them, grappled with the complexities of shaping their professional paths amidst shifting opportunities. We trace Miller's involvement in key organisations in the US, with a specific focus on his close associations with influential figures in the Chicago sociological milieu, such as Robert E. Park and William I. Thomas. We show how the intellectual landscape in the initial decades of the twentieth century featured a noticeable shift in mainstream sociology, pivoting away from reformist activism towards a scientific orientation, marked by a dedication to formulating robust theoretical frameworks for research. Although Miller's career today seems separated from the core of what would be designated as the Chicago school proper, this chapter posits that his research programme uniquely connected issues of race and ethnicity in the US with colonial systems of global domination.

In Chapter 2, 'The old pedagogue', we set out Miller's approach to education and how he established a distinctive sociological

Introduction: 'One who knows' 11

pedagogy along pragmatist lines, including sociology as a form of 'publicity'. Miller's teaching career was lengthy and exhibited a high degree of continuity in his interests. He was affiliated with noteworthy educational institutions in the US, ranging from the Ivy League to historically Black colleges and progressive liberal experiments. Throughout, he was a prolific public speaker for various political and practical causes, predominantly related to anti-nationalism, race issues, immigration and international relations. We also show how Miller's extensive public and political engagements for various causes (political problems of Central Europe, Korea, Southeast Asia, India) were consistent with his pedagogic programme that underscored his commitment to the practical application of knowledge. In all these contexts, he showed interest in the dialectic of oppression and freedom, and revolutions against domination, particularly when it involved one racialised group claiming superiority over another. The chapter explores his classroom practices, which included site visits to various sociologically significant locations. We suggest that Miller's interpretation of sociology's purpose, in relation to education, citizenship and progressive politics, contributed to diminishing his role and status in American sociology during a period of heightened professionalisation.

In Chapter 3, 'Race relations and immigration', we show how Miller made a distinctive contribution to the sociology and politics of race relations. He was among the earliest sociological critics of eugenics and its role in US social science, and he developed a unique approach to race relations and the position of subject minorities through a critical analysis of European empires. His approach complemented that of Du Bois, with whom he had a close relationship. We trace Miller's critique of eugenics during and after his PhD thesis at Harvard, as well as the idea of 'Americanization' as a policy for immigrant assimilation. We show the distinctiveness of his approach within North American sociology, particularly in the milieu of Chicago sociology with which he was affiliated. Specifically, we discuss his contribution to the Cleveland Survey on immigrant children in the school system and his advocacy for reforms based on an understanding of the needs of marginalised communities. Notably, Miller's arguments about the disorganisation of the Cleveland school system aligned him with library reformers and public-school educators who understood the special needs of the 'new' immigrants. This interaction played a formative role in Miller's subsequent academic and political activities, especially in his commitment to cultural pluralism.

In Chapter 4, 'Americanisation, assimilation or pluralism?', we show how in 1918, Miller was appointed to head the division on Immigrant Contributions in the Carnegie Corporation's 'Methods of Americanization' project. This was initially considered a pinnacle in his sociological career. However, he departed midway to take part in the Czechoslovak independence movement. This chapter unravels the threads of the Carnegie project, revealing its complexities and ill-fated trajectory. The project succumbed to the discourse of assimilation prevailing in the post-World War I era, endorsed by figures such as Park and Thomas. Contrary to this trend, Miller's research on immigrant populations from subject nationalities in Europe, initiated in the Cleveland Survey and continued in the Carnegie project, took a divergent path. Examining Miller's role as the director of the Mid-European Union, we interpret his political engagements as a continuation of his earlier advocacy for 'oppressed peoples'. Through this experience, Miller crafted a distinctive approach to 'Americanization', based on the concept of 'proportional patriotism'. In the process, he developed a global perspective on domination and oppression through advocacy for a plural and multicultural America. The chapter concludes with reflections on *An American Dilamma* (1944), written by Myrdal at the end of Miller's career. It also considers the alternative approach to race relations outlined by both Du Bois and Miller in the 1920s and 1930s and their contribution to the ongoing debate on the legacy of Myrdal.

In Chapter 5, 'Empire and international relations', we explore Miller's contributions to geopolitical issues after the First World War, especially regarding post-imperial peace in Europe and beyond. Miller's theoretical formulations on inter-group relations and his political activism against racial political orders shaped a global perspective on domination which placed minority rights at its core. The chapter investigates Miller's political activities during his tenure as Director of the Mid-European Union and his support of the Korean Independence movement. His advocacy for international cooperation and 'un-national' political arrangements sought a post-imperial global order after the First World War. Miller's extensive travels to global sites of interest (such as India, Russia, China, Korea, Syria, Turkey and Palestine) informed his theory of the 'internationalisation' of groups and inspired prospects for a future grounded in plural sovereignty and the possibility of a cosmopolitan global order. This chapter identifies Miller's relevance to contemporary issues of race, empire and minority rights, particularly in the face of the resurgence of ethno-nationalisms.

In Chapter 6, 'From conflict at Fisk to dismissal', we examine two pivotal events in Miller's life and university career – his role in resolving the Fisk University strike in 1924–25 and his subsequent dismissal from Ohio State University in 1931. Between these events, Miller dedicated a substantial amount of time to extensive study trips abroad. His return to Fisk in 1925 included decisive interventions driven by his sociological commitments to racial equality and the self-determination of oppressed groups. Serving as the head of the Committee on Administration at Fisk University, he argued that there was a global issue of suppressed and oppressed peoples, including African Americans, emphasising the need to look beyond the situation of oppression to a wider equality for all. We also touch on Miller's growing interest in the East, particularly in the prospects of pluralism in India and China. Miller's speech at the start of the Salt March, a contributing factor to his dismissal from Ohio State University, his meeting with Gandhi, public speeches in Korea, and other episodes from his travels are contextualised within his claims to a plural global order. The chapter concludes with a discussion of the conflict over racial integration at Black Mountain College and Miller's involvement in debates about the admission of Black students.

In Chapter 7, 'A political sociology of domination', we provide a systematic presentation of Miller's arguments in his two major books, *Races, Nations and Classes: A Psychology of Domination and Freedom* (1924) and *The Beginnings of To-morrow: An Introduction to the Sociology of the Great Society* (1933). In contrast to the preceding chapters, where we traced how Miller applied his positions in various public engagements, we now present them in a formal manner to underscore their distinctive character. The primary point of comparison centres around the concept of the 'public', as set out by Charles Horton Cooley, Walter Lippman, John Dewey and Graham Wallas. We explore a convergence with Durkheim's approach in *Professional Ethics and Civic Morals* (1957). The core theme of *Races, Nations, and Classes*, we argue, is the concept of 'inter-group relations of domination', which offers a systematic framework for addressing social and political conflict based on the differentiation of the horizontal and vertical dimensions of groups. The central theme of *The Beginnings of To-morrow* revolves around the idea of plural cosmopolitanism, with Miller being the first to address the idea within a sociological framework. The chapter concludes by illustrating how Miller applied this framework in his practical engagements with civil society organisations.

1

Forgotten sociologists and roads not taken

Herbert Adolphus Miller is a marginal, and largely forgotten, figure in the history of sociology. He exists on the radar as an outer satellite of the Chicago school of sociology, albeit with little direct connection by training or appointment. He is named as author with Robert E. Park on one of the landmark books of its early period, *Old World Traits Transplanted* (1921), although even his role in this came to be sharply qualified as a consequence of a controversy over authorship. He does not feature in most histories of sociology, even of the Chicago school, except, at best, as a footnote, and as someone who did not quite make the cut, with his main claim for recognition coming to be denied. Floyd House, for example, in his text on the *Development of Sociology*, notes cryptically in relation to a discussion of the work of W. I. Thomas, 'it is an open secret that Old World Traits Transplanted, published over the signatures of Robert E. Park and H. A. Miller, was the product, chiefly, of the work of Thomas' (House, 1936: 284).

Nonetheless, Miller was part of the Chicago sociology milieu sharing its roots in pragmatist philosophy, much as did Park. For example, his PhD at Harvard between 1902 and 1905 was undertaken with Josiah Royce and William James. He was also active within the settlement movement, and progressive politics more generally, alongside other pragmatists. Jane Addams had established the first settlement at Hull House in 1889 and, together with Graham Taylor in 1897, set up the Chicago Commons, serving immigrant populations (Schneiderhan, 2011). Miller was involved with the latter and was also closely connected with Mary E. McDowell, who established the University of Chicago Settlement House in 1894.

Many of the Chicago settlement women were more radical on issues of race than was typical of the men of Chicago sociology, with Addams, in particular, treating race relations as involving oppression and domination (Diner, 1970), as would Miller. Indeed, the sociology and politics of race relations were central to his work, including as an educator at 'historically Black colleges'. He was the first appointment in sociology at Fisk University between 1899 and 1902 (Wright II, 2010) before beginning his PhD at Harvard, and he developed a connection with Wilberforce University during his period at Oberlin and later at Ohio State. Park, a gradualist on issues of race, is, nonetheless, renowned for his work in this area, encompassing an early involvement at Tuskegee Institute (Matthews, 1977) and a later relationship and position after retirement at Fisk University (Raushenbush, 1979). Although largely unremarked in the secondary literature, Miller's involvement at Fisk was both crucial and central to the development of what came to be seen as a distinct tradition of sociology there (Wright II, 2010; 2020).

Despite these connections – and, as we shall see, notable engagements in political causes associated with anti-racism and opposition to imperialism (both Western and Japanese) – Miller has been written out of the historical record. How and why this has occurred, we shall argue, provides important insights into the history of sociology and how its role in the academy and public life was constructed with lessons for the present, too.

A career at the margins?

Forgotten figures have become a new topic within the sociology of knowledge. As Neil McLaughlin (1998) has suggested, there is now less confidence in the idea that marginality is to be explained by individual characteristics (for example concerning the quality of the work, and so on) and there is more interest in how the nature of institutions and academic networks serve to render an individual marginal. For their part, Alex Law and Eric Lybeck (2015: 3) comment, 'it is important to understand who, when, where, and why sociologists became excluded from the canon, how they became "failures"'. Of course, that also raises issues of how and why they come to be 'rediscovered' and why it matters that they should. In the case of Miller, we will suggest that his fate is bound up with the way in which Chicago sociology itself developed and professionalised, such that the very nature of what would otherwise appear to be his propitious networks meant that Miller came to be aligned with academic practices and political leanings that were being displaced by those of the Chicago school at the centre.

Forgotten figures are uninteresting if they never did burn bright. McLaughlin's (1998; 2021) account of Erich Fromm's fate within the Frankfurt school circle, for example, depends, in part, on his public recognition in the early period of the school's US exile. Fromm's transgressions, in McLaughlin's telling, are straightforward – his pursuit of opportunities of income from private therapeutic practice and unwillingness to forego salary when the funding of the Institute for Social Research in exile appeared perilous – and his fate determined by a miscalculation of the consequences.[1] In contrast, the moment at which Miller appears to be most connected – his seeming collaboration with Park on the writing of *Old World Traits* – is the moment when the connection is severed. Nor does it appear to be occasioned by conflict. His light, it seems, just faded. Or, at least, was cast into shadow by how sociology was otherwise being constructed.

Although never appointed at the University of Chicago, Miller spent a significant part of his career – between 1914 and 1924 – at Oberlin College (near Cleveland, Ohio) which was itself within the Chicago sphere of influence (and that of the settlement movement).[2] Indeed, many Chicago academics had parents who had been at

1 Fromm parted company with the Institute in 1939. There was evidently also the basis of a rift in the Institute's failure to publish a manuscript based on a 1929 survey of German workers Fromm had conducted with Hilde Weiss, a survey which used the F-scale that would later be used in Adorno's (1950) study of the Authoritarian Personality. There were also intellectual differences with Adorno over the significance of Freud (see Funk, 2019; McLaughlin, 2021). Fromm received $20,000 in severance, equivalent to around $440,000 at present values, a significant blow to the finances of the Institute.
2 Before his appointment at Oberlin, Miller taught at its sister college in rural Michigan, Olivet, between 1905 and 1914. Both Oberlin and Olivet began as coeducational and historically integrated colleges (see Smith, 2016).

Oberlin (as in the case of future president of Chicago University, Robert Hutchins), or had themselves been educated there (as in the case for George Herbert Mead). Thomas had himself taught at Oberlin between 1889 and 1893 before moving to Chicago. Miller appeared to be well connected – he met Thomas in 1911, shortly before Thomas met Park. According to a note appended to the box of his papers held at Temple University, Miller took a course at Chicago in 1911 with Thomas, who also arranged for him to visit Bohemia (Czechoslovakia) in 1912 'to study an alien culture'.[3] In a letter to Kimball Young about his name being removed from *Old World Traits*, Thomas was unforthcoming about the circumstances, but clear about his relationships with Park and Miller, that they 'were my friends and acted friendly'.[4]

In 1924, Miller moved to Ohio State University in Columbus, which was, at that time, the largest sociology department in Ohio. There is some suggestion of disquiet about his political involvements and pedagogic practices involving racial mixing at Oberlin (or, at least, knowledge of them followed him to Ohio State).[5]

3 Descriptive Inventory of the Personal Papers of Herbert Adolphus Miller: Biographical Note. Temple University, Samuel Paley Library, Conwellana-Templana Collection. It is also confirmed by Miller in his 'memoirs', albeit without dates. In a letter from Moscow to his wife in 1925, Miller also recalls an earlier trip to Moscow in 1912 as part of the same trip. Letter from Miller to Miller, Temple University, Samuel Paley Library, Conwellana-Templana Collection, Folder D. Mary E. McDowell provided introductions to Tomáš Garrigue Masaryk and Alice Masaryk in Prague.
4 Letter from Thomas to Young, 4 May 1930. Cited in Chapoulie (2020: 374, n. 178). Thomas was accused of having an affair with the wife of a US army officer serving overseas, and of travelling with her across state lines for immoral purposes, as proscribed by the Mann Act (see Abbott and Egloff, 2008: 221). The charges were dropped, but not before he was sacked by the University of Chicago and his reputation besmirched.
5 The suspicion that Miller had been disliked at Oberlin and 'was about to lose his position there' (Sabine, 1931: 469) featured prominently on the list of reasons given by the Ohio State University's Board of Trustees to justify Miller's dismissal. The president of Ohio State himself visited Oberlin and personally conceded to Miller that 'no question had ever been raised in any way as to my dismissal from Oberlin'. Letter from Miller to Tyler, 26 May 1931. Cited in Sabine (1931: 467).

In 1931, proceedings to dismiss him from Ohio State were begun in a case that was taken up by the American Association of University Professors (Sabine, 1931). Following his dismissal, he undertook visiting lectures for a fee organised on his behalf by the Speakers' Forum of Columbus – an adjunct of the Foreign Policy Association, of which Miller was an early and active member. He did this for two years before his appointment as a lecturer at Bryn Mawr in 1933, where he taught sociology in the department of social economy until his retirement in 1940. Thereafter, he held a number of visiting positions, including a year at Temple University and at Beloit College and Pennsylvania State University, hired on a semester-by-semester basis. He ended his career at Black Mountain College in Asheville, North Carolina, where he taught between 1943 and 1947. Black Mountain was set up on 'Deweyan' principles of education as an experimental artists' community and college in 1933 after the dismissal of John Rice from Rollins College (Reynolds, 1998).

In short, Miller was connected with noteworthy educational institutions in the US – from the Ivy League to historically Black colleges and progressive liberal experiments. Through it all, he was active in professional sociological organisations. These included the Ohio Sociological Society (of which he was president in 1932, the year of his formal dismissal from Ohio State University, though that event is not mentioned in its journal)[6] and the American Sociological Society (ASS) and was chair of several of its committees (including one on international relations) and member of the executive committee at the time of his sacking. The ASS was founded in 1905 and a large proportion of its early roster of presidents and officers was from the Chicago sociology department.

---

6 The *Bulletin of the Ohio Sociological Society* did not publish in 1931 and its first issue of 1932 – volume V(I), published in May out of the Ohio State University Sociology Department – ran to just three pages of news. It reported laconically that 'Dr J. E. Hagerty has resigned as head of the Department of Sociology at Ohio State after thirty years of active service.' Hagerty was very active in defence of Miller, but it seems that the latter was stoic in not using his presidential position to advocate in his own cause. The *Bulletin* is archived on JSTOR.

Throughout his career Miller was active in the meetings of both societies, discussing substantive matters relating to race and immigration as well as sociological pedagogy. He was also a founding member of other associations involved with international relations, most specifically the successor organisation to the League of Free Nations Association, the Foreign Policy Association (where he was a critic of empire, including the British empire, one of the reasons given for his dismissal from Ohio State University). Yet, his contribution is lost to the history of sociological thought and its promise of public education for democracy.

Sociology and its professionalisation

The history of sociology in the US is often told as a history of distinct phases of development. The first involves the appointment of key professorial positions in universities, initially linked to substantive issues of the development of the industrial economy and social reform. These were what Herman and Julia Schwendiger (1974) have called the 'sociologists of the chair'. Next was the development of key 'departments' offering a density of focus on sociological matters, including distinct research programmes and research monographs, rather than the writing of texts for the teaching of courses for students planning to go into positions in social work and other forms of public administration. The most important of these departments were associated with Chicago, Columbia and Harvard (Camic, 1995).

Broadly speaking, these developments occurred from the last decades of the nineteenth century and into the first decades of the twentieth centuries through the inter-war period. It is routinely described as a process of professionalisation, but it has a highly gendered and racialised history, as we shall see in much greater detail later. As Aldon Morris (2015) and Earl Wright II (2020) have argued, the Atlanta University sociology laboratory set up by W. E. B. Du Bois in 1897 has a legitimate claim to be the first 'school' of sociology, just as his *Philadelphia Negro* (Du Bois, 1899) has claim to be US sociology's first major monograph study, pre-dating Thomas and Znaniecki's *Polish Peasant in Europe and America*

(1918–21) by a good twenty years. Universities in the US (with the exception of those now designated as 'historically Black') were racially divided throughout the period and, while Black sociologists could undertake graduate study in historically White institutions, they were not appointed to tenured faculty positions there (Wilson, 2006). In the same way, just a handful of women would receive their PhDs from universities like Chicago, and fewer still would be employed in their sociology departments (Deegan, 1988).

In the period after the Second World War, following the dramatic expansion of higher education, the development of sociology came to be associated with what Nicholas Mullins has called distinct 'theory groups' (Mullins, 1973). This designation followed developments in the sociology of science after Thomas Kuhn's (1962) account of the 'structure of scientific revolutions'. If not exactly organised in terms of successive paradigms, sociology could at least be understood in terms of competing quasi-paradigms. There is some overlap in the identities associated with the different phases of development, such that departments became associated with particular theoretical positions and key figures. For example, 'structural-functionalism' – one of Mullins's theory groups – is associated both with the Harvard Department of Social Relations and with the figure of Talcott Parsons. Another of his theory groups, defined in competition with structural functionalism, 'symbolic interactionism', is associated with the Department of Sociology at Chicago and with Herbert Blumer as a key figure.

At the same time, the designation of a position as a 'theory group' allows the enrolment of sociologists from other universities into a group associated with a primary location. This is a process that is also facilitated by the key institutional feature of departmental organisation, the graduate programme and its production line of PhD students, with some placed locally and others dispersed to spread the message. This was especially marked in the case of Chicago Sociology, where Park set up a Society for Social Research among faculty members and advanced graduate students in 1920 (Bulmer, 1983). It organised regular meetings and lectures, an annual summer institute and published a bulletin. By 1927/28 it had 53 local and 97 out-of-town members. The identity of a theory group, then, is partly constituted by its core ideas, but also by its programmes of training and the placing of its graduates, including within the peer-review process of journals and other means of gatekeeping, such as positions within grant-giving bodies.

The latter agencies also demonstrate a similar pattern of professionalisation in the mid-1920s away from the patronage of specific benefactors – frequently female, as exemplified by Mrs Russell Sage (Crocker, 2006), Laura Spelman or Helen Culver – to the conversion of such patronage into philanthropic trusts like that of the Rockefeller or Carnegie Foundations (Lagemann, 1989). These were then coordinated through the Social Science Research Council, itself a project of the Chicago political science professor Charles E. Merriam, and representatives of the American Economic Association, the ASS and the American Statistical Association, among other organisations. These developments would help to align the policy interests of the foundations with the 'scientific' interests of professionalising social scientists and disciplinary entrepreneurs, like Merriam. It also moved funding into the hands of a new professional bureaucracy of administrators and away from the direct involvement of their female patrons, although the latter remained important figures.

These developments, their patterns and interconnections, are evident in retrospect, less so at the time. Nonetheless, they were part of what sociologists, Miller included, had to negotiate in the construction of their careers and the different opportunities that came to them. We will discuss their role in Miller's career in more detail throughout this book. However, as Stephen Turner (2007) has argued in his discussion of the career of Charles Ellwood, the story of key departments, like that of Chicago, is also the story of how they managed to cultivate and curate these opportunities. As departmental centres of sociology emerged with privileged access to research funding, so a professoriate at other universities was left to generate income through teaching and public writing and lecturing. Turner describes Ellwood's career in these terms. He was a 'public intellectual' with a high reputation, but marginal to the disciplinary self-understanding that emerged in the period following the Second World War and, in consequence, now largely disregarded despite his significance in his own times.

In part, this is because the later theory groups were conscious not only of their present and future, but also of their past and how to narrate it to their advantage. This is a process that Andrew Abbott (1999) has called the 'manufacturing of a tradition'. While pre-war sociologists mixed together at meetings of associations and, to some degree, read each other's work, only some of that work would be incorporated into their narratives of disciplinary identity construction. For example, symbolic interactionism came to be identified as the focus of a 'second Chicago school' (Fine 1995). This included the incorporation of George Herbert Mead as a founding figure of 'symbolic interactionism' on the basis of his affiliation with the University of Chicago, where he taught philosophy. As Daniel Huebner (2014: 3) wryly notes, 'he became known in a discipline he did not teach for a book he did not write'.[7] In fact, Charles Horton Cooley has the greater claim to have initiated ideas in social psychology, such as the 'looking-glass self', that would go on to influence symbolic interactionism. He taught at the University of Michigan alongside John Dewey and is closer to the older mode of sociology than being the initiator of a school. Ellsworth Faris was one of the few (along with Herbert Blumer who was a graduate student at Chicago in the late 1920s) to have developed Mead's ideas alongside those of Dewey and Cooley. However, it was the latter who was more widely read, including by Miller.

The 'second Chicago school' required a 'first Chicago school', something that was delineated by Robert E. L. Faris, the son of Ellsworth Faris, who had become head of the department of sociology in 1925. Robert Faris (1967) set out the key figures among the Chicago sociology professoriate from its first professor and head of department, Albion Small, through Thomas, Mead, Park, Ernest W. Burgess, Robert E. L. Faris, William F. Ogburn and Louis Wirth, identifying its key period as lying between 1920 and 1932. The legacy of Small is largely understood in terms of his prowess in university politics and the great gift he provided to the department of the first sociology journal, the *American Journal*

---

7 The manuscript of *Mind, Self and Society* (1934), Mead's most influential book in sociology, for example, was prepared after his death from the lecture notes of students transcribed over a number of sessions.

of Sociology, which was established in 1895, through which Chicago could exert its influence across the discipline. In effect, Thomas is seen by Faris as a crucial interstitial figure, along with Park. Thomas left Chicago in 1918, though Faris is discreet about the circumstances. He describes him as going on to undertake 'research in New York on Americanization' (in effect, taking over from Miller on his segment of the Carnegie project, although, as we shall see, Thomas already had a role as general adviser to the project).

Park remained at Chicago. Having been recruited by Thomas in 1914, he continued in the department and, for Faris (and others), became a kind of intellectual guru in the department despite a relatively modest output. According to Faris, Chicago school sociology developed substantive research programmes, associated with the ecological structure of the city, urban behaviour (including issues of social disorganisation) and social psychology. Despite the assertion of Park's influence, these are much more the areas defined by Burgess, Wirth and Faris senior. Nor are they areas in which Miller might lay claim to be making his contribution, albeit that he appears in some footnotes as following the Chicago interest in 'disorganization'. However, where Park and Thomas argued that the process of migration disorganised immigrant communities, Miller argued that those communities were disorganised by public policy.

It is not until the 1970s and after that a spanner gets thrown into the works of the manufacture of sociological histories. This is the period when feminist historians of the discipline, like Mary Jo Deegan, began to raise questions about the erasure of the Chicago women from the story of the Chicago school. At the same time, there were similar arguments about the erasure of Black sociologists. Paradoxically, this was also the period in which the first Chicago school's contribution to race and ethnic relations came to be foregrounded with major studies by Fred Wacker (1983), Stow Persons (1987) and, most recently, Jean-Michel Chapoulie (2020). In other words, the period when 'canonisation' began to be disrupted is also associated with a new canonisation of the Chicago sociology of race.

The problem of 'race'

We are conscious of the risk of anachronism in presenting an author whose views now seem more advanced than those of others at the time. Martin Bulmer (2017), for example, has criticised (unfairly in our view) both Morris and Deegan for misrepresenting the Chicago school, and Park in particular, in their claims of the distinctiveness of the contributions of Du Bois and the women of the Chicago settlement movement, respectively. Bulmer makes a methodological point that 'the history of one's discipline should not be written to convey a certain view of the present concerns of the discipline ... The history of sociology should portray figures in the discipline as they were' (Bulmer, 2017: 24). In this respect, he is following Quentin Skinner's (1969) principles for intellectual history of avoiding 'anachronism' and 'prolepsis'. Ideas from the present should not be projected into a past where they were absent, or arguments from the past misrepresented as anticipatory of arguments in the present. It is hard to disagree. But, however problematic it may be to Skinner or Bulmer, sometimes once-disregarded arguments in the past do resonate with present concerns and, in doing so, speak directly to problems in the construction of sociological knowledge claims. In what follows, we do not present Miller's views out of their time and place.

Following Thomas Fallace (2011: 104ff.), we can identify three broad approaches to race within the mainstream US academy at the start of the twentieth century. The first was that of eugenics, where inherited biological traits were understood to differentiate racial groups in terms of a hierarchy of superiority and inferiority. This influenced popular discourse on racial mixing and 'replacement' and was bound up in xenophobic concerns about immigration in the last part of the nineteenth century and through into the 1920s. The second, more moderate, view was that, while there were some inherited traits characteristic of groups, most group characteristics were environmental in character and determined by different ways of life or cultures. However, this argument was typically presented in terms of the superiority and inferiority of cultures which were then represented in a developmental sequence. This was the dominant position within the Chicago school of sociology, forming, for example, a core organising principle of Thomas's *Source Book for Social Origins* (1909).

On this basis, Africans were identified as representing a 'lower' culture, with African Americans understood as being also deracinated in cultural terms by enforced transportation to the US, and only partially integrated into Anglo-American culture when involved in a 'civilising process' of participation in the plantation household (Park, 1918). Southern and middle Europeans were distinguished from northern Europeans, who were either directly of 'Anglo-American' culture or easily assimilated to it, especially where their religious heritage was Protestant. Primarily, however, the culture of southern and middle Europeans was understood to be a 'lower' peasant form of their home national culture. The question was how they were to be assimilated to the dominant Anglo-American culture. This was a central theme of Thomas and Znaniecki's study, *The Polish Peasant in Europe and America* (1918–20), alongside the disintegrative and demoralising effects of the process of migration prior to eventual assimilation. It would also be the main theme of *Old World Traits Transplanted* (1921), written by Thomas, but attributed to Park and Miller.

This understanding was applied to the position of African Americans after the Civil War. Park had already travelled to Europe as amanuensis to Booker T. Washington in pursuit of the 'man furthest down' (the findings were published in 1912 under that title), which purported to find that in Sicily and central Europe there were groups in worse conditions of life and mores than African Americans. There was a problem of rural culture in Europe that was mitigated by urban life, but it was rural populations that provided the bulk of new immigrants to the US. The situation of African Americans in the South was argued to be similar to that of the European peasant. No longer exposed to the 'racial etiquette' of the plantation household, as a consequence of being freed into sharecropping, they were, in effect, Chicago sociologists argued, incorporated into a similarly backward peasant culture. Prior to his post with Washington, Park had been secretary to the Congo Reform Association, set up by missionaries to challenge the brutal practices of King Leopold II of Belgium in his personal colonies in the Congo. However, he was far from being a critic of empire and regarded the 'civilising' mission of Rhodes in British Africa positively while also coming to criticise the 'moralising' reformism of his erstwhile colleagues at the Congo Reform Association (Mathews, 1977; Lyman, 1992; Zimmerman, 2010).

Fallace (2011: 105) identifies a third position; this was a 'multicultural and pluralistic view of race [which] expressed full cultural and biological equality among the races'. He associates it with Du Bois and Franz Boas. Even here there were ambiguities with regard to other advocates ostensibly of the same position. Horace Kallen (1924), for example, was an ardent defender of Jewish traditions against assimilation and an advocate of Zionism, but he did not include African Americans in his pluralist democracy. Miller, we will argue, is straightforwardly of this third position, albeit that his association as co-author of *Old World Traits* would otherwise seem to place him in the second group. His advocacy of the plight of 'oppressed peoples' in Europe (including Jews) and his work with immigrants to the US from those groups might seem to place him closer to Kallen. However, he was unequivocal in including African Americans, alongside Jews, among the 'subject and oppressed peoples' that were the focus of his interest. Indeed, in a letter he wrote to Du Bois, he outlined that his interest in the position of immigrants in the US derived from his prior interest in the situation of African Americans.[8] He explicitly challenged the 'myth of racial inferiority', whether on psychological or sociocultural grounds, as being equally a product of the modern period (Miller, 1922).

Overlapping circles

Miller's biography and his trajectory within sociology, then, place him within what were, at least initially, overlapping circles. It is this

8 Miller wrote, 'for a good many years I have been devoting myself to the study of minority peoples in Europe. My interest in them, however, originated from an effort to get perspective for the study of the race problems.' Letter from Miller to Du Bois, 16 December 1924. W. E. B. Du Bois Papers (MS 312), Special Collections and University Archives, University of Massachusetts Amherst Libraries.

overlap that leads us to associate him with the milieu of Chicago sociology. However, as sociological positions became consolidated in the development of the discipline, the circles begin to move apart and Miller's contribution came to be marginalised or, at least, separated from the core of what would be designated as the Chicago school proper, even though it coincides with his involvement in research on the 'Americanization of immigrants' which was itself central to the consolidation of the school.

As we will see, Miller had a joint commitment to sociology as a science, designed to distinguish what was possible from what was necessary, and to democratic engagement with the possible. While the balance between the two may be different in Miller than in other sociologists at the time, the substance of the distinction is relatively uncontroversial, especially given the wider influence of pragmatist philosophy in the development of US sociology. Despite similar general philosophical views about the relation of science and politics, then, it was his *scientific* approach to race and immigration that provided for a different politics, one that was increasingly at odds with that of other colleagues.

We can draw a parallel with the trajectory of Du Bois and other Black sociologists. As various writers have suggested, Du Bois's sociological arguments were neglected within mainstream sociology, notwithstanding their significance and substance (Green and Driver, 1976; Bhambra, 2014; Morris, 2015; Wright II, 2020). After the end of post-Civil War reconstruction in the 1870s, the imposition of segregation under Jim Crow laws in the South, along with de facto segregation elsewhere in the US, meant that Du Bois was denied appointment at the centres of White sociology. At the same time, while his work was (typically) represented as specific to the experiences of Black Americans, it was not taken up by Chicago (or other) sociologists of race relations. His political work became more urgent to him and he left academic sociology behind, thereby reinforcing his neglect by mainstream sociology which, until recently, regarded him primarily as a political figure, where his work was referenced at all (Green and Driver, 1976; Morris, 2015).

The organisation of the Chicago school contributed to the marginalisation of Du Bois and the subordination of other sociologists of colour (Baldwin, 2003: 405). In part, this followed from an absence of fit with Park's own understanding of race relations as primarily an issue of the South and its system of 'caste', an issue to be resolved by a process of gradual assimilation following migration to northern cities (Wacker, 1983; Persons, 1987). It also derived from Park's earlier relationship with Washington, from whom he derived his gradualist views on race as well as a consciousness of the antipathy between Washington and Du Bois (Matthews, 1977; Lyman 1992). For other sociologists of colour, marginality to the White mainstream was a consequence of the segregated nature of higher education.

The Chicago department did train significant sociologists of colour – among them, for example, Charles S. Johnson and E. Franklin Frazier – but they took up positions in historically Black colleges, specifically Fisk University in Nashville (and later at Howard), and not at Chicago (where a colour bar existed *de facto*, somewhat in contradiction of Park's view of a gradual overcoming of racial prejudice). They maintained the 'official' Chicago position on race relations as being an issue of gradual assimilation and, although they became increasingly critical, their statements were muted (Blackman, 2023). Park, himself, went to Fisk after his retirement from the University of Chicago and visited for part of the year from 1936 until his death in 1944. Frazier's theoretical approach to race and the role of colonialism became noticeably closer to the third of the positions described by Fallace only after he left Fisk University to join Howard University in 1934 and after Park's death, though he retained respect for his mentor (Platt, 1991).[9] Johnson worked tirelessly to pursue significant reforms through his association with the National Urban League, but he

---

9 This is so notwithstanding the Whiggish tendency of Chicago school historiography to make all positions in the sociology of race relations emanate from Park. Thus, Everett C. Hughes has commented that 'much later [Frazier] wrote a book on *Race and Culture Contacts in the Modern World*. It follows Park's work rather closely by perceiving race relations as a product of the colonial expansion of Europe' (Hughes, 1979: 187). This implies a criticism of colonialism and neglects Park's favourable evaluation of imperialism and its civilising consequences (see Matthews, 1977; Zimmerman, 2010; Magubane, 2014; Blackman 2023).

was significantly more cautious than Frazier, even after the death of his mentor.

Jean-Michel Chapoulie describes this configuration when discussing what he understands to be the Chicago school's unique contribution to the study of ethnic and race relations in American sociology, which, he suggests, was rather limited before 1950 and organised around just a few universities. The circle, or 'theory group', involved the University of Chicago at the centre, a group at University of Hawaii (involving Chicago-trained sociologists), a separate group around Howard Odum at the University of North Carolina and, finally, at 'the traditionally African American Universities Fisk (in Nashville, Tennessee) and Howard (in Washington)' (Chapoulie, 2020: 229).

Significantly, Chapoulie does not include Du Bois among those contributing to the field, despite his association with Fisk and his landmark study *The Philadelphia Negro* (1899). Indeed, major contributions by Du Bois bookend the period considered by Chapoulie. For example, *Black Reconstruction* (Du Bois, 1935), while published toward the end of the period discussed, had been prefigured by an important article setting out its core arguments and criticism of the Dunning school of historiography in the *American Historical Review* (Du Bois, 1910).[10] Nor does Chapoulie discuss Miller as even a minor figure, except to restate the authorship tangle involving *Old World Traits*. Yet Miller (1916) had completed a study of the schooling of immigrant children in Cleveland, which was the basis of his selection to direct the research on 'immigrant contributions' for the Carnegie Trust's Americanisation studies (in which series *Old World Traits* was published). Significantly, as we shall see, Miller was also a crucial figure in the resolution of a profound crisis at Fisk University in 1924–25 in which Du Bois was also a major protagonist. This was a resolution that established that institution for the development of the very social-scientific

---

10 Alrutheus Ambush Taylor (1924) is otherwise credited with the first challenge to the Dunning school of historiography. Taylor was appointed at Fisk in 1926 and, at the end of his life, wrote a detailed, unpublished history of the institution which is very favourable to Miller's role at Fisk (Taylor, 1952).

contribution that Chapoulie identifies with the Chicago school. It is as if the clarification of the ambiguity over the authorship of *Old World Traits* clears the way for Thomas's contribution to be finally recognised and the *Polish Peasant* study to be given its place as a landmark in US sociology (Abbott and Egloff, 2008). At the same time, this lays the ground for the start of Chicago sociology proper and, with that retelling, Miller is removed from his place within it.

Miller became a forgotten sociologist, we will suggest, as a consequence of Chicago (and wider) sociology's eschewal of reformist activism and its turn to 'science' and a concern with the elaboration of proper theoretical conceptualisations of research. In that sense, he is easily seen as representing an earlier moment in the development of Chicago sociology when social research, reform and progressive politics were united. He is, then, collateral damage in the evolution of its 'collaborative circle', to use Michael Farrell's (2001) term. Miller is a satellite that left the orbit and gravitational pull of the core members of the circle. Yet we do not think that explanation is sufficient. Farrell suggests that there are social structural conditions for collaborative circles, but he has little to say about the racialised and gendered conditions that might apply; these are central to the story of the 'first' Chicago school as it comes to be called in the period of its formation after the First World War (Fine, 1995). The displacement of female sociologists by assigning them to the settlement movement and of Black scholars to the segregated academy extended to others who continued to work in the older way as part of their collaborative circles.[11]

Farrell's account (and that of McLaughlin) identifies the special creativity and innovation of the core group as it rebels against orthodoxies to create its own distinctive position. The implication is that this is the story of the formation of the Chicago school, too. The figure of Du Bois should be sufficient to remind us that those who are excluded might have significant claims to originality. Du Bois was never part of the collaborative circle, while Miller fell away. We shall suggest, too, that Miller represented a richer development of a Chicago sociological theory grounded in pragmatism

---

11 Deegan (1988) nicely captures the idea of the Chicago women of the settlement movement as a collaborative circle ahead of that coinage.

than is found within the core group by extending its social psychology to issues of power and domination. In addition, he was alone among the White sociologists of the pre-war generation of Chicago sociologists inspired by pragmatism to steer it towards a position connecting race relations and colonialism (on which Dewey, for example, remained rather timid; see Fallace, 2011).[12] We will see that Miller withdrew from his role in the Carnegie study in order to take up the position of director of the Mid-European Union, a body advocating for the rights of oppressed peoples, especially those organised under the dual monarchy of Austria and Hungary, or oppressed within the German empire (May, 1957). However, as we shall show, his interest in oppressed peoples was central to his involvement in the Carnegie Study, not a diversion from it.

Just as Du Bois developed a global (and post-colonial, *avant la lettre*) angle to his work through the idea of an *international* 'color-line', so, too, did Miller develop his arguments about domination to address problems of colonialism and empire, initially in the context of Slavic nationalism.[13] It was a strategic decision on the part of core Chicago sociologists to align what they suggested was but a temporary colour-line in northern cities with a general process of immigrant assimilation. As Stow Persons (1987: 34) suggests, the main Chicago sociologists conflated race and ethnicity with a rural–urban distinction and, in that way, represented African American migration to the north as posing problems of 'adjustment' similar

---

12 Green and Driver (1976: 323) cite Miller as denying Du Bois's sociology and referring to him in *Races, Nations and Classes* as an 'editor' and 'agitator', but this ignores the fact that Miller is strongly endorsing his leadership in this text and discusses his sociology elsewhere. As we shall see, Miller and Du Bois had a close connection, deriving from their common involvement with Fisk.
13 Miller's admiration for Du Bois is clear from a letter asking for an autographed photograph to be displayed in his study among 'photographs of persons who are symbolic of my special interest. They are Paderewski. President Masaryk. Syngman Rhee, President of the revolutionary Korean governments, and some others.' Letter from Miller to W. E. B. Du Bois, 26 January 1925. W. E. B. Du Bois Papers (MS 312), Special Collections and University Archives, University of Massachusetts Amherst Libraries.

to that of European peasants migrating to the US. They were involved in recommending that African Americans would be better to remain in the South and were involved in the Chicago Urban League's actions in the first years of its founding to achieve that end (Strickland, 1966).

In contrast, Miller continued to have an interest in both race and immigration, what connected them, and how they differed. In that context, we will suggest that he made advances in sociological theory beyond those at the core of the collaborative circle, albeit advances that fell on deaf ears. Indeed, at each stage of his career, Miller's sociological positions were distinctive and different from those of other Chicago sociologists while being rooted in similar concerns. His advocacy was also distinctive, but it was based on his science. Most emphatically, the latter was not what is now pejoratively termed 'advocacy research' (Athens, 2020).

We are not arguing that the positions of Park and other members of the circle described by Chapoulie were 'racist' (Kivisto, 2017; Athens, 2020); indeed, they were 'progressive' when compared with the eugenic position that was widely held both in public and academic circles, including among those associated with the wider progressive movement in politics, like John R. Commons (1907). It is also possibly moot among sociologists today whether the second or third position outlined by Fallace (2011) is scientifically the more adequate. The third position *may be more akin to some current sensibilities in sociology*, but our argument does not depend on 'retro-fitting' Miller to it. His arguments for cultural pluralism and equality are, however, unequivocal and aligned with the position under development by Du Bois and other advocates of the 'new Negro' (Locke, 1925; Baldwin, 2003).

In this book, we shall set out the development of Miller's thought and its connections with a pragmatist pedagogy for sociology and a programme of research that led him to connect issues of race and ethnicity in the US with colonial systems of global domination. Inevitably, in setting out these arguments, there will be some repetition. Miller flies so far below the radar that we have had to circle around the topics that concerned him to show that the episodes in his life added to something that is more than a sum of their parts. Having suggested the integration of those parts, we will disaggregate them in the following chapters to show the richness of his sociology in all its detail before, in the final chapter, reuniting them again in discussion of his political sociology of domination.

2

The 'old pedagogue'

Not much is known about Herbert Adolphus Miller's early family circumstances, except what can be gleaned from the obituaries by Negley Teeters and his fellow students at Dartmouth College, where he studied for his first degree between 1895 and 1899. When he was employed late in his career at Bryn Mawr it was announced that, on his retirement, he planned to write a memoir, but nothing came of it. Certainly, there are few documents relating to his personal life in the archives at Oberlin or at Temple (where most of the material provided to Negley Teeters came to be lodged). Teeters had planned to write about Miller, but did not do so apart from supplying the obituary for the *American Sociological Review* and a later article on the Mid-European Union for the *Hartwick Review* (Teeters, 1951, 1966). Nonetheless, from these sparse materials a picture emerges, one which is reinforced by Miller's later accomplishments.

Miller's father was of Swedish background and his mother's family was Welsh. He was born on 5 June 1875 in Tuftonboro, New Hampshire, on his maternal grandparents' farm. There is some indication that family circumstances may have been straitened. His parents moved to Massachusetts when Miller was one, but he and his mother returned to the farm after his father died when he was 8 years old. At the age of 16 he was enrolled in Brewster Academy, a boarding school, free for local young people, where he prepared for entry to Dartmouth College in 1895. Dartmouth College had been set up in 1769 to train Native American students for the ministry but had developed in the nineteenth century as a regular college, narrowly avoiding incorporation into the University of New Hampshire. By the time of Miller's enrolment, it was on the cusp of a transition to become a major Ivy League college following substantial endowments during the period of his studies there.

From his first year at Dartmouth, Miller taught at local district schools, earning the nickname 'Ye Old Pedagogue' from his classmates, shortened to 'Peddy'. His path as an educator, it seems, was set early and his commitment remained undimmed throughout his life. In a letter to W. E. B. Du Bois, written in December 1934, shortly after the latter had given up the editorship of *The Crisis* to take up a position at Atlanta University, Miller wrote, 'I hope you are well and enjoying your work. Teaching is after all the most satisfying thing one can do. I know from experience after two years of "retirement"'.[1] This 'retirement' was a period of unemployment following his dismissal on political grounds from Ohio State University in 1931.

In this chapter, we will set out how Miller established a distinctive sociological pedagogy along pragmatist lines, including sociology as a form of 'publicity'. Throughout his extensive career, he was a dedicated lecturer, offering insights into the principles of sociology, the dynamics of immigration, and race relations. But his ideas about education went beyond the classroom. Whether in his academic pursuits or his political and practical endeavours, Miller consistently prioritised education. He worked to raise awareness about critical issues close to his heart, including cosmopolitanism, minority rights and domination. In the process, he engaged with diverse audiences, delivering hundreds of public talks to countless organisations. His commitment to fostering understanding and dialogue remained a constant theme in his life's work.

A significant part of his pedagogic practice unfolded through his 'laboratory' approach to sociological issues, organising field visits to important 'sites', whether they be prison, reform school or settlement house. This also included 'racial mixing'. The latter

1 Letter from Miller to Du Bois, 11 December 1934. W. E. B. Du Bois Papers (MS 312) Series 1A, General Correspondence, Special Collections and University Archives, University of Massachusetts Amherst Libraries.

would come to be part of the controversy surrounding his teaching. His methods, driven by his unwavering dedication to sociological education, stirred controversy and eventually led to his dismissal from his professorship at Ohio State University.

The enduring significance of Fisk University

We can guess that Miller's earliest sympathies were liberal within the constraints of his time and the New England context. There seems to be nothing to indicate his future dedication to the amelioration of race relations. In contrast, the teaching in sociology and philosophy at Dartmouth firmly reinforced the idea of a racial and civilisational order with the White 'race' at its apex. Indeed, the principal teacher of sociology and advocate of social biology there, David Collin Wells, was committed to racial segregation and opposed to the education of women on the grounds that it reduced the fertility of middle-class women and thereby diminished the White 'racial stock'.[2] Miller would find similar ideas dominating at Harvard when he went there to study for his PhD in 1902.

There is no explanation that we can find for Miller's decision, on graduating from Dartmouth in 1899, to take up a position teaching philosophy and athletics, but also sociology, at Fisk University in Nashville. Fisk was one of what became known as the 'historically Black colleges', though, in truth, it was itself an integrated college operating in an academic system that would otherwise remain segregated until the 1960s. The appointment at Fisk would prove decisive, both for Miller personally and for Fisk University itself. On the face of it, though, it appears to be a brief interlude prior to him leaving after three years to undertake a PhD at Harvard.

Earl Wright II suggests that, despite being limited to just three years, he gained from the experience 'a particular insight into the Black world that possibly impacted his 1924 book and definitely altered his view of the ex-slaves during his tenure at the Nashville school' (Wright II, 2010: 49). Similarly, Teeters, a graduate student

---

2 See for example Collin Wells's (1907) advocacy of Social Darwinism in the *American Sociological Review*.

of Miller at Ohio State University at the time of his dismissal, comments that Miller's experience there convinced him that biological accounts of race were wrong (Teeters, 1951). The impact was indeed significant. In his second year at Harvard, he won the Bowdoin Prize (a prize also awarded to Du Bois when he was at Harvard) for an essay on the 'Comparative Psychology of the Negro'. It begins with a statement that the so-called race problem 'is more than one of caste, which is a purely artificial division, though most of the practical treatment of the problem in all countries is colored by caste feeling. This is pre-eminently true in the United States where the Negro as an ex-slave is not justly valued as a human being because of the almost universal impossibility of judging him without the prejudice which has resulted from his previous condition of servitude.'[3] This was an early intimation of his interest in the sociological consequences of domination for both the oppressor and the oppressed.

In fact, Miller's appointment at Fisk gave rise to a connection that was both more personal and more profound. He met, and would later marry in 1903, Elisabeth (Bessy) Cravath – 'her with whom I have travelled through many years and many lands, with growing joy and understanding' (as the 1933 dedication to *The Beginnings of To-morrow* declares). She was the daughter of the first President of Fisk University, Erastus Milo Cravath. President Cravath was from a significant abolitionist family – his parental home in upstate New York had operated as a station on the 'underground railway' – and, following service in the Civil War, he became a field agent for the American Missionary Association (AMA) and worked with the Freedmen's Bureau in Georgia and Tennessee setting up schools and colleges, including Fisk (Lewis, 1993: 58ff). He was educated at Oberlin, as were his children Paul and Elisabeth. Oberlin was itself an integrated college set up by the AMA. However, as Christi Smith (2016) has argued, by the end of the nineteenth century, the commitment to integration on the part of the AMA had faded, with Oberlin, in particular, ceasing to be an

---

3 This was written under the not very convincing pseudonym 'Gustavus Adolphus'. Temple University, Special Collections Research Centre (SPC) MSS SP 055, Folder J.

integrated college in the face of new competitive pressures within US higher education. Moreover, the AMA itself was less inclined to work with Black-led civil rights groups, while the broader professionalisation of higher education had its impact on historically Black colleges, too, and made them more dependent on maintaining their support from local White philanthropists and businesses even as activist groups chafed at the slow pace of change.

In these respects, President Cravath was a connection to a more radical past of interracial cooperation that would not be reproduced by subsequent generations of (White) leaders at the colleges. This was also confirmed in an unpublished history of Fisk University by Alrutheus Ambush Taylor, who was appointed there in 1926. He wrote that Cravath had acted without 'compromising his belief in the fundamental equality of individuals before both God and man. Resolutely he had sought to help the Negroes secure the enjoyment of every right, human and legal, which was accorded to the most favored peoples' (Taylor, 1952: 452). This was a commitment that would be attenuated in subsequent presidents of the university.

President Cravath died in 1900, but his children – and by extension Miller – continued their association with Fisk. Miller formed a connection with Du Bois, Fisk's most illustrious alumnus, at least in part based on the latter's affection and respect for Cravath. Indeed, Du Bois wrote a eulogy at the unveiling of a stained-glass window in Cravath's memory in the university church in 1909 – 'He meant in his soul to make Black men American citizens, equal in every respect with their fellows and with every right that belongs to free and independent human beings.'[4]

Cravath's son, the prominent New York lawyer Paul Cravath,[5] served as Chair of the Board of Trustees until the 1930s although

---

4 Du Bois, W. E. B. (William Edward Burghardt), 1868–1963, Erastus Milo Cravath, ca. 1909. UMass Amherst, W. E. B. Du Bois Papers, Series 3, Articles. Special Collections and University Archives, University of Massachusetts Amherst Libraries.

5 Paul Cravath was a very distinguished figure, responsible for designing the organisation of US law firms that is still in existence today. He also became involved in the development of what Priscilla Roberts (2005) has called the US Anglophile tradition of foreign policy at the same time as Miller

he largely accommodated the resiling from the radical traditions of Fisk represented by later presidents. However, Miller maintained connections with Fisk and regularly gave series of lectures there. In fact, in a crucial episode to which we will return in a later chapter, Miller chaired a committee convened to settle a student protest that erupted in 1924–25, following a commencement speech by Du Bois, against the then incumbent president. This committee would identify a new president – the sociologist Thomas Elsa Jones – and appoint new Black faculty, including Alrutheus Taylor and Charles S. Johnson (Lamon, 1974; Taylor, 1952), a development that would also secure the influence of Chicago sociology over sociology at Fisk.

We will set out in later chapters the nature of Miller's substantive and distinctive arguments on race, immigration and international relations. Our purpose in outlining the significance of his experiences at Fisk is to establish how the issues of race relations domestically in the US and globally came to be the fulcrum against which his pedagogic practice took purchase. We suggest that his substantive arguments set him apart from his colleagues as sociology professionalised, but so, too, did his pedagogic commitments. Nor did they deviate across his various appointments, first, following Harvard, at Olivet College between 1905 and 1914, then at Oberlin College between 1914 and 1924, and Ohio State University from 1924 to 1932.

was developing his criticisms of European overseas empires. Cravath's extensive archive was edited and published by the partners of his law firm, but the letters and documents associated with his foreign-policy ventures were left out and the archive itself destroyed. Cravath self-published his letters from India extolling British rule, but none of these were to his brother-in-law. Only a few letters from Miller to Cravath survive. We know that family relations were cordial because Cravath stepped in privately to supplement his salary when Miller was appointed at Bryn Mawr to a lowly lecturer position following his dismissal from Ohio State University. Marion E. Park to Paul Cravath, 5 May 1938. Herbert Adolphus Miller Papers, Bryn Mawr College Special Collections.

The purposes of sociology

After graduating from Harvard, with a strong background in philosophy, psychology and ethnology, Miller embarked on a sociological career at a time when the discipline was in its earliest formation and when most of those identifying with the new discipline had migrated to it from other subjects. According to Albion Small, first chair of sociology at the University of Chicago, sociology was a discipline without 'a problem, a method, or a message' (Small, 1905: 2). Sociologists were 'those who call(ed) themselves sociologists' (Turner and Turner, 1991: 9). In many ways, what, in a different context and with a different purpose, Talcott Parsons (1937) called the founding '1890–1920' generation of sociologists revealed what Roscoe Hinkle has called 'extraordinary variation, if not total heterogeneity, in the central problems, assumptions, concepts, arguments, and structure of the field' (Hinkle, 1980: 56). Parsons suggested that there was an underlying coherence that could be found in a group of European thinkers of the 1890–1920 generation, but that was a pitch for his own vision for the discipline. More evident in the US at the time was a strong influence of Spencerian political and conservative ideas against social reform (Breslau, 2007), together with a preference for empirical methods. This paved the way for the gradual rejection of reformism and the abandonment of claims for social amelioration within the agenda of American sociology (Platt, 1996). Concurrently, a predominant expectation within professionalism emerged at the turn of the century, characterised by the insistence of universities, along with their conservative presidents and trustees, that 'their employees avoid controversial subjects and opinions' (Smith, 1994: 22).

The 'newcomer's dilemma' (Camic, 1995: 1008) for sociology of creating its own distinct identity hinged on the ability of the discipline to differentiate itself from existing more established disciplines and, at the same time, prove its scientific status. This was particularly acute, as Dorothy Ross (1979: 125) has pointed out, in the 'competitive university and professional context' that obtained at the time. At the University of Chicago, Small opted for an expansive strategy to propel sociology into a top social science.

The institutional success of Chicago sociology, involving the establishment of the *American Journal of Sociology* in 1895 and the American Sociological Society (ASS) in 1905, underpinned a move from 'education to expertise' (Buxton and Turner, 1992), and solidified the image of sociology as an empirical science. Noticeably, this also brought about a more restricted conception of social inquiry, a fact that was later made even more intense with the professionalisation and growing specialisation of research, although, as we shall see, Miller participated in two major research projects, the Cleveland Survey in 1915 and the Carnegie Research Project on Methods of Americanization in 1918.

These changes in disciplinary focus were not unconnected to issues of practical applicability, but, primarily, they introduced a politics of knowledge grounded in the separation of knowledge claims and reformist aims, albeit that the separation was viewed asymmetrically. Those who were committed to a reformist programme for sociology, for example, did not disagree with the grounding of action in science. For sociologists influenced by pragmatism, the purpose of research was to distinguish what was necessary from what was possible, with action directed at the possible. This was a theme first set out by George Herbert Mead (1899) as the 'working hypothesis in social reform'. It was, he argued, necessary to distinguish socialism with its *a priori* construction of an ideal world in thought, from a (social) scientific understanding of the world as it is and the possibilities inherent to it that might be discovered through a reflective consciousness directed at reform.

Despite initial doubts stemming from philosophical discussions about pragmatism, Miller came to believe in its constructive influence within sociology, finding sympathy with the idea that its pragmatic principles could lead to a more insightful and applicable understanding of sociological phenomena:

> As a student of William James, I used to resist his pragmatism; but as a sociologist, I soon became convinced that any other method is futile. No universally complete principle about society whose complexity is so infinite can be laid down. Pragmatism insists that the truth appears only so far as it proves to work and its working proves it to be truth. If we examine the ordinary interpretation of social phenomena, we shall discover that our social philosophy has been largely dominated

by theories that are *not working* and therefore are not true. We do know, however, some things that work; and if we can classify the principles that are known to work, we shall have some positive law to which we can make practical adjustments, and by so far progress can take place. (Miller, 1921b: 335; original emphasis).

Broadly, Miller framed his approach along these pragmatic lines, voicing a hope 'to substitute progress for chaos' (Miller, 1924a: xvii), and an expectation 'to reform the world' (Miller, 1924a: 172). Miller also explicitly placed focus on egalitarian and democratic goals (Miller, 1916). Significantly, he did not emphasise the role of *observation* so much as that of *dialogue* and 'talking' to those who were the subjects of research. To this end, he devised a classroom practice that involved site visits to prisons, schools, settlement houses, places of worship, and so on, including visits to historically Black colleges to encourage racial mixing among students. In the period after his graduation from Harvard, Miller wrote extensively on pedagogic matters for the ASS and in talks at its meetings. This also influenced his political engagements and his public talks to a wide-ranging set of community and civic groups.

In 1913, while at Olivet College, Miller spelled out his definition of sociology's purpose at an informal conference held at the annual meeting of the ASS at Minneapolis.[6] Essentially, he saw it as being in line with the core ideals of pragmatist pedagogy, connected to the aims of education, citizenship and progressivism:

> All of us can tell of the great influence that our teaching has had on our students. They tell us how sociology has turned the world over for them, but we have got to make sociology respected by scholars, which is not the case now. Sociology ought to supplant psychology as the basic study of pedagogy. Psychology deals with method while sociology deals with purpose, the one looks backward and the other forward, and if there is any single requirement for education it is that of preparing for the future. If sociology cannot command respect in any other way, it should 'butt in' and offer its services. Sociologists ought to be leading speakers at state teachers' associations but they

---

6 The topic of discussion was 'What are the best contributions sociologists can make at the present toward the conditions of life in the United States, particularly the central portion of the country?' (Gillette, 1914: 29).

are rarely called upon. They should be called into the counsel of state educational systems as other experts are called in from various departments, and outline the aims of education in fitting children for citizenship in the society in which they are going to live. Sociology cannot adequately make its contribution to society merely by influencing students; it should exercise its prerogative in guiding the thinking of society toward a fulfilment of its possibilities. (Miller, 1914d: 35)

Miller's perspective on sociology as an educational process that transcended mere academic influence resonated with the ambition of many early American sociologists to secure a respected position for their discipline. However, his advocacy for sociologists to actively engage in educational discourse and policy formulation parallels broader pragmatist commitments to effect societal change through informed and participatory decision-making. Instead of an 'American quest for objectivity' (Bannister, 1987), it was the purpose of finding practical applications through shaping collective realities that was at the core of Miller's conception of sociological knowledge. It would be a theme throughout his life, including his involvement in the Foreign Policy Association, which was set up in 1918 and designed to extend democratic debate about foreign policy through public meetings in US cities (Allen, 2023).

This understanding of sociology's purpose arose from broader interdisciplinary connections and was also developed in Miller's years at Olivet, where he expanded his pragmatist sociological approach. In 1905, after graduating from Harvard, where he was among the last PhD students of William James, Miller joined Olivet College as an assistant professor of philosophy. He started teaching basic courses in psychology and philosophy, working under President Ellsworth Gage Lancaster. Within a year, he became a full professor in philosophy, and by 1910, a professor of philosophy and sociology.

Miller's teaching agenda was moving continually in the direction of social science, through his activities in the Department of Applied Economics (where he taught the course on political economy), and later branched out into a broader set of sociology courses. The Olivet College Catalogue shows the school's commitment to the expansion of sociology, with Miller leading the way. He chose topics covering broad areas like social evolution and society's structure in 1906–1907,[7] and more specific topics like child labour, alcohol issues, public health, crime and poverty in 1912–13.[8]

In terms of the disciplinary differentiation, and the division of labour among the core social sciences, Miller gave priority to connections between sociology and psychology over expanding into the territory of economics. In another informal session of the ASS, Miller wrote,

> it seems to me that some of the work that we try to do does belong more distinctly to the economist. Thus matters of relief are more economic than sociological. To be sure, sociology must describe a standard, but the practical problem of dealing with economic problems may belong to the economist more than to us. In other words, it seems to me that we have appropriated rather more than belongs to us. The social work of women's clubs, settlements, and all sorts of municipal organization are called sociology. It certainly is no nearer related to the kind of thing we are dealing with yesterday as sociology than physics is related to chemistry. (Miller, 1914e: 166)

Miller's cultivation of his sociological outlook found its crucible in the space of the sociology seminar. Here, he began the practice of taking students to important sociological sites, forming the basis for his teaching approach. The launch of the Sociology Seminar in 1911–12 announced plans for visits to places like the Michigan state capital, Lansing, including the Industrial and Blind Schools, State Health and Vital Statistics departments, as well as the State Penitentiary in Jackson.[9]

In 1914, Miller became a head of a tiny department of sociology (three full-time positions) at Oberlin College, which was within the Chicago circle of influence. He came there with endorsements from Professors Thomas and Small of the University of Chicago, and Professor Cooley of the University of Michigan.[10] Long before

---

7 *Catalogue of Olivet College for 1906–1907*. Printed for the College by Frank N. Green, Olivet, MI, February 1907: 29.
8 *Catalogue of Olivet College for 1912–1913*. Printed for the College by Frank N. Green, Olivet, MI, February 1913: 71.
9 *Catalogue of Olivet College for 1910–1911*. Printed for the College by Frank N. Green, Olivet, MI, February 1911: 62.
10 *Oberlin Alumni Magazine* X(10), 1914: 346.

the formal crystallisation of the Chicagoan notion of the city as a social laboratory (Park and Burgess, 1925), Miller had begun his headship with pressing for 'vitalizing the work through making connections with Cleveland. With a large city so near at hand as a laboratory the facts and principles can be made much more vivid by immediate observation.'[11] The success of the announced strategy was immediate. As it is reported a year later, 'the resulting increase of interest in the department is shown by an increase of sixty-seven in its registration for the coming year'.[12] In contrast to the 'master of all (social science) disciplines' manner of teaching at Olivet, Miller's portfolio of lectures was decidedly more sociological (Introduction to Sociology, Social Organization,[13] Social Problems,[14] Physical and Mental Factors in Social Evolution, The History of Sociological Theory). At Oberlin, Miller started to give special topic courses on Immigration and the Immigrant and, after 1917, also on The Race Problem, which was announced as a course that 'studies the Negro as an example of the race problem

11 Annual Reports of the President and Treasurer of Oberlin College for 1913–1914, *Bulletin of Oberlin College* New Series 103, Oberlin, OH, 1914: 138. This is also recorded in the Report of the Dean from Miller's first year in the office, where the distance from a larger centre of population is seen as an obstacle to making the work of the department vivid: 'Mr. Miller expects later to demand one or two trips to Cleveland or elsewhere by each student. A fund to pay the expenses of lecturers who are experts in their field is mentioned as the greatest need of the department at this time.' *Annual Reports of the President and the Treasurer of Oberlin College for 1914–1915*. Published by the College, Oberlin, OH, 30 November 1915: 161.
12 *Annual Reports of the President and the Treasurer of Oberlin College for 1915–1916*. Published by the College, Oberlin, OH, 30 November 1916: 186.
13 Cooley's *Social Organization* and Wallas's the *Great Society* were the set texts.
14 The course description says, 'no textbook is used but each student must subscribe for the Survey, a weekly magazine, and expect to make two study trips to Cleveland or their equivalent elsewhere'. *Bulletin of Oberlin College*, New Series 121. *College of Arts and Sciences: Announcement of Courses for the Year 1916–1917*. Published by the College, Oberlin, OH, 16 May 1916: 166.

with special reference to America'.[15] The attendance in his lectures remained consistently high throughout the Oberlin period, mainly attracting female students (for instance, in 1918, the lectures on the Race Problem drew 1 male student and 22 female students while the Immigration and the Immigrant drew 4 male students and 23 female students).[16]

There is no indication that Miller orchestrated student research activities in a style similar to the Chicago department. In the recollections of Margery Wells Steer, a member of Oberlin College's Class of 1923, however, there emerges a portrayal of her experiences under Miller's tutelage.[17] Steer illustrates the transformative impact of Miller's pedagogical approach through episodic accounts of her sociological experiences. She recalls the immersive nature of Miller's instruction, which extended beyond the confines of the classroom: 'The air age was still in the future and such things as semesters abroad were unthinkable. But Mr. Miller managed to get us out of the classrooms and off the campus, all the way to Cleveland, the Mansfield Reformatory, and other fascinating places too numerous to list. His classes were never dull and he opened many doors for me through which I glimpsed a world of new interests and unsolved problems' (pp. 3–4).

Miller's teaching methods transcended conventional boundaries, leading students on expeditions beyond the campus. Journeys to various locales, including the Mansfield Reformatory and other compelling sites, were meticulously orchestrated to stimulate students' sociological insights. Steer's narrative captures the atmosphere of intellectual exploration fostered by Miller's guidance, positioning him as a mentor who deftly kindled curiosity and deepened understanding.

15 *Annual Catalogue for 1916–17*. Published by Oberlin College, Oberlin, OH, 31 January 1917: 232.
16 *Annual Reports of the President and the Treasurer of Oberlin College for 1917–1918*. Published by the College, Oberlin, OH, 30 November 1918: 219.
17 Oberlin File RG21. VII. Writings by Oberlinians. Series B. Subseries: Diaries. Folder: Margery Wells (Steer), 1973. Box 3, Oberlin College Archives.

The challenging nature of Miller's instruction shines through in Steer's anecdotes – 'My mother began to have misgivings about what college was doing to my sunny outlook on life ... I went on to assure that I'd try not to get contaminated' (p. 14). Notably, he orchestrated invigorating debates, such as one between Norman Thomas and Raymond Robbins on the themes of socialism and capitalism.[18] Steer's accounts highlight Miller's aptitude for curating a dynamic educational environment that invited guest speakers, and encouraging dialogues that enriched students' academic experiences. Further, Steer wrote about Miller's habitual theme: 'The man that forgets his old fatherland will never make a good citizen here. Be loyal to the good in the old as well as to the better in the new world' (p. 14). Finally, she commented, 'Mr. Miller is going to Washington to reconstruct the universe' (p. 15).

Steer's recollections also provide glimpses into Miller's engagement with sociological fieldwork. The Race Problem class, for instance, prompted students to immerse themselves in diverse cultural contexts, attending gatherings such as the 'colored Holly Roller Church [sic]', not for conversion, but to glean sociological insights. Additionally, Miller's design of trips to sites like the Jewish synagogue and various churches underscored his commitment to experiential learning, allowing students to engage with difference at first hand.

Miller's dedication to practical engagement is also exemplified through Steer's descriptions of sociology trips to institutions such as the county jail, the police court and the Warrensville Farm (a workhouse facility that also acted as a sanitorium and place for the disabled and elderly). Such excursions unveiled the intricacies of societal structures and the challenges faced by marginalised populations. Miller's pedagogical prowess lay in his ability to bridge theoretical constructs with real-world observations, cultivating in students a deep appreciation for the complex interplay of social forces.

---

18 Norman Thomas was a Christian Socialist who would go on to be presidential candidate for the Socialist Party of America, and Robbins a labour economist and progressive who advocated for diplomatic relations with the Soviet Union.

Steer's reminiscences provide a glimpse into the indelible influence of Miller at Oberlin College during the 1920s. His pioneering pedagogy, characterised by experiential learning, dynamic fieldwork and interdisciplinary engagement, resonated profoundly with his students. Indeed, Steer's recollections etch a portrait of Miller as an educator who surpassed conventional teaching norms. He guided students towards critical engagement with society's problems and nurtured a passion for sociological inquiry that endured far beyond their classroom interactions. It might appear that Miller was treating Cleveland as a social laboratory in a manner akin to Robert E. Park's approach. However, unlike Park's directive to 'get the seat of your pants dirty in real research',[19] Miller's approach was centred not so much on methods, but rather on fostering self-reflective impacts on students as dedicated citizens who internalise values of cultural pluralism, collective involvement and a dedication to democratic participation.

Sociology and international relations, war and its aftermath

In between his appointments at Olivet and Oberlin, Miller had a brief interlude in 1911 in which he took a course with William I. Thomas at the University of Chicago. This also introduced him to the milieu of the Chicago settlement houses and Mary E. McDowell, in particular. She had founded the University settlement house and introduced Miller to the local population of immigrants from Bohemia. Thomas, in turn, encouraged this interest and recommended a field trip to Europe. In 1912, Miller travelled to Prague with a large delegation of American Bohemians and received an invitation to spend a week in Moravia with Tomáš Garrigue Masaryk, a visit most likely engineered by McDowell, who had a close relation with Masaryk's daughter Alice who had studied social work in Chicago.[20] The discussions with Masaryk on the social and political problems of central

---

19 Robert Park talking to students at the University of Chicago in the 1920s, cited in Brewer (2000: 13).
20 From the Masaryk visit he went on to visit Poland, Russia and Finland.

Europe made a lasting impression. The intended case-study approach to the Bohemian question developed alongside academic activism and practical politics.[21]

At a meeting of the ASS in Minneapolis, in 1913, Miller suggested that 'the force of nationalism in Central Europe was becoming so strong that sooner or later the map of Europe would have to be changed to recognise it' (Miller, 1914c). What he termed a 'rising nationalist individualism' embodied psychological aspects and much of the abstract meaning that Miller assigned to nationalism – where the group seeks to secure its own individuality – yielded a very effective political framework to address minorities under the Habsburg empire.

After the start of the war, Miller was active in raising awareness about the battle against German hegemony. He published a number of non-academic articles (Miller, 1915, 1917), gave many public lectures and joined committees being established among Czechs in America (and Cleveland in particular) to pursue the national cause. These engagements were primarily educational. At the outbreak of war, Miller and his Oberlin students designed 'The New Map of Europe: Approximate Boundaries of Peoples'. The map proved to be an extremely efficient tool for raising awareness about German hegemony over oppressed nationalities. Most famously, it was put on display in summer 1918, in a very large format, in front of the New York Public Library and at various places on Fifth Avenue.

For Miller, the war years marked a period of frenetic educational activity. As a snapshot of these activities, the list from Oberlin's yearly report in 1914 shows that Miller delivered public talks to more than 50 organisations, primarily focusing on topics such as nationalism, immigration, education, minority rights and race (figure 2.1). Upon his arrival at Oberlin, Miller assumed the role of adviser to foreign students and advocated for a more inclusive approach. The excerpt from the yearly report reads: 'For the sake of the highest scholarship results, Professor Mosher specially urges

21 In the end, the study of the Bohemian immigrant did not parallel the methodological robustness of Thomas's study of the Polish peasant. Miller did an enormous educational job in support of the subject minorities and later on got engaged in practical politics, as we shall see in later chapters.

> 82 REPORT OF THE PRESIDENT
>
> tended the meeting of the Classical Association of the Middle West and South at Nashville, in April, and was elected Secretary and Treasurer of the latter organization.
>
> LUTZ, PROFESSOR HARLEY L.
>
> Addresses in Wellington and Elyria, and some speaking for the suffrage and prohibition amendments.
>
> Attended the meeting of the American Economic Association, at Princeton, in December, the State Tax Conference, at Columbus, in February, and the meeting of the Ohio College Association, in Columbus, in April.
>
> Taught in the Summer School of the University of Chicago.
>
> Was awarded the Toppan Prize by Harvard University for doctoral thesis on "State Control Over the Assessment of Property for Taxation, with Special Reference to the State Tax Commission."
>
> LYMAN, PROFESSOR EUGENE W.
>
> Seven lectures on "The Ethical and Social Aspects of Religion," at the Congregational Assembly, Frankfort, Mich.
>
> Conducted a class on the "Teachings of Jesus," at the Y. W. C. A. Student Conference at Eaglesmere, Pa., and the Bible study at the Massachusetts Christian Endeavor Institute, at Sagamore Beach, Mass., during the summer.
>
> College Preacher at Amherst College, February 28th; preacher on the Day of Prayer for Colleges at Lake Erie College, Painesville, O.; supplied pulpits at Toledo, Elyria, and elsewhere.
>
> MACLENNAN, PROFESSOR SIMON F.
>
> Paper on "Neo-Realism, Pragmatism and Idealism," before the Ohio College Association, at Columbus, in April.
>
> MARTIN, PROFESSOR CHARLES B.
>
> Attended the annual meeting of the College Art Association, at Buffalo, in April.
>
> MILLER, PROFESSOR HERBERT A.
>
> Addresses, lectures, and sermons, as follows: "The Cause of the War," at the Methodist Church, Oberlin; "The Modern Way of Glorifying God," and "Social and Religious Significance of the War," before the College Y. M. C. A.; "Social Problems," before the Promotion Committee of the College Y. M. C. A.;

Figure 2.1 Extract from Oberlin Catalogue

FACULTY

"The Change in Woman's Duties," before the College Equal Suffrage League; Equal Suffrage speech at Amherst; "Socialism and the Church," First Church, Oberlin; "Habit," Rust Methodist Church, Oberlin; "Other Race Prejudices," before the Douglas Club, Oberlin; "Nationalism," and an illustrated lecture on Bohemia and Russia, before the Cosmopolitan Club, Oberlin; "Advantage of Difficulties," Chapel talk before the State School for the Deaf, Columbus; Discussion before the University section of the Conference of Charities and Correction, Columbus; "The Soul of the Immigrant," "The Immigrant and Democracy," and "Points of a Good Job," before the Men's Forum of the Second Church, Oberlin; "Health and Heredity," before the W. C. T. U., Oberlin; "America and the Foreign Student," before the Association of Cosmopolitan Clubs, Columbus; "Women and War," before the Woman's Bible Class, Olivet, Mich.; "The Femininist Movement," before the New Century Club, Detroit, Mich.; "Why Study Socialism," Oberlin Socialist Club; "Religion and Duty," before the Colored Men's Christian League, Oberlin; seven lectures on sociological subjects, at Fisk University; three lectures before the Woman's Civic Class, Norwalk, O.; "The Contribution of the Slav," before a joint meeting of the Slavonic peoples of Cleveland; "National Freedom," before a meeting in behalf of the Servian Red Cross, Cleveland; "Righteousness," before the Polish Mission, Cleveland; "The Present Significance of John Hus," at Cleveland, celebrating the 500th anniversary of the martyrdom of Hus; "Democracy," and "Customs and Traditions," at the Hiram House Settlement, Cleveland; "The Limits of Socialism," before the Jewish Young People's Socialist League, Cleveland; "Responsibility for Jewish Ideals," at the Hebrew Free School Synagogue, Cleveland; "South Slavonic Freedom," before a joint meeting of the Servian, Croatian, and Slavonian Leagues of Cleveland; "Some Problems of Democracy," at the A. M. E. Church, West Chester, Pa.; "Play and Playgrounds," before the Playground Assembly, West Chester; "Contemporary Religious Expression," at the Friends meeting, and "Purpose of Higher Education," before the High School, West Chester, Pa.; "Race Ideals," at an assembly of colored girls of the Pennsylvania Girls' Refuge Home, Darlington, Pa.; "The War and America," before the staff and honor girls of the Refuge Home; Chapel talk, Tennessee Agricultural and Normal College; talk before the National Convention of the Hungarian Sick and Benefit Association, Turn Hall, West Side, Cleveland;

Figure 2.1 continued

REPORT OF THE PRESIDENT

Equal Suffrage speeches at the Coast Guard's Station, Stone Harbor, N. J., and in Pennsylvania at Downingtown, Parksburg, Newtowne Square, West Chester, Milltown, Berwyn, Mt. Pleasant, and Mendenhall; sermons: "The Promise of Tragedy," at Second Church, Oberlin, and "Democracy and Religion," at the Congregational Church, Olivet, Mich.

Spent eight weeks of the summer studying the foreign population of Cleveland.

Attendance at the following meetings: Ohio Conference of Charities at Columbus, in November; Association of Cosmopolitan Clubs, at Columbus, in December; American Sociological Society, Princeton, N. J.; National Association of University Professors, at New York, in January, and a meeting of Fisk University Trustees, at New York, in February.

MOORE, PROFESSOR DAVID R.

Addresses as follows: At First Methodist Episcopal Church, Elyria, on the "Awakening of China," December; "The Partitioning of Africa," at the Oberlin High School; "Yuan Shi Kai," at the Congregational Church, Bellevue, O.; "Italy and the War," at Oberlin, in July.

Attendance at the meetings of the American Historical Association and the American Political Science Association, at Chicago, in December; and at an informal meeting of History teachers, at Toronto, Canada, in December.

MOORE, ASSOCIATE PROFESSOR EDWARD J.

Lecture on "The Solar System and Its Place Among the Stars," at Chatham, O., in February; address on "X-Ray Spectra and the Newly Discovered Series Relation between the Elements," before the Physics Club of the University of Chicago, in July.

Elected a Fellow of the American Association for the Advancement of Science in December.

Taught at the University of Chicago during the summer, giving a course in advanced General Physics, and one in advanced Optics.

Assistant Professor of Physics in the Extension Division of the University of Chicago.

MOSHER, PROFESSOR WILLIAM E.

Address on "Germany and the German War," before general audiences at Penfield and North Monroeville, O.; on "The Present

Figure 2.1 continued

a faculty of picked scholars and teachers and a group of homogeneous picked students, limited in number. Professor H. A. Miller, on the other hand, with larger social and national needs in mind, urges that our present student body is too homogeneous and the distinct effort ought to be made to bring in larger numbers representative of the immigrant populations of the country.'[22]

A significant part of the Oberlin tradition, cosmopolitanism, was, on Miller's analysis, challenged by the demographics of the student body:

> One problem is that of the remarkable uniformity of type of our students. They are fine students with sane backgrounds and purposes but they do not represent America ... The geographical cosmopolitanism of Oberlin is merely the means of securing provincialism. I have just had the pleasure of reading ninety odd autobiographies from one of my classes in which the social background was described. It was amazing how true to type they were. Middle class, large Protestant families with ideals and Christian purposes send their children to Oberlin to get good things in harmony with the family ideals ... Oberlin is a place for the alumni to send back its children ... Oberlin graduates in whatever professions go as missionaries, but they cannot go *back* to the groups that need them most. My recommendation in regard to this is that as soon as possible scholarships be provided to make a special appeal to different types. I read the other day that a Hungarian in Cleveland had persuaded a German college in Iowa to offer scholarships, and then he had got, I think twelve, Hungarian high school graduates to go to Iowa.[23]

Consistent with his pragmatist methodology and 'making connections', in his proposed Oberlin strategy Miller firmly believed that by embracing a more inclusive representation, a broader impact could be exerted. This influence, in its scope, would stem from the

---

22 *Annual Reports of the President and the Treasurer of Oberlin College for 1915–1916*. Published by the College, Oberlin, OH, 30 November 1916: 35–36.
23 *Annual Reports of the President and the Treasurer of Oberlin College for 1915–1916*. Published by the College, Oberlin, OH, 30 November 1916: 196–197.

tackling of a wider spectrum of societal challenges embedded within the diverse fabric of America.

Towards the end of his time at Oberlin, Miller found himself at the zenith of his career. He wrote the well-received book *Races, Nations and Classes* (1924) and assumed the role of chairman of a Committee on International Relations of the ASS, alongside board members Jane Addams, Jerome Davis and Albion Small. In 1924, Miller moved to Ohio State University in Columbus, which was, at that time, the largest sociology department in Ohio. During a convocation address delivered in 1925, Miller unveiled his new agenda, centred around the 'rumblings of international movements' and the 'international aspects of patriotism' (Miller, 1925: 5). He expressed strong opposition to the 'particularism' seen in religion, science, state and race, and advocated for the examination of group egotism within inter-group relations. Drawing from William James's concept of 'encyclopaedic ignorance', he suggested that the 'scope of each science is arbitrarily limited' (Miller, 1925: 3). Miller emphasised that neither religion, science, state nor race can offer universal solutions. He highlighted two commonalities among individuals: 'We all, however, have two things in common, the necessity of living in contemporary society and the urge to find the significance of our own lives' (Miller, 1925: 3).

This announcement was not only a critique of the educational ideas of Europe and America, but also 'an introduction to the sociology of internationalism which will be an essential mark of the education of the future' (Miller, 1933: 18).[24] Miller joined Ohio State with the intention of developing his arguments for a global cosmopolitan sociology, including through study trips abroad. Between 1925 and 1931, these involved visits to the Soviet Union and Baltic States, central Europe, the Middle East, Southeast Asia and India. In all these contexts, he was interested in the dialectic of oppression and freedom and revolutions against domination, especially where this involved one racialised group claiming superiority over another.

24 'Western education has been experimental and pragmatic. It is now leading the West to try to find out what is going on elsewhere' (Miller, 1933: 107).

The Department of Sociology at Ohio State University was undergoing a phase of expansion at the onset of Miller's tenure. During this period, there was a substantial increase in faculty turnover, and the number of awarded graduate degrees tripled between 1925 and 1930. Under the leadership of James A. Hagerty, who had served as chair since 1903, the department was actively developing programmes geared towards the training of social service professionals. It is noteworthy that Hagerty's commitment to the practical application of knowledge resonated strongly with Miller, as reflected in his lecture content. Miller's instructional focus narrowed down to encompass his enduring scholarly interests, namely 'The Race Problem', 'The Immigrant' and 'Adjustment of Alien Groups.' At graduate level, he conducted seminars on topics such as 'Sociological Theories', 'Cultural Types and Intercultural Processes' and 'Group Composition of American Society'.[25]

Miller embarked on two extensive international journeys. The first, spanning seven months in 1925–1926, saw him traverse 19 European countries, while the second, lasting for a remarkable 15 months from 1929 to 1930, took him on a global expedition. These journeys contributed to his international reputation, making him the most internationally recognised scholar among social scientists at Ohio State (Sabine, 1931). Additionally, Miller spent a semester teaching at Yenching University in Peking and delivered lectures at Shanghai University and at universities in India and Syria. A noteworthy aspect of Miller's impact was his mentorship of a significant number of Chinese, Korean and Indian students at Oberlin and at Ohio State. Many of these students maintained contact with him even after returning to their respective home countries. This aspect of Miller's pedagogic programme underscores his commitment to the practical application of knowledge, aligning with his pedagogical approach that emphasised 'site visits' to enact 'practical adjustments to truths discovered in action' (Miller, 1924a: xvii). We will discuss the nature of these trips in a later chapter. However, a widely reported speech in Bombay in March 1930 associated with

---

25 *Ohio State University Bulletin* XXIX(16), 1925: 220. Published by the University at Columbus.

Gandhi's march protesting a tax on salt imposed by the British precipitated procedures at Ohio State University for his dismissal.

Understandably, this affair had a detrimental effect on Miller's sociological career and, irrespective of vast public support, contributed to the marginalisation of his positions in the discipline. Essentially, Miller's understanding of the disciplinary purpose in the 1930s differed much more significantly from the standard (professional) positions within the discipline than had been the case in the 1910s or early 1920s. In the main, it had been the move away from pedagogy to research practice, a transition that Miller saw as restrictive.[26]

Three thousand students signed a petition in support of Miller after the final decision to dismiss him. In a letter to the editor of *The Nation*, a former student of Miller's wrote,

> This case is of public concern because it involves one of the finest teachers ever available to an American University. Miller has never had any use for cut-and-dried formulas in education. He was always cynical about the grading system revered by orthodox pedagogues. He would never stand over a lazy student with any sort of whip. The main point is that Miller has the power of being fascinatingly interesting to alert pupils, of making education adventurous, of stirring his students to seek new facts and appreciations for themselves. He was a pioneer in the educational method of taking students directly into contact with the institutions they were investigating. If he occasionally minimized the more formal outlines of his courses, he always had on tap an amazingly wide knowledge, flavored with a mellow and essentially tolerant philosophy. A mind would be hopeless if it did not grow under his stimulus. Entirely apart from his extra-curricular interests and public services, Miller's unique value as a teacher is the greatest loss to the student body of Ohio State.[27]

---

26 The discipline in the 1930 'drew increasingly sharp lines between scientific (meaning quantitative) knowledge and other kinds of writing ... The sociologists who were subsidized and wrote primarily for the narrow audience of professional sociologists wound up dominating professional sociology, and the public intellectuals ... died as professional outcasts' (Buxton and Turner, 1992: 378–379).

27 Devere Allen, *The Nation*, 5 August 1931: 135.

After the affair, Miller undertook visiting lectures for a fee organised on his behalf by the Speakers' Forum of Columbus, an adjunct organisation of the Foreign Policy Association, of which he was an early and active member. This was for two years before his appointment at Bryn Mawr in 1933, where he taught sociology in the department of social economy until his retirement in 1940. At Bryn Mawr, Miller was highly engaged in promoting public understanding of international events during the rise of fascism. He frequently reported on the situation in Czechoslovakia and the challenges faced by small nations. The *Bryn Mawr Bulletin* comprehensively documents his involvement in international relations, including his discussions on topics such as the Jewish question, the growing threat posed by Germany in Czechoslovakia, and other imperial ambitions.

After Bryn Mawr, he held a number of visiting positions, including a year at Temple University and at Beloit College and Pennsylvania State University, hired on a semester-by-semester basis. He ended his career at Black Mountain College in Asheville, North Carolina, where he taught between 1943 and 1947.

During the Second World War, Miller immersed himself in an educational job that he later declared as the most fulfilling experience of his entire career (Teeters, 1951). In 1940, he assumed the role of director for the American Seminar for Refugee Scholars, an initiative organised by the American Friends Service Committee in Wolfsboro, New Hampshire, the town where he had attended school. This seminar spanned from the summer of 1940 to 1944 and provided assistance to hundreds of scholars seeking refuge in America due to political and racial discrimination. The primary objective of the seminar was twofold: first, to establish an informal democratic community, and second, to facilitate the rapid integration of these scholars into American society while fostering a deeper understanding of American democracy and history, with a particular emphasis on American educational principles and methodologies.[28] Miller orchestrated the entire programme as a collaborative effort

---

28 See Hertha Kraus, 'Experimenting in Group Services. The Friends' American Seminar', 1942. Temple University, Special Collections Research Centre (SPC) MSS SP 055. Folder K. Black Mountain College Papers, pp. 1–12

in Americanisation. His underlying ambition, articulated in his broadcast talk 'America's Gain, Europe's Loss', was to interpret newcomers to the American community and underscore the idea that it was America that should extend gratitude to these newcomers.

The programme, characterised by its intensity,[29] offered scholars the opportunity to study 'creative writing, history, government, psychology, sociology, economics, biology, physics, mathematics, modern languages, home economics, and methods of music and secondary education with university students from ten to fifty years their juniors' (Kraus, 1942: 10). This curriculum mirrored Miller's lifelong aspiration to dismantle barriers related to race, nationality and religion (Kraus, 1942: 12). Miller's lectures for the seminar participants covered 'subjects necessary for the newcomer to know: 'democracy, racial groups, immigration, the negro, education, geography, and community life in America' (Kraus, 1942: 11).[30] These were all subjects that held profound significance for Miller throughout his lifetime.

In the summer of 1943, he brought the seminar to the picturesque surroundings of Black Mountain College in Asheville, North Carolina, on the request of the college and as part of his appointment there. This was a fitting last stage of Miller's academic career. The college was set up in 1933 as a liberal experiment grounded in John Dewey's principles of progressive education. Its establishment was spearheaded by John Andrew Rice, Theodore Dreier and associates, who had faced dismissal from Rollins College, Florida, in a case similar to that of Miller at Ohio State University. The incident involving Rice and others was also elevated to the American Association of University Professors, which, while vindicating them, could not reinstate their positions (Lovejoy and Edwards, 1933). In fact, the issues at Rollins involved a clash over pedagogic

---

29 The participants were occupied from 7.30am until late in the evening. Together with his wife Bessy, Miller operated the New Hampshire Unit of the seminar. He also supervised, and lectured for, the other unit located in Maine.

30 Miller also delivered the commencement address in which he inducted participants into the 'Durham Clan of the American Seminar Tribe of the Federation of Human Understanding' (Kraus, 1942: 11).

principles, rather than politics and, perhaps, indicated the difficult personalities of the protagonists (Duberman, 1972)

The founders articulated Black Mountain College's purpose as being 'to establish an educational institution that would avoid the pitfalls of autocratic chancellors and trustees and allow for a more flexible curriculum' (p. 2). The overarching goal, as set out by Eva Díaz (2014: 2), was to 'educate a student as a person and as a citizen', aligning with Miller's own convictions. Notably, the absence of course requirements, grades, accredited programmes and a mandated curriculum further resonated with Miller's educational philosophy. Upon Gorman Mattison's invitation to join the college staff, Miller responded with enthusiasm: 'I am sure that I would be very happy in Black Mountain. The American seminar of which I have been director for three summers has had some of the same technique that you practice.'[31]

In fact, the novel arrangements for running the college – a faculty board, student representation and no trustees – proved to be precarious. The arrangements were also overlain by a 'Quaker' idea of government by consensus, ill-suited to large personalities. Rice interpreted the sense of a meeting to mean the sense represented by a consensus among the 'intelligent', rather than decision by majority vote when the community was divided (Duberman, 1972: 72). Resentments, exacerbated by lower pay than was available elsewhere, and the fact that newer faculty appointments often intended their period of stay only to be short-term, meant that conflicts, when they arose, were profound. Ironically, there were more dismissals, resignations on principle and failures to renew contracts than at a regular college with conventional governance.

Rice himself was forced to tender his resignation in summer 1942, shortly after the school had embarked on a self-build programme to create a new 'campus' in close proximity but down the hill from the large building they had rented since 1933.[32] Tensions quickly

---

31 Letter from Miller to Gorman Mattison, 7 November 1942. Miller Faculty File. Temple University, Special Collections Research Centre (SPC) MSS SP 055. Folder K. Black Mountain College Papers, p. 42.
32 Significantly in the light of concerns about community sensitivities toward integration, the original building was called Robert E. Lee Hall. It was

arose within this second phase of Black Mountain College, centring on the provocations of a new faculty member, Eric Bentley, who quickly gathered a group around him, opposed to 'Quakerism' and the older members of faculty around Dreier, and including Anni and Josef Albers and other European emigrés. Paradoxically, the 'radicals' – as Duberman sees them – were conservative in terms of pedagogy, reflecting, perhaps, their intention of moving back into mainstream education.

During Miller's tenure at Black Mountain College there were, at its largest, 26 instructors and 75 students. Miller also served as a registrar, overseeing student admissions. His contract underwent renewal on an annual and then semester basis, reflecting the financial difficulties of the college. The conditions of his employment were modest, encompassing room and board for Miller and his wife, minimal compensation and a monthly cash stipend of $50. His responsibilities extended beyond the classroom, as is evident in the contract confirmation of 1945, which stipulated, 'As part of your duties, you will give extension courses and lectures in western North Carolina, and on our own campus will give a weekly news summary and commentary.'[33] The latter summary and commentary was provided more widely in the form of a radio programme. Significantly, western North Carolina brought Miller close to the state border with Tennessee and the old stamping grounds of his PhD. Fisk University, too, was just 350 miles west of Ashville.

Black Mountain College did not admit Black students, in deference to the sensibilities of the local community. This was something which chafed with Miller and something for which he advocated, albeit with caution. In his inaugural address to the college community, he argued, 'Speaking sociologically, it is inevitable that we white races are going to have to learn to live in equality

---

owned by the Blue Ridge Assembly of the Protestant Church, which had only used it for summer meetings and was willing to rent it out for a low fee in order to retain access in the summers.

33 Letter from W. R. Wunch to Miller, 17 April 1945. Miller–Dreier Correspondence. Temple University, Special Collections Research Centre (SPC) MSS SP 055. Folder K. Black Mountain College Papers, p. 18.

with the colored races.'[34] His courses encompassed an introduction to the scientific study of society and a more advanced study of the sociological makeup of America, and later additions such as Social Problems, American Minorities and World Minorities. His wider public engagement continued. In correspondence with Dreier, Miller detailed his extensive public engagements and his aptitude in navigating the demands of what was termed 'the accelerated program'. He wrote, 'I am doing a good deal of speaking, having spoken at the Lions Club both in Hendersonville and Asheville, as the representative of the Black Mountain Club and I am going to speak at Mars Hill College this week on Thursday. I have spoken many times at the Moore General Hospital. Also I am especially invited to the City Hall tonight in connection with the hearing in the matter of the highway.'[35]

George Zabriskie, Miller's colleague from Black Mountain, later reminisced that Miller was an ardent proponent of what is now known as civil rights, but a cloud hangs over his role at Black Mountain, one that we will not be able to dispel until a later chapter, when we will be able to consider how it intersects with circumstances at Fisk University. In 1942, Eric Bentley and others advocated for the immediate admission of Black students and that possible community tensions should be confronted head-on. Miller took the side of the Faculty Board to err on the side of caution while advocating measures to address the underlying failure of integration. As with his earlier role at Fisk, Miller was cast again in the role of diplomat. The circumstances were equally fraught, as we shall see, albeit on a smaller scale. The fallout from the episode was dramatic, with Bentley and others resigning in September 1944. The College then entered its third phase (Duberman, 1972; Díaz, 2014), with Miller continuing for a further two years until September 1947 (the College would finally close in 1956). Duberman's evaluation of Miller's role is dismissive, 'a retired historian who had himself

---

34 *Black Mountain College Bulletin* 1(2), 1943: 4.
35 Letter from Miller to Dreier, 6 May 1946. Miller–Dreier Correspondence. Temple University, Special Collections Research Centre (SPC) MSS SP 055. Folder K. Black Mountain College Papers, p. 1.

worked many years for egalitarian causes but now, in his seventies, and in the Black Mountain context, was viewed as a conservative' (1972: 180).[36]

Conclusion

Miller's educational activities with students or wider publics were diverse, taking him to a multitude of locations and platforms aligned with his interests. Whether he was at Camp Sherman, where he delivered talks to soldiers as a pacifist, instilling in them a sense of purpose against oppression, or at the Philadelphia Hall, where he contributed to the dissolution of the Austrian empire, or delivering his speech in Bombay in which he addressed the application of religion to practical problem-solving, or during his tenure at the refugee seminar, where he, again, sought to uncover the genuine spirit of Americanisation, Miller consistently viewed his role as primarily educational, aimed at finding practical solutions when groups, nations, races or classes confronted problems.

In his journey, Miller crafted a pragmatist pedagogical approach that placed a premium on contextual comprehension and active engagement surrounding themes of freedom and democracy, in opposition to domination and ideas of superiority. Education, in his view, served as a method for advancing social progress and reform. His approach emphasised the importance of dialogue and interaction with diverse perspectives and audiences. This fostered self-reflection and the internalisation of democratic values.

Broadly, Miller's pragmatist pedagogy diverged from mainstream professional positions in sociology. At its core, the emphasis on the education of judgement took precedence over prioritising research practices. His commitment to exploring real-world contexts,

---

36 Duberman does not discuss the Refugee Scholars seminar that Miller brought to Black Mountain College, but, as we have seen, he was generally dismissive of the Quaker influence at the college and would have put Miller in that bracket, at the same time as he acknowledges that the 'radical' faction was conservative on matters of curriculum and pedagogy and critical of the experimental methods of the college (see Ates, 2022).

embracing cultural diversity and advocating for citizenship reflected his belief in guiding students towards active engagement with the problems of the 'great society'. In his pursuit of this goal, Miller balanced his academic and public uses of sociology with a reflective consciousness and integrity.

3

Race relations and immigration

In Chapter 1, we discussed Thomas Fallace's (2011) characterisation of approaches to race within the mainstream (White) US academy at the start of the twentieth century. Our purpose there was to identify the distinctiveness of Herbert Adolphus Miller's position on race relations in order to establish his significance as a sociologist and in justification of a book-length treatment of his life and writings. Fallace's discussion was directed at the very milieu in which Miller participated, that of pragmatist philosophy and progressive politics, especially the work of John Dewey. It was not until the 1920s, he argues, that Dewey came to adopt a position of racial equality, while leading figures in progressive politics – perhaps most notably, John R. Commons (1908) in his book on race and immigration – were explicitly racist.

As we saw, Fallace identifies three positions. Social biologists – among them Miller's teacher at Dartmouth, David Collin Wells – adopted a eugenic position, in which supposedly distinct racial groups were rendered in a hierarchy based on personality disposition and intelligence, with White, north European-descended populations at the apex. Most White sociologists in the US, and elsewhere, at the turn of the twentieth century adhered to this position. A more moderate view was that observed differences among groups were a consequence of differences in cultural development, rather than inherited traits. This involved the construction of a hierarchy of cultures associated with civilisational traits, which also involved representation of the superiority of 'Western' culture over others. Pragmatist sociologists and philosophers were distributed across both positions, with Dewey initially aligned with the second.

As we have suggested, this second position was the one most commonly found within the emerging Chicago school of sociology and was promoted by W. I. Thomas in his *Source Book for Social Origins* (1909). The first of the approaches was associated with vehement opposition to 'race mixing' in order to maintain the 'racial stock' of the nation, and also to restrict the immigration of supposedly inferior races. The second of the views identified possible problems of immigration from 'backward' cultures, but carried the possibility that individuals could become 'encultured' by assimilation with the dominant culture. Sometimes the two approaches were combined in the figure of the 'mulatto', or mixed-race individual, which became significant within Chicago sociology, for example in the arguments of Edward Reuter (1918). Here, the frequently forced circumstances of race mixing were elided and the emphasis was on the influence of the traits associated with the 'superior' race in improving the stock of the 'lower' race.

We are not arguing that the positions of Robert E. Park, Thomas and other members of the Chicago circle were 'racist' (Kivisto, 2017; Athens, 2020). They were 'progressive' when compared with the eugenic position that was otherwise widely held in both public and academic circles, including among those associated with the wider progressive movement in politics. Miller's position *may be more aligned with current sensibilities in sociology*, but our argument does not depend on 'retro-fitting' him to it. As Julian Go (2020) has argued, sociology across the period – whether in the US or Europe (see also Bhambra and Holmwood, 2021) – was organised through an 'imperial episteme', which operated to exclude those who were critical of empire and its systems of domination. However, those voices did exist, including within the White academy.

We suggested in the last chapter that Miller's association with Fisk University and the Black experience in the South was both longstanding and formative in the development of his sociological views on race and immigration. From his earliest writings he was an advocate of the third position identified by Fallace which the latter associates with W. E. B. Du Bois and the anthropologist Franz Boas. This was a 'multicultural and pluralistic view of race [which] expressed full cultural and biological equality among the races' (Fallace, 2011: 105). As we shall see, Miller's arguments for cultural pluralism and equality were unequivocal and developed across his career. They were aligned with the position also being developed by Du Bois and other advocates of the 'new Negro' (Locke, 1925; Baldwin, 2003).

Around the time of his dismissal from Ohio State University in 1931–1932 and believing it to be a consequence, in part, of lobbying by the local chapter of the Ku Klux Klan, Miller (1931a) wrote about his views on race for the magazine of the NAACP, *The Crisis*. He was not given to public complaint, least of all about his own dismissal, but this article was something of a *cri de coeur*. He declared his commitment to race mixing, not as a means of improving a racial stock, but as an index to the decline of a prejudice that continued to blight the lives of fellow Americans. In this chapter, we will set out the early development of Miller's views on race relations and immigration which he came to associate with problems of empire.

Race and eugenics

Miller went from Fisk to Harvard in 1902 to study for a PhD in the psychology department. Apart from its prestige as an institution and the significant status of William James, with whom he studied, this was not otherwise a propitious choice for Miller. It was not only that eugenics was strongly represented, but, as Adam Cohen has argued, 'Harvard was more central to American eugenics than any other university. Harvard has, with some justification, been called the "brain trust" of twentieth-century eugenics' (2016a: n.p.). This was so across the university and in its highest echelons. President Charles Eliot (in office from 1869 to 1909) was an advocate of racial purity and was vice-president of the First International Eugenics Congress, which met in London in 1912. He also helped organise the First National Conference on Race Betterment in Michigan in 1914.

Strong advocacy of eugenics by significant members of the professoriate continued well into the 1920s, directed towards immigration policy and against racial mixing, as well as advocacy of the sterilisation of the 'feeble-minded' (Hansen and King,

2013; Cohen, 2016b). These views were entrenched within the university, including in the psychology department. Robert W. Yerkes, for example, developed IQ tests, including one administered in 1917 – the 'Army Alpha and Beta Test' – to one and three quarter million servicemen. The findings were published in 1921 and purported to show that 40 per cent were 'feeble-minded' with the highest proportion of those so designated being among Black servicemen.[1] The results were absurd, albeit widely cited and accepted, despite the efforts of Walter Lippmann to debunk them in a series of seven articles on 'the mental age of Americans' in the *New Republic* in October and November 1922. Yerkes was a 'rising star' in the psychology department during the period of Miller's studies. He had completed his PhD on intelligence testing and was appointed as an 'instructor' in the year that Miller joined.

Miller's thesis was on the topic of 'The race problem and psychophysics'. His PhD was awarded in 1905. He was encouraged by William James to devise an intelligence test as part of his dissertation research. As might be expected, when operating in a context where eugenics was endorsed by more senior faculty as being scientific, Miller was careful to pay obeisance to its potential, at the same time as arguing that it had been misused. In particular, he was concerned that it had been used to propose that differences among (racial) groups are indications of inherent capacity rather than environmental circumstance. Tests, he believed, had hitherto been administered to groups in very different circumstances, with the unwarranted conclusion that discovered differences expressed within them were indications of inherent racial differences rather than differences in circumstances.

The test that Miller developed was along a number of dimensions.[2] It was administered to three 'racial' groups – African

---

1 The results were published in 1921, when Yerkes asserted that while the 'average white mental age' was 13.08 years, the 'average mental age for negroes' was 10.41 years and almost 89 per cent of all Blacks who took the test were classified as 'moronic' (Galloway, 1994: 3).
2 The tests were: '(1) quickness and accuracy of perception; (2) disconnected memory, both auditory and visual, as tested by figures and letters exposed

Americans, Native Americans and White Americans – all in similar circumstances of disadvantage. The White Americans included Highlanders from Kentucky and Tennessee as well as other rural locations. On this basis, Miller found no differences among the groups and the sexes. In particular, he argued that 'race problems develop from the lack of common ideals and not from psychophysical differences. The cause of the difference in ideals is the accidental existence of external differences which stand for the symbols of the sameness of kind' (Miller, 1905: 99).[3] An article derived from the thesis was published in 1906 in *Bibliotheca Sacra*, the oldest theological journal published in the US by the Dallas Theological Seminary. Du Bois included Miller's article in the section on Negro Health and Physique as part of Atlanta University's social studies and also as a source for the resolutions of the eleventh Atlanta conference for the study of the Negro problems (Du Bois 1906). Franz Boas had been invited to provide the commencement address at the conference (Liss, 1998).

It is in the conclusion to the *Bibliotheca Sacra* article that Miller first made the argument that it is necessary to separate what is 'universal' and 'essential' from what is 'accidental'. Science is concerned to establish the former, and it enables the identification of what is 'accidental' as a possible focus of action. Racial differences fall into the latter category and are a product, for Miller, of the operation of prejudice and the absence of mixing. He wrote, 'the purpose of education and social progress is to make the accidental give way to the essential, and to let each individual stand for his [*sic*] true worth to society; then the problems as they now confront us will cease to exist' (Miller, 1906: 363).

>   and read; (3) logical memory, tested by reproducing a story; (4) rational instinct, as shown in the immediate detection of fallacies; (5) suggestibility, as shown by the judgment of the size of equal circles on which there were numbers of different denominations; and, finally, (6) color preference' (Miller, 1905: 50). For a discussion of the wider interests of psycho-physics in taste and aesthetics, see Fretwell (2020).
> 3 This may be contrasted with Howard Odum (1913), who purported to discover very significant differences between White and Black children in New Jersey and Philadelphia, findings which reinforced local policies of school segregation into the 1950s.

In effect, Miller proceeded 'dialectically' to show that whereas eugenics encouraged social control and the representation of social problems as deriving from 'poor stock', a proper scientific analysis demonstrated that the solution would lie in social reform, education and inclusion. It is a theme continued in later articles (Miller, 1914b, 1927), where he set out the scientific significance of eugenics at the same time as pivoting to indicate that its real value was pointing to the role of 'environment' in the determination of social problems and, therefore, to the role of education and social reform in changing environments.

In his doctoral thesis on theories of stratification in US sociology, Roscoe Hinkle (1952) identifies the compelling force of eugenics throughout the 1920s deriving from Yerkes's army IQ tests.[4] He has a brief discussion of Miller, but he fails to notice that a powerful and effective critique had been mounted by him a decade before the army tests had been administered. In a later reflection, Miller described the circumstances in which he used the tests:

> Twenty-five years ago, at the suggestion and with the help of Dr. R. M. Yerkes, who later was largely responsible for the Army Tests, I devised in the Harvard psychological laboratory a series of tests, and, with money secured by William James, I made a trip South, giving the tests to hundreds of Negroes, mountain whites, and the Indians at Hampton and Carlisle. Although I won the Bowdoin Prize and wrote a doctor's dissertation from the material, its one essential value to me was to convince me that, as a method of group classification, it was utterly useless. All the developments in recent years have not dissuaded me from this opinion. They have their value, but it is not in this field, and yet on the basis of the Army Tests, Professor McDougall undertook to prove that America is not safe for democracy, and many other people having lost their Biblical fundamentalism have substituted intelligence tests as a new religion. (Miller, 1931b: 345)[5]

---

4 Ironically, Hinkle's thesis was submitted while he was at Miller's former department at Ohio State University.
5 William McDougall was an English professor of psychology who took up a position at Harvard in 1920 and then at Duke in 1927. He published the eugenic tract, *Is America Safe for Democracy?*, to which Miller refers in 1931 (Pattie, 1939). Miller's reference to fundamentalism is a significant theme in his psychology of domination, as we shall discuss later.

The Cleveland Survey

After the completion of his thesis, Miller took up an appointment at Olivet College in 1905, a small liberal arts college in Lansing, Michigan and a former scion of Oberlin College. Here he devoted himself to his pedagogic practice in pragmatist sociology outlined in the previous chapter, before an appointment to Oberlin in 1914 where he became involved in the newly proposed Cleveland survey. This was initially planned to be similar to the Pittsburgh survey which had begun in 1907 (Cohen, 1991). The latter was directed by the 'social entrepreneur' Paul Kellogg, who had also become editor of the magazine, *Charities and the Commons*, in which the surveys were published in a series of 35 articles between January and March 1909, and subsequently in other books and articles up to 1914 (Chambers, 1971; Cohen, 1991).[6] The publications in *Charities and the Commons* became the occasion for a change of its name in 1909 to *The Survey*. It would become an important vehicle for the publication of Miller's work under the auspices of the later Carnegie project on 'Methods of Americanization' begun in 1918 and for social research and the promotion of social reform more generally through into the early 1950s.

The Pittsburgh survey is widely seen as an important moment in the development of social research, both as a culmination of an activity that had begun with Du Bois's *Philadelphia Negro* (1899) and as a turning point. Martin Bulmer, for example, argues that it marked the moment when sociology in the academy turned away from research embedded in reformist aspirations to become more rooted in 'professionalism' and that it was 'orthogonal to academic sociology, rather than a linear ancestor' (Bulmer, 1996: 15). On this understanding, it would seem that Miller hitched his career to a wagon that was on a different path even before he became part of the very Carnegie research project that would provide a different

---

6 Kellogg's very considerable flair probably contributed to the idea of the *Survey* magazine being more about 'publicity' (in the best and pragmatist sense of that word) rather than 'science', notwithstanding the research basis of its articles (Chambers, 1971).

trajectory for Park and Thomas, who were involved alongside him. Yet, as Mary Furner (2000: 407) suggests, it was their political interests (those of class, gender and race), not *professionalism*, that frequently separated out 'survey' reformers from other researchers. And, of course, by that token, academic sociology was not without its own 'politics', even if it was suppressed. Nor could it exclusively claim the mantle of scientific objectivity, as we shall show in the example of Miller.

Furner's conclusion is severe, but apt, that 'Bulmer's account raises important issues by setting Chicago-school sociology up as the paradigm for "objective" social science. Beyond the static quality of this analysis, there is its lack of concern with the substance of that particular sociology, which in this reviewer's eyes must be viewed as ideological in the extreme, as it slotted Chicago's diverse immigrant cultures (and rural migrants everywhere, and in its later applications all Third World people living in "traditional cultures") into a cultural continuum stretching from initial "disorganization" to ultimate (except for American blacks) assimilation' (Furner, 2000: 407–408).[7] It is precisely the significance of Miller, we suggest, that he disrupts this Chicago narrative and did so though the different conclusions he reached both about Black Americans and the immigrant population of Cleveland.

In the last chapter, we saw that the more general process of 'professionalism' in education undermined the radical political ambitions of the Black colleges. In part, the survey movement was a response to the professionalisation of the management of municipal

---

7 Furner's conclusion mirrors that of Stanley Coben (1975: 608), who writes of the 'aura of despair' that hung over Chicago sociology: 'The chief theme of studies conducted at the University of Chicago's Department of Sociology the first real school of sociology became the social disorganization rampant in the city. Rapid change of many kinds, the Chicago sociologists discovered, weakened traditional social controls, broke down feelings of community and group solidarity, and fragmented society. Evidence of social disintegration crime, divorce, mental illness, social deviancy, and race and ethnic conflict were subjected to intensive investigation. Poverty, graphically described in the monographs emanating from this research, accompanied the fragmentation as either cause or effect within ethnic and racial ghettos, and among individuals described by the sociologists as "marginal".'

affairs. This is something that George Herbert Mead had noted in his 1899 essay on the working hypothesis in social reform. The expansion of public utilities and municipal ownership had changed the character of local government, which 'has become a business concern, which enters into the business world on a basis that is determined by the latter' (Mead, 1899: 367). The survey movement was intended as a means of informing publics and creating new forms of publicity to counter the incorporation of local government into business-dominated models of efficiency.

In January 1914, Fred Goff, a philanthropic entrepreneur, set up the Cleveland Foundation as a public trust institution with an evident aspiration to avoid the vulnerabilities of big private philanthropic organisations and their corporate trustee structure. The risks of 'capture' were serious. Only a year after the official establishment of the foundation, Goff had to go to New York to defend its position at hearings conducted by the Federal Industrial Relations Committee in the aftermath of the Ludlow Massacre on the Colorado coalfields.[8] All charitable foundations had come under suspicion on the grounds that they might, as reported in the *New York Times*, represent an effort to 'perpetuate the present position of predatory wealth through the corruption of the sources of public information'.[9] The coal-mining company involved in the Ludlow Massacre was owned by the Rockefeller family, and this cast suspicion on the Rockefeller Foundation and its interest in funding studies on labour unrest. Goff's community-based institutional model provided an opportunity to fend off such allegations and held up a different understanding of research, civic debate and reform, one aligned with the aspirations of pragmatism and distinct from the orientation to business efficiency that Mead had warned against.

At the outset, Goff envisioned an all-encompassing municipal survey similar to that for Pittsburgh. The Cleveland Foundation hired Allen T. Burns as the paid director of a five-member Survey Committee. Burns was himself a significant figure. He was licensed

---

8 This was a mass killing of miners and their families by the state national guard and company militia on 20 April 1914 during protracted strikes on the Colorado coalfields that took place across 1913–1914.
9 'To Investigate all Foundations', *New York Times*, 17 December 1914, p. 6.

as a Baptist minister, but turned towards social action and involvement in the settlement movement at Chicago Commons, from where he was appointed first Dean of the Chicago School of Civics and Philanthropy between 1907 and 1909.[10] The School had been established under a different guise in 1903–1904 to teach the first courses in social work associated with the University of Chicago. The relationship was fraught and the university withdrew support in 1905, after which it continued under the auspices of the Chicago Commons settlement house. It was finally incorporated into the university in 1920, with the Chicago sociologists maintaining their distance. Burns left the University of Chicago in 1909 to become secretary of the Pittsburgh Civic Commission, with administrative responsibility for the Pittsburgh survey conducted by Kellogg (Cohen, 1991). He then moved to the Cleveland Foundation in 1914 as Director of Surveys, with the intention of setting up surveys similar to those of Pittsburgh (Tittle, 1992). However, the Committee eventually put a halt to Goff's original extensive plan and opted for 'investigating one topic of societal interest at a time' (Tittle, 1992: 48). At the same time, the orientation to 'business efficiency' came to dominate over Goff's initial aspirations (Miggins, 2014).

The Committee identified three major topics: public education, recreation and the administration of justice. A number of surveys were devoted to each topic. High drop-out rates from schools called for immediate action in educational matters. Goff and Burns hired the director of the Russell Sage Foundation's division of education, Leonard Ayres, a statistician who had made a name for himself as a proficient organiser of large-scale studies. The Cleveland school surveys were, by far, the largest ever made of a public school system at that time. Twenty-four surveys and a summary were published, with Miller appointed to conduct one on the problems of immigrant children within the school system. Ayres's approach epitomised a notion of reform through research in a bid to pin down principal factors that 'determine the quality of results and efficiency of work of a school system' (Ayres, 1917: 49).

---

10 Information about the life and career of Burns is derived from a privately published memorial, Friends and Relatives of Allen T. Burns (1954).

In consequence, his ideas of school reform rested on measurable factors and turned the spotlight on the criterion of 'efficiency' in educational matters.

The Survey Committee, dominated by businessmen, initiated a number of public debates on the recommendations for action. The debates voiced recurrent criticism that the business orientation was forcing out the educational work and excessively dominated the school system. In a response, Ayres (1917: 57) maintained that 'the fact remains that the business management is so markedly efficient that it constitutes one of the real and important assets of the educational situation'. Ultimately, 'the search for the one best system' (Miggins, 1986) concluded that the way to overcome the educational troubles would be through the reinforcement of business models that would 'promote efficiency' and 'facilitate uniformity'.

The tension between 'social survey activism' and established local interests, and the victory of the latter is something also described for Pittsburgh by Stephen Turner (1996). The victory of the same interests in Cleveland would be exemplified by Ayres's large-scale reorganisation of the public-school system in the name of efficiency on the basis of the surveys. It left Kellogg's magazine, *The Survey*, as the beacon for those interested in aligning social research and active social reform, as the philanthropic foundations withdrew to the funding of academically oriented social research associated with departments like that of Chicago sociology.

The school and the immigrant

Ayres's summary report made no reference to Miller's contribution, *The School and the Immigrant* (1916). Miller saw educational problems as reflecting wider social pathologies related to the issues of immigration. In the Cleveland area, the rapid demographic change and large concentrations of urban immigrants had palpable effects on racial, gender and social class divisions. On Miller's understanding, efficiency measures represented a problematic response as they stood in the way of reforms based on an understanding of the needs of marginalised communities.

The issue for Miller was not how to secure integration and uniformity, but how to use the cultural heritage of immigrant groups to facilitate their participation and achievement within the school system. His contribution demonstrated high drop-out rates from 'steamer classes' (designed to teach English to recently arrived children and adults), as well as underachievement in schools. He found the failure of the adult English classes puzzling because such classes had proven successful in recently incorporated American territories – for example, in the Philippines and Port Rico (*sic*) (Miller, 1916: 76). The problem was a failure of action and the absence of a proper curriculum and training for the teachers (Miller, 1916: 83–84).[11] But, if Cleveland had the highest proportion of non-English speakers compared with other large cities (31 per cent against 23 per cent in New York, for example – Miller, 1916: 22), this was not an argument directed only at language. It was also an argument to facilitate naturalisation and participation in political life.

As we have seen, Miller's dictum (in both research and in teaching) taken from pragmatism was the importance of talking to others and understanding their perspective. The dominant approach to Americanisation had not allowed for different cultural identities and only reinforced 'segregation' by pathologising what were, for Miller, 'normal tendencies'. He maintained that 'to blame immigrants for their own segregation is unjust' (Miller, 1916: 56). Families did not wish their children to 'grow away' from them, and it was precisely when they did that a problem of 'disorganization' arose.

Thus, Miller wrote, 'as a matter of fact, we find within these various colonies a neighbourliness and social organization sadly lacking in much of our modern society. A teacher should know something of the social life to be found within these various groups, both in order that she may understand her pupils better and that she may be able to use these social forces to the advantage of the school and the community' (Miller, 1916: 56). Instead of invoking patriotic

---

11 It was exacerbated by the fact that evening classes for adults were funded on the basis of enrolment, rather than attendance – by the end of a term only about one-fifth of the enrolled class would be in attendance (Miller, 1916: 98–100).

sentiments for public schools, he argued that, 'in order to understand the social and educational problems of the different foreign groups, it is necessary to study their origin and history' (Miller, 1916: 54). Many of the immigrants, Miller argued, 'come from subject races and they come here primarily for freedom' (Miller, 1916: 55–56).

In addition, he recommended the teaching of home languages and the use of curriculum material from home cultures, something that would be developed within the Cleveland Library system. This would mitigate the poor achievements of foreign-language-speaking children in schools and their high drop-out rate. It was also important because many of the immigrant groups came from countries where attempts had been made to impose another language upon them (Miller, 1916: 42). Paradoxically, for Miller, the teaching of home languages and cultures would facilitate 'Americanization', once the latter was properly understood and associated with the 'spirit of freedom' that had motivated migration. He also recommended that public schools could be used out of hours by the different national groups to encourage both self-expression and identification with the school system.

The aspiration to change the Cleveland educational system – according to Miller, *it was it that was disorganised*, not the immigrant communities – had a practical element that aligned him with library reformers and public-school educators who had an understanding of the special needs of the 'new' immigrants. These were often women steeped in the social-reform traditions of the settlement movement. According to Plummer A. Jones, 'their mission was not to instil American ideas and ideals into the immigrants but to teach immigrants to read and speak the English language and to prepare them for the required citizenship exam, an approach that was pragmatic rather than political' (Jones, 2013: 251). A significant figure in library activism, Eleanor Ledbetter, who was a member of the Cleveland Americanization Committee, and later took part in the Carnegie research on Americanisation, referred to Miller as 'probably the best informed man in the country regarding immigrant backgrounds' (Jones, 2013: 259). She looked to him as a mentor for a different approach to Americanisation.

The tensions between business efficiency and progressive reform came to a head in Cleveland when Burns was forced to resign in 1917 after political opposition to another report that had seemed to uncover the existence of a new red-light district and which became part of a mayoral electoral battle (Tittle, 1992: 78). Burns undertook an evaluation of some settlement houses that were supported by the Carnegie Trust before he was asked to administer a new Americanisation studies programme under its auspices, to which he would appoint Miller in 1918. Clearly, Burns valued Miller's approach and contribution to the Cleveland school survey, yet his contribution otherwise has been sidelined. There are only sporadic references to it in the histories of educational reforms in America. His colleague in the Carnegie Americanization project, Frank Thompson, made only one brief mention in his report on *Schooling of the Immigrant*, referring to it simply as being 'mainly critical' (Thompson, 1920: 54). Thompson grounded his own study in the 'official' attitude towards education: 'it is to our credit that in our schools we have never made invidious comparisons with respect to the children of the immigrant; we have received them on a basis of equality and made them feel that there were no distinctions on account of accidents of birth and economic condition' (Thompson, 1920: 73). Miller had provided extensive evidence to the contrary in Cleveland. He was responsible for research on 'immigrant contributions' and yet there would seem to be no interaction between him and Thompson.[12] This indicates, perhaps, that the divisions that had beset the Cleveland studies would also become evident within the Carnegie project.

Conclusion

In the next chapter, we will discuss Miller's role in the Carnegie project, the nature of the work he undertook as part of it, and how

---

12 Grace Abbott, for example, who would also be appointed to the project to undertake a study of the immigrant and the courts (she later had to withdraw because of ill health), had earlier affirmed Miller's arguments in her study, *The Immigrant and the Community*: 'In our zeal to teach patriotism, we are often teaching disrespect for the history and tradition that the ancestors of the immigrant parent had their part in making ... this often means disrespect for the parent himself' (Abbott, 1917: 226).

he came to leave midway through. As we have seen in this chapter, Miller stood to the side of mainstream positions in sociology. His contributions were largely neglected, but where they were remarked, they were also frequently misrepresented. For example, in an article published in 1943, C. Wright Mills criticised a prevailing professional ideology of 'social pathologists' in which Miller is mentioned in three footnotes (albeit in one, it is to the editor of the series in which Miller's book on *Races, Nations and Classes* (1924) was published). Social pathologists, according to Mills, operate from a perspective of 'social disorganization'. As we have argued, this is a position repudiated by Miller, although, as we shall see in the next chapter, it is put forward by Thomas in his treatment of the 'two-step' process of disorganisation followed by assimilation which he associates with the migrant processes. Mills also argued that the social pathologists failed to address large social structures, when, as we shall see, Miller patently was concerned with the structures of domination associated with race, class and nation, a position he sets out in the light of his experiences associated with the Carnegie project, to which we now turn.

4

Americanisation, assimilation or pluralism?

The Carnegie Corporation research project on Methods of Americanization looks at first sight to be the highpoint of Herbert Adolphus Miller's sociological career. He was appointed to head one of its research divisions and was identified, together with Robert E. Park, as author of one of its ten reports, *Old World Traits Transplanted* (1921). It would emerge that he left halfway through the period devoted to the field research, which was completed by William I. Thomas. This was something known within Chicago sociology circles, but not formally acknowledged until much later and the publication of a selection of Thomas's writings by Volkart (1951). The reasons for Miller leaving the project and how they bore upon the research he had already undertaken, however, have not been addressed.

The overall Carnegie project was itself ill-fated. It was set up in a highly-charged atmosphere shortly after the US had entered the First World War in April 1917. As we have already seen, there were concerns about the mental and moral 'fitness' of troops that had given rise to Yerkes's Army Alpha IQ testing, but there had also been a fervid debate about immigration that preceded it. This was associated with the Dillingham Commission in 1911, which had concluded that 'new' immigration from southern and eastern Europe represented a threat to the nation (King, 2000). The war on the Western Front ended in November 1918, before the planned completion of the research and before the publication of the bulk of the studies, which occurred in 1921 when circumstances were very different.

The project was initially mooted with Allen T. Burns in November 1917 and approved by the Board to begin the process of recruitment of research staff in January 1918. Burns divided it up into ten themes, or Divisions, each with a Division Head who were all appointed by March 1918. The intention was for the field research to run for 18 months, with reports delivered by December 1919. Miller was given responsibility for a report on Immigrant Contributions (later to be renamed Immigrant Heritages), with Park made responsible for the Division on the Immigrant Press and Theatre (Park, 1922).[1]

A final summary report by Burns, as Director of the Project, was planned but not published, although he gave several talks, including one on 'American Americanization' (Burns, 1920). Here he argued for policies different from those associated with the forced 'Germanification' of minority populations in those parts of Europe subject to German domination, which he likened to some existing approaches to Americanisation. He also promoted positive examples of the self-organisation of immigrant communities in America (there was a separate Division on Neighborhood Agencies and Organizations under John Daniels).[2] The invitation for the talk from the Education Department of the Municipal Court in New York cites his role as Director of the Carnegie Corporation's Americanization project, but Burns, himself, makes no mention of any of its studies.

The problem, as far as one is represented within the files of the Carnegie Corporation, was that there were delays involving four of the reports, with one of them – William M. Leiserson's report on Industry and the Immigrant – not cleared for publication by a small group of reviewers until May 1923.[3] Most of the reports had been delivered by their due date of December 1919, with

1 Americanization Studies, 1918–1945. Carnegie Corporation of New York Records. Rare Book and Manuscript Library. Columbia University Libraries. [Series III: Grants, 1911–1994, Subseries III.A., Box 41, Folder 4–6.]
2 A shortened version was published under a different title in the *Annals of the American Academy of Political and Social Science* (Burns, 1921).
3 The review committee – Talcott Williams, Raymond B. Fosdick and Dr Edwin F. Gay – evidently regarded some of the studies too partisan. Leiserson was a progressive economist who would go on to be an adviser to Franklin D. Roosevelt.

the remainder delivered by April 1921. But the review process and publisher delays held up the completion of the series. The contract with the publisher, Harper & Brothers, had also been written on terms problematic to the Corporation. It placed too much reliance on a marketing strategy that favoured a staged release of titles to maintain public interest, at the same time as public opinion was shifting. Burns was not paid by the Carnegie Corporation after April 1921 and yet was responsible for supervising the remaining volumes to publication, alongside his responsibilities in his new field of work. He was unable to write his summary until the series would be complete and was anxious to do so.[4] He was working on it up until January 1924 when he was told that the series would be closed without his summary volume, despite it having been advertised in all the series notifications. In hindsight, then, it was not just Miller whose reputation faded; that seems also to be the fate of the Carnegie project itself, and Burns too.[5]

4 The Carnegie Corporation Archive on the Americanization project indicates that reviewers thought that some of the books in the series were of 'uncertain quality', which delayed the publication of the set. Burns indicated that he had a summary report available to publish in January 1924, but by then the Corporation was in discussion with the publishers about ceasing publication.
5 Burns left the employment of the Corporation. His career then turned almost exclusively towards work for charitable bodies. After a short interlude as Chair of the Labour Adjustment Board of the Rochester, NY clothing industry, he was appointed in 1922 as executive director of the National Information Bureau, advising on charitable appeals, as part of which he went to Russia (together with Graham Taylor) as part of a three-person Commission on Russian Relief. He held this position in combination with the American Association for Community Organizations, which was linked with the Bureau. In 1926 he became executive secretary of the successor and independent body, the Community Chests and Councils of America, Inc., in 1926 and continued with that organisation until his retirement in 1942. See Friends and Relatives of Allen T. Burns (1954).

Restoring Thomas

We suggest that there is something more to the fate of the Carnegie project than the story of a project that went wrong and whose overall contribution was less than the sum of its parts. This was especially so where two of its parts – the contributions of Park and Thomas – would come to be incorporated into the narrative of Chicago sociology. Miller's fate is emblematic of a different story, one where public policy was increasingly dominated by eugenic concerns and more robust forms of assimilation that Burns dubbed as 'Germanification' and where he was left outside as others adapted to these new norms.

The Carnegie Americanization studies are not widely remarked in the secondary literature on US immigration policy, which is much more concerned with the xenophobic Dillingham Commission and its 42-volume report published in 1911 (King, 2000; Mirel, 2010). The major study of Americanisation as a public policy by George Hartmann (1948) has just two very brief mentions of it. This is so notwithstanding that the author identifies two moments of intense political concern; specifically, the last decades of the nineteenth century leading up to the Dillingham Commission and 1915–1916, when war in Europe had accelerated the pressures to inculcate patriotism.[6] The Dillingham Commission had recommended stringent measures for controlling against poor 'stock', promoting eugenic arguments about 'unfit races' and arguing for a rigorous assimilation to 'American values'. These were actions which were already in train in many cities and were gathered under the proselytising efforts of the North American Civic League for Immigrants. Different cities had 'Americanization Committees' (Hartmann, 1948) and incorporated educators, librarians and social workers under that drive, as

---

6 It is discussed more fully in William C. Smith's *Americans in the Making: The Natural History of the Assimilation of Immigrants* (1939). As might be anticipated from the subtitle, Smith adopts the Chicago school approach in outlining a two-stage process of assimilation and aligns *Old World Traits* with that argument.

we have seen, but not always as willing participants (Jones, 2013). This was 'German Americanization' in action.

An emphasis on assimilation is evident in the title of the Carnegie project – 'The Study of Methods of Americanization or Fusion of Native and Foreign-Born' – albeit that the focus on identifying *appropriate methods* of Americanisation potentially steered away from identifying *social problems* associated with immigration (Lagemann, 1989). At the same time, it gave scope to researchers, like Miller, with a different orientation implicitly to contest the very idea of Americanisation through a critique of the current methods used by the many city committees on Americanisation that had been formed. This is what Miller had done in his discussion of schooling in Cleveland and, presumably, it was the basis of his recruitment by Burns. Yet the Carnegie project appears to have missed its moment. US entry into the First World War in early 1917 was decisive in bringing the war to an end in November 1918, with Allied victory. This was well before the publication of any of the studies, which were delivered into a very different political environment. After the war, public opinion settled into support for what Burns (1920) had called 'German Americanization', rather than the 'American Americanization' he advocated. It had also hardened against a more progressive policy, in part as a consequence of the 'race riots' that occurred in 1919 in a number of cities, including Chicago (Waskow, 1966).[7]

---

7 Charles S. Johnson was jointly responsible for the Chicago Commission on Race Relations' investigation into the Chicago 'race riots' of 1919, which was published as *The Negro in Chicago* in 1922. It was a comprehensive study for which Johnson – then a graduate student in the Chicago sociology department – was responsible for the research. The co-organiser was Graham Romeyn Taylor, son of the founder of the Chicago Commons settlement house and himself actively involved in it and the survey movement. Park is widely credited with guiding Johnson, and Winifred Raushenbush was first employed as an assistant in the writing-up period. The study tends to be identified when discussing the contributions of African American sociologists at Chicago, but left out of the main histories of Chicago sociology of the period, including those of Fred Wacker and Stow Persons focused on race and ethnic relations. For an exception, see Bulmer (1981). Johnson was constrained to support the position of the Chicago Urban League.

It has to be admitted that the Carnegie Project no longer holds much interest, except perhaps for historians of the Chicago school, and, even then, it is superseded in importance by the publication between 1918 and 1920 of the five-volume *Polish Peasant in Europe and America*, by Thomas and Florian Znaniecki, which has come to be regarded as a landmark in US sociology (Abbott and Egloff, 2008). *Old World Traits*, it would seem, is merely a transposition of ideas and methods from the *Polish Peasant* to a broader set of immigrant groups, albeit on a significantly reduced canvas. The identification of Thomas as the major contributing author of *Old World Traits* served to reinforce his standing at the same time as attention was directed towards the *Polish Peasant* study as his principal achievement.

The Carnegie Corporation itself also shifted its direction of effort away from a direct engagement with social and public policy towards funding the professionalisation of social research, following the appointment of a new Director, Frederick Keppel, in 1923 (Lagemann, 1989). Significantly, this involved funding a new Social Science Research Council which had been set up with the involvement of Chicago social scientists in 1923. It was also funded by, and consolidated the activities of other foundations, such as the Rockefeller Foundation and Russell Sage. It became active in promoting appropriate methodologies for social science involving critical appraisals and symposia on exemplary studies, including, in 1939, a volume on *The Polish Peasant* by then Chair of the Chicago Department of Sociology, Herbert Blumer (1939). This rehabilitation of Thomas and his 'reincorporation' into the post-1920 Chicago school continued with an SSRC-funded Committee on Thomas's Contributions to Social Science, which published a volume of his papers on social behaviour and personality (Volkart, 1951), with collateral damage to Miller's reputation.[8]

The Volkart volume published the concluding chapter from *Old World Traits*, alongside which it was announced that the book, 'while published over the names of Park and Miller, was primarily

---

8 The year before, Everett C. Hughes had begun to publish the collected papers of Robert E. Park, with a first volume on *Race and Culture: Essays in the Sociology of Contemporary Man* (Park, 1950).

the work of Thomas' (Volkart, 1951: 259), confirming the claim of Floyd House cited earlier. The date of publication has some significance, albeit unremarked – it was the year Miller died. Volkart referred readers to a confirmatory letter from Burns.[9] It is widely understood that the reason was the sex scandal associated with Thomas's name. Milton Gordon (1975), in his review of a republication of the series of Carnegie studies, devotes much of his review to *Old World Traits*. The repressed attribution of authorship is finally rectified on the title page, but the book itself, he suggests, is only of historical interest. He writes that it was before its time in its opposition to racist ideas, but by the 1970s it was fully in the mainstream, and 'merges imperceptibly with the climate of thought and opinion which produced the civil rights movement of the 1950s, '60s and '70s' (Gordon, 1975: 473).

This judgement is rather sanguine in the context of what Thomas had written in the chapter reproduced in the Volkart volume. This included a description of the 'material value' found in the use of forced labour and temporary migrant labour in America and Germany respectively. Thomas states that we know that 'this attitude has a bad effect both on the aliens and the culture of the group which receives and uses them as mere things. If visitors are disorderly, unsanitary, or ignorant, the group which incorporates them, even temporarily, will not escape the bad effects of this'

---

9 There is no discussion of the episode in the material collected in the Carnegie Corporation archive on the Americanisation project. The exchange of letters takes place in November 1951 when Burgess refers to a 'recent' meeting in St Louis with Burns when he discussed the matter and asks him for an 'authoritative statement' in one sentence for the publication committee, that the book was 'actually written by W. I. Thomas, but for reasons that do not need to be entered into, it appeared under the name of Park and Miller' (Burgess to Burns, 22 November 1949). Burns replies, 'How'll this do. The volume Old World Traits of the Americanization Studies was primarily written by W. I. Thomas though at the time it was considered to have it appear under the authorship of Park and Miller who also worked on the volume. I am very glad that Prof Thomas is to receive credit for his invaluable contribution' (Burns to Burgess, 24 November 1949). Burgess, Ernest. Papers [Box 3, Folder 3], Hanna Holborn Gray Special Collections Research Center, University of Chicago Library.

(Thomas, in Volkart, 1951: 263). Thomas goes on, 'every country has a certain amount of culturally undeveloped material. We have it, for instance, in the Negroes and Indians, the Southern mountaineers, the Mexicans and Spanish-Americans, and the slums. There is a limit, however, to the amount of material of this kind that a country can incorporate without losing the character of its culture' (Thomas, in Volkart, 1951: 263). While Thomas opposed 'quick and complete Americanization', this is far from the commitment to cultural pluralism evinced by Miller (significantly, the 'culturally undeveloped material' includes three of the groups whose equality Miller had espoused in his PhD).

Gordon celebrated the restoration of Thomas as author and described the story as 'fully told' in the new introduction to the reprinted volume, which referred to the scandal that had impacted on Thomas's reputation. However, the scandal had taken place in April 1918 and, seemingly, had not impeded Thomas's involvement in the project until the point of publication some three years later. There is no record of why the decision to remove his name was taken, and those involved in the studies were in place throughout.[10] The story, however, is far from fully told.

Unpicking the story

Winifred Raushenbush, biographer to Park and employed by him in October 1918 as assistant on his Immigrant Press research (and

10 It seems most likely that it was at the behest of the publisher, whose concerns about sales of all the books in the series is recorded throughout the Carnegie Corporation files on the Americanisation project. Certainly, the report was delivered in December 1919 under the name of Thomas, recorded in the minutes of the Conference of the advisory committee, which included Henry S. Pritchett, the President of the Carnegie Corporation. A contract with Harper & Brothers was signed by the Vice-Chairman and Treasurer of the Corporation on 7 June 1920 with the names of Robert E. Park and Herbert A. Miller entered as authors. Americanization Studies, 1918–1945. Carnegie Corporation of New York Records. Rare Book and Manuscript Library. Columbia University Libraries. [Series III: Grants, 1911–1994., Subseries III.A., Box 41, Folder 4–6.]

later as a research assistant preparing the data analysis for the report on the Chicago race riots in the six months prior to its publication in 1921), offers a description of the circumstances, though it is not reliable.[11] She notes (correctly) that Miller withdrew from the project in 1918, citing a notice in the November *American Journal of Sociology* to that effect, and that he had taken up work for the 'League of Central European Nations' (what was more generally known as the Mid-European Union). He had become director of it and would be based in Washington and Pittsburgh. The organisation published its aims at the end of October 1918, though there was considerable activity leading up to that point. What is at issue is how that earlier activity related to the Carnegie study, where Miller was Director of the Division on Immigrant Contributions.

Raushenbush describes Park as taking over from Miller, and that 'he knew there would be difficulties. Miller had employed a large staff, started many projects, and spent a considerable share of his $14,700 budget … [Park] probably would not have taken on the study of immigrant heritages if it had not been possible for him to employ his friend William I. Thomas, then living in New York to assist him' (Raushenbush, 1979: 88). Although Thomas's appointment seemingly happened in close proximity to the scandal, there is significant evidence that it was not directly the occasion of it. The newspaper story of Thomas's arrest was on 12 April and he resigned from the university on 16 April. Abbott and Egloff (2008: 221) cite correspondence between Thomas and Mrs Ethel Sturges Dummer, who had funded the *Polish Peasant* study, dated 9 April, a few days before the incident, describing his appointment to the Carnegie project.[12] Although Abbott and Egloff do not speculate on the

---

11 See, for example, Chapoulie (2020: 374–375, n. 148). Raushenbush wrote her account of Park in later life, shortly before she died. In fact, she had been taught by Miller at Oberlin and, on her graduation in 1916, he had recommended her for a teaching position at a historically Black college (most probably, Wilberforce, with which he also had a connection), which her father had not wanted her to take up. See Gross (2008: 68, n. 18).
12 Abbott and Egloff (2008: 221) comment, 'Thomas's work for the Carnegie Foundation antedated the episode and thus was not cooked up by his friends to give him work, as has been sometimes assumed.' Letter from

reasons for Thomas's appointment, or what exactly it was to which he had been appointed, they do not seem to involve Miller's role. In fact, the records of the Carnegie Corporation show that Thomas was involved right at the start of the overall project in March 1918, when he was appointed as 'General Consultant'. The records provide monthly details of salaries and other expenses and his does not seem to have been a salaried position. The project also had an advisory committee that met regularly, but Thomas was not at those meetings (and not marked as absent).[13] No one appears to have been perturbed by the scandal associated with Thomas until three years later, when his name was removed from the contract of publication.

Although Miller is linked by authorship to Park, his connection otherwise was most clearly with Thomas, who had encouraged his interest in Bohemia and assumed Miller's motivations to be similar to his own with Poland and Polish immigration. While Raushenbush claims that Park took over from Miller as Director of the Division and that he employed Thomas, the archive suggests something different. The nature of Thomas's active role, and its starting date, are clear from the monthly salary record. This sets out the salaries of directors and field officers involved in each of the Divisions. Miller is listed from March through to November 1918, when both his and Thomas's names are listed. Thereafter, it is Thomas's name that appears. Park is listed separately for the Division on the 'Immigrant Press and Theatre' (along with Raushenbusch's name – as it was then spelled – as field officer). Clearly, they were two separate projects with two Directors acting independently of each other. As we have indicated, the name of the Division for which Miller and Thomas were responsible was not initially called

Thomas to Dummer, 9 April 1918. In Thomas's testy exchange with Kimball Young over his biography some truth to the standard version is conceded: 'You know darned well how much I had to do with "Old World Traits Transplanted," but do you expect me to tell you for publication? The men concerned there were my friends, and acted friendly. I needed the money' (cited in Throop and Ward, 2007: n.p.).

13 Americanization Studies, 1918–1945. Carnegie Corporation of New York Records. Rare Book and Manuscript Library. Columbia University Libraries. [Series III: Grants, 1911–1994., Subseries III.A., Box 41, Folder 4–6.]

'Immigrant Heritages', but 'Immigrant Contributions'. It only changed when Thomas took over as its Director. The significance of this will become apparent.

Raushenbush comments on the large staff employed by Miller, with the implication that this was a concern for Park. The number of field officers was, however, fewer than on other projects.[14] There is evidence that there were difficulties with some of the field officers that reflect less well on the change of direction. For example, Eleanor Ledbetter, the librarian at Cleveland Public Library who had developed a strong working relationship with Miller through their common interest in the Slavic communities in Cleveland, as we have seen, joined the Carnegie project in November 1918, according to the salary records. However, she left in January, citing, according to Jones, 'a conversation she had with Helen Horvath, a local Americanization teacher and Hungarian immigrant, about what was involved. Horvath had reacted negatively to what she viewed as patronizing and offensive survey questions proposed by Robert Ezra Park, an associate of Herbert Adolphus Miller on the Carnegie Corporation Americanization study' (Jones, 2013: 257).[15]

A document called 'Life Histories and Questionnaire' was produced for the 'Division of Immigrant Heritages' (as it was now

14 An extra subvention of $5,000 is recorded in the October minutes of the sixth conference of the advisory committee, but this attracts the note, 'on the grounds that the importance and extent of inquiry require $5,000 additional appropriation'. Americanization Studies, 1918–1945. Carnegie Corporation of New York Records. Rare Book and Manuscript Library. Columbia University Libraries. [Series III: Grants, 1911–1994., Subseries III.A., Box 41, Folder 4–6.]
15 Plummer A. Jones kindly provided us with a copy of her letter to the Librarian at Cleveland Public Library, where she wrote, 'I submitted to [Mrs Horvath] Mr Park's outlines of the work he wants done. Mrs Horvath, as an immigrant felt about them exactly as I had expected, and said she would be much offended if I, as an investigator, were really to ask her those questions. I was gratified to have this confirmation of my own judgement, which satisfied me completely that I have done well in resigning. Now to get back home.'

named) in January 1919.[16] This document was certainly written by Thomas (and endorsed by Park) and was likely the document under criticism by Horvath (and Ledbetter). It is made up of three parts. The first sets out a prospectus for the study of behaviour, rather than immigrant contributions, and it does so by setting out the kinds of documents relevant to determine values and attitudes associated with 'four wishes'. The latter are classed as the 'desire for new experience', the 'desire for security', the 'desire for recognition' and the 'desire for response'. It also sets out the familiar argument of Thomas concerning 'disorganisation' – in which he places 'revolutionary attitudes' (including nationalist attitudes) as a form transitional between the old (peasant) culture and the new (American) culture. These distinctions appear in *Old World Traits*, representing a direct transfer of arguments (and indeed ethnographic material) from the *Polish Peasant*. The document also sets out material that could be used to represent values and attitudes – letters, diaries, life records prepared by individuals, and so forth, and existing autobiographies, much as are also presented in the former study. Finally, a proposed life-history questionnaire survey is presented, although there is no evidence that it was used and no findings from it are reported in *Old World Traits*.[17]

16 Americanization Studies, 1918–1945. Carnegie Corporation of New York Records. Rare Book and Manuscript Library. Columbia University Libraries. [Series III: Grants, 1911–1994., Subseries III.A., Box 41, Folder 4-6.]
17 A shorter version of a similar survey is presented at the end of an earlier article by Thomas (1912) on 'race psychology' which serves as a model for the document presented to inform the study of immigrant heritages. A similar reaction to that of Ledbetter is provided by Du Bois in response to a questionnaire administered as part of the Chicago Commission on Race Relations (1922) inquiry into the 1919 Chicago race riots. The study was undertaken by Charles S. Johnson and advised by Park. The methods used, including a questionnaire, are similar to those described by Thomas and are reported in the chapter on 'Public Opinion in Race Relations'. W. E. B. Du Bois set out a severe critique of it in the January 1921 issue of *The Crisis*: 'If a professed enemy of black folk and their progress had set out to start a controversy so as to divide negroes and their friends in counsel and throw the whole burden of such nasty outbreaks of race hate as the East St Louis,

The alignment with the *Polish Peasant* following Thomas taking over as Director of the Division is comprehensive. What has also gone unremarked in discussions of the episode, however, is that this was also associated with Florian Znaniecki who, according to the monthly salary returns, worked as a field officer on the project for six months from January through to July 1919. He replaced Ledbetter, whose work for the project – a manuscript on the Jugoslavs – receives just one citation in the final report in a footnote. Significantly, the same is true also for Miller – a manuscript on the Bohemians receives just one citation. While this may give some credence to Raushenbush's intimation that the direction of the project under Miller was problematic, it is surprising that there is little discussion of the war and nationalism, either in the questionnaire document, or in *Old World Traits* itself. The issue, as we shall see, is not simply the failure to include unpublished drafts, but also material written and published by Miller in the course of the project and with the approval of Burns. Indeed, the new questionnaire document has the flavour of a reorientation of the project in the light of the end of the war.

Evidence for this interpretation is provided by the fact that the advisory committee had called an emergency day-long meeting in February 1919 to discuss a Government Memorandum on Americanization, which had been circulated to the Directors of the Divisions.[18] This began with the comment that 'the recent war was the most effective agency for Americanization ever applied in the United States'. It also set out the importance of 'the deep community of interest between the natives and the great majority of the recent immigrants of the United States. Our country's war for world liberty included the long sought liberty for the peoples from which the most immigrants have lately come.' The Memorandum went

---

Washington and Chicago riots upon them, he would have framed just such a questionnaire as has been sent out by this Commission' (Du Bois, 1921: 102).

18 Letter in January for meeting 15 February. Americanization Studies, 1918–1945. Carnegie Corporation of New York Records. Rare Book and Manuscript Library. Columbia University Libraries. [Series III: Grants, 1911–1994., Subseries III.A., Box 41, Folder 4–6.]

on to describe this as epitomised by banners in a 'Czecho Slovak' parade in Cleveland. It also stated that the American government would continue to be involved in the countries from which immigrants came and that this was a source of potential risk in terms of discontent among the immigrant population. It proposed a bureau dedicated to bringing about the 'co-operation of the foreign born'.

The Memorandum was understood by Burns and the advisory committee as a pivot towards methods of Americanisation suitable to the peace. This reinforced the position of the North American Civic League for Immigrants and its role within the Bureau of Education, displacing the more moderate orientation of Burns and leading to the Carnegie Corporation's increasing sense that the project had been misplaced.

The impact of war

When Ledbetter commented on her concern about the new direction of the now redescribed Immigrant Heritages Division, she was reflecting an understanding she shared with Miller and derived from their mutual interests and criticisms of the dominant ideas of Americanisation. When Miller withdrew from directing the Division he had been involved in Slavic nationalist movements in Chicago and Cleveland for a number of years. This was a consequence of his involvement with the Chicago settlement movement and his friendship with Mary E. McDowell, to whom he was most probably introduced by Thomas. The Czech sociologist and social work academic, Alice Masaryk, had stayed in the University settlement between 1904 and 1905, and her father Tomáš (also a sociologist, philosopher and future president of a newly independent Czechoslovakia) was a visitor to the university and to the settlement in 1902,[19] and briefly in 1907, during a lecture tour

---

19 In 1902, Tomáš Garrigue Masaryk visited the University of Chicago at the invitation of the president William R. Harper, who offered him $2,000 for a series of 24 lectures for a non- academic audience. The number of attenders fluctuated between forty and sixty. Later, Masaryk summarised the main

for Czechoslovak immigrants. Miller first met with them both on his trip to Czechoslovakia in 1912.[20] Together with McDowell, Miller was active in petitioning the Austrian authorities for the release of Alice Masaryk after her arrest on charges of sedition in 1915. Tomáš Masaryk was elected President/Chairman of the Mid-European Union when Miller was appointed director and, in his memoir, describes it as 'meeting pretty often to discuss all the ethnographical and political problems of the smaller mid-European peoples' (Masaryk, 1927: 237).

In 1926, at the request of a publisher in Prague, Miller wrote a memoir on his work with the Mid-European Union for publication for the local audience. Miller delivered his manuscript in July 1926,[21] and wrote a letter to Masaryk asking him whether he would write an introduction. Although there is evidence that the Czech translator continued her work on the manuscript as late as 1928, Masaryk never sent his introduction and Miller's memoir was not published in the Czech language.[22] The English manuscript contains descriptions of the activities of the Union, as well as extracts from the minutes, alongside his commentary and account of its relation to the Americanisation project.[23] We will discuss the substance of

topic of his Chicago lectures as 'the philosophy of the history of a small nation' (see Kovtun, 1988: viii).

20 Miller went to Bohemia in 1912 with a large delegation of American Bohemians. He spent three weeks in Prague and received an invitation to spend a week with Masaryk, who was then spending his summer vacations in Moravia. Miller also names McDowell as the person who helped him establish contacts with the Masaryks (Miller, 1940: 74).

21 In a letter dated 12 July 1926, Miller writes that he has just sent off the completed manuscript of his story 'An American Sidelight on the Czechoslovak Revolution', indicating that it had been due in Prague on 1 June for translation and publication during the summer. Letter from Miller to Hinman, 12 July 1926. Herbert A. Miller Papers, Folder Correspondence – Miscellaneous, Box 1, Oberlin College Archives, RG 30/23.

22 See Švec (2006: 316) and letter from Miller to Masaryk, 17 July 1926. Correspondence, Folder 58, Archive of the T. G. Masaryk Institute, Prague.

23 It is referenced by Negley Teeters (1951) in his obituary of Miller, and he deposited a set of papers associated with Miller in an archive at Temple University (together with notes of areas where it seemed to have

the activities of the Mid-European Union and Miller's role in it in the next chapter. Here we will discuss how Miller became involved in it and how it took his work in a direction further away from the mainstream understandings of Americanisation and into a direct engagement with international relations. In short, while the Carnegie project prepared for domestic peacetime relations among ethnic groups within the US, Miller was beginning to confront the obstacles to peace in the treatment of subject minorities and, from there, to the problematic role of imperialism.

Miller describes arriving at Oberlin on the outbreak of the First World War in August 1914 and being told by a Czech friend that many Czechs in the Austrian army would contrive to be captured and enlist in the Serbian army to fight against Austria. He also describes being asked to write his first article (for the *North American Review*) on 'Nationalism in Bohemia and Poland' (Miller, 1914a) – 'this was my first contribution toward an understanding in America of the deep and unquenchable aspirations of the oppressed nationalities involved in the war' (Miller, 1926, ch. II: 2). It also led to him joining committees being established among Czechs in America (and Cleveland in particular) to pursue the national cause. He also met with McDowell to join her campaign to free Alice Masaryk. This resulted in her release, although, as he stated, 'the full credit belongs to Miss McDowell' (Miller, 1926, ch. II: 4).[24]

It is easy to misunderstand Miller's orientation to the war and to 'Americanisation' in that context, not least because he seems to have combined a deep distrust of patriotism and a commitment to cultural pluralism with advocacy of the participation in the

> missing pages. Teeters (1966) wrote a short summary of the memoir for the *Hartwick Review*, but it contains no details of Miller's account of the relation between Miller's work with the Mid-European Union and the Carnegie project.

24 The statement is characteristically modest. He appears in all the letters to the Austrian Ambassador as joint signatory. Herbert A. Miller Papers, Series I Correspondence, Box I, Folder – Correspondence between Miller and Woolsey, 1916, Oberlin College Archives, RG 30/23. The larger network of campaigners comprised very prominent friends of the Masaryks such as Charles Crane, Julia Lathorp and Adolph Sabath (see Crawford Mitchell, 1980: 85–91).

war of units in the US military drawn from immigrants to the US from oppressed European minorities. Indeed, in his manuscript he describes that 'in my deep abhorrence of war I had not approved of declaring war against Germany' (Miller, 1926, ch. II: 4). However, he felt the call that had been made to academics to use their special knowledge to help government in the war effort, but 'there seemed such an impractical value to my knowledge that I remember remarking to a friend that so far as I could see, the only contribution I could make in the present crisis was to do as good teaching as I could in the hope that some day it might have some value' (Miller, 1926, ch. II: 5).

By autumn 1917, before his appointment to the Carnegie project, in line with his pragmatist pedagogy, Miller felt that 'as a sociologist, I should try to see an army camp which was a distinct social phenomenon' (Miller, 1926, ch. II: 5). He contacted the YMCA to arrange a talk at Camp Sherman in Ohio where 30,000 troops were in training: 'Not assuming that I had anything to say to white troops, I wrote asking if they would not like to have me talk to the Negroes since for many years I had taught at Fisk University. I proposed as the title of my talk, "How the Germans Treat Subject Peoples". What I really wanted to acquire was a perspective to show that the treatment of Negroes in this country was not at all unique and thus arouse, I hoped, their enthusiasm' (Miller, 1926, ch. II: 5). Instead, he was detailed to speak to White troops, but also to commissioned officers in charge of 10,000 immigrant soldiers. This was over four days in January 1918. He was immediately asked to return to discuss 'European Nationalities'.

He returned on 24 January, just four days after the War Department had offered honourable discharge to all those who requested it so that they did not have to fight against 'fellow countrymen' (German immigrants had been classed as 'enemy aliens' in December 1917). Despite being 'then as anti-militarist as I am now' (Miller, 1926, ch. II: 7), Miller describes organising talks with men of different nationalities – Poles, Czechoslovaks, Roumanians and Jugoslavs. In an article, 'America's Lost Division', published in *The Survey*, he wrote that 'when it was explained to those men that America's fight for freedom was the same as their own long struggle for freedom, the result was nothing short of amazing'

(Miller, 1918a: 307). Nearly all refused the offer of discharge. Yet the War Department compounded what Miller had thought to be their original error by declaring that they would serve only in non-combat roles, thereby indicating a continued prejudice against them, and providing them with tasks that were stigmatised by their association otherwise with fatigue duties (i.e., punishment).

Miller's approach stressed *freedom from oppression* and its association with underlying and unrealised (American) values of freedom, not patriotism as such. Significantly, Du Bois expressed a similar ambivalence to the war, regarding participation in it as necessary to the furtherance of African American claims for equal citizenship. They should participate as Americans and, as participants, should be granted the same rights and respect as other citizens. As Karen Fields puts it, for Du Bois, 'along with a double-consciousness went what can be called "double death" – dying once for America and once for Afro-America' (Fields, 2012: 251). His experience of the failure of this strategy took him in more radical directions,[25] as it did for Miller with regard to his subsequent critique of the pathologies of nationalism. Miller advocated internationalism reconciled with a 'proportionate patriotism': 'It is my claim that already more than half of the values that give reality to our lives are internationally in existence and that the possibilities of pluralistic sovereignty make it entirely possible to be loyal to them. Most specific patriotic claims are anachronous' (Miller, 1921: 143).

We know from Miller's account that he became director of the Mid-European Union after a preliminary meeting of interested parties over a luncheon on 3 October 1918, where the participants were provided with two articles by Miller from *The Survey*, 'The Bulwark of Freedom' and 'The Emergent Democracies', as well as

---

25 In his later autobiographical reflections on this time, Du Bois wrote, 'I am less sure now than then of the soundness of this war attitude. I did not realise the full horror of war and its wide impotence as a method of social reform. Perhaps, despite words, I was thinking narrowly of the interests of my group and was willing to let the world go to hell if the black man went free ... Possibly passive resistance of my twelve millions to any war activity might have saved the world for black and white' (Du Bois, 1995 [1940]: 407–408).

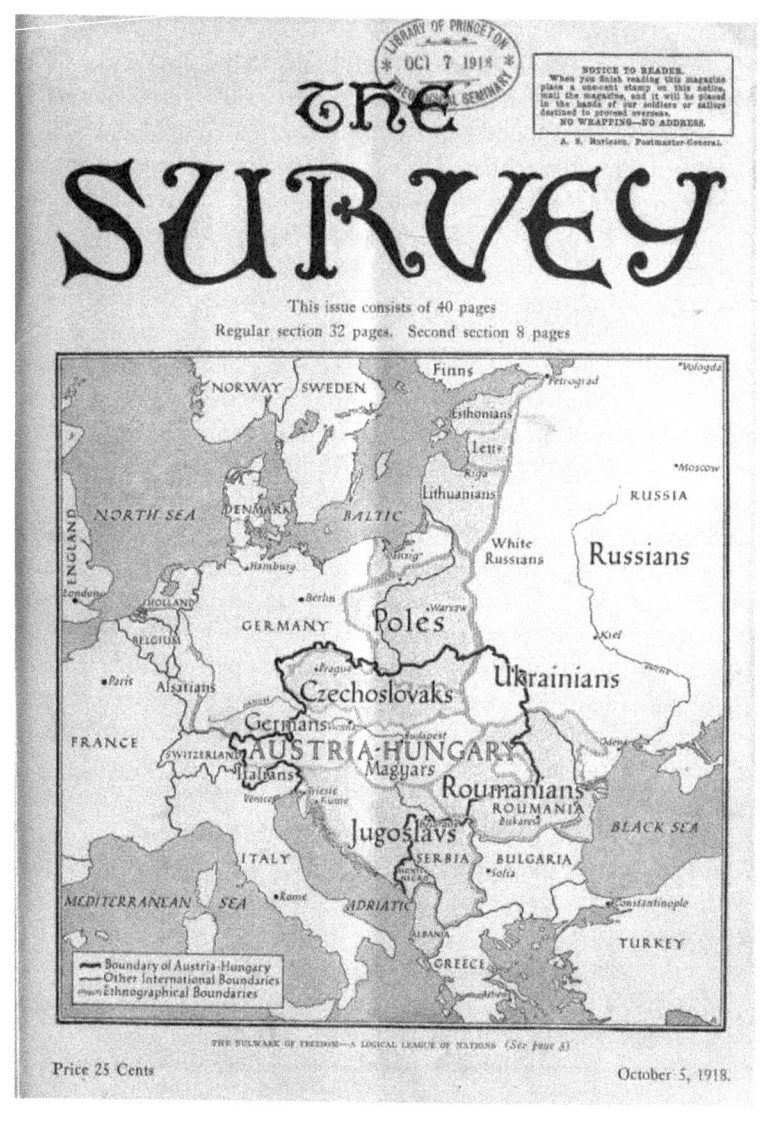

Figure 4.1 Map: The bulwark of freedom

a map of European subject nationalities located in the territories of the 'Central Powers'.[26] They resolved formally to establish the Mid-European Union. The event was promoted in the newspapers and in *The Survey*. Earlier in April 1918, Paul Kellogg had convened a small group to advocate for the rights of minorities, which would be designated six months later as the League of Free Nations (Chambers, 1971: 72–73). Burns was a member of the Founding Group and subsequently of the smaller executive committee.[27] Like Miller, Kellogg was disappointed by the direction of policy after the war and the compromise on the rights of minorities that came to be enshrined in the League of Nations when it was established in 1920 and the global claims of European empires were endorsed.

The founding of the Mid-European Union began a period of intense organisation, which occasioned Thomas taking over Miller's Division of the Carnegie project. The implication is that he had been too busy outside the project – and, indeed, had misdirected his activities for some time, if Raushenbush is to be believed – but closer examination reveals that those activities were understood by Miller (and Burns) to be *part of the project*, not separate from it. Miller had also been involved in a hectic period of organisation under the initial authority of the US Government Committee of Information – a body to which Burns, on behalf of the Carnegie project, also reported – which involved contacting churches serving immigrant populations and benevolent societies, as part of the job of 'filling the gap' between Czechs and Jugoslavs by contacting Roumanian and Greek organisations (Miller, 1926, ch. III: 3).[28]

---

26 The Central Powers were those of the German Empire, the Habsburg dual monarchy of Austro-Hungary, the Ottoman Empire and the Kingdom of Bulgaria. It is this map that is reproduced in the first edition of *Old World Traits*.
27 Its founding is described in *The Survey* by Kellogg, together with the ringing statement, 'we stand for absolute freedom of religion, of civil liberty, of cultural development of the weaker peoples within the stronger nations, and of the native peoples of the undeveloped regions of the earth' (Kellogg, 1918: 251).
28 In its context, Miller meant making connections between the middle-European countries and those further east and south.

The Committee on Public Information had been set up, under the journalist George Creel, by Wilson in April 1917 to direct war propaganda to 'hold fast the inner lines', as Vaughn (1980) puts it. It was a controversial body that came to be criticised as an agency that began a government-directed attack on progressive and liberal opinion in the US, despite it being formally abandoned at the end of the war (Hedges, 2010). Its activities were also aligned with actions under the Espionage Act (1917) and the Sedition Act (1918) that were directed at peace activists, militant labour organisations and ethnic minorities. In this context, association with it could undermine progressive credentials.[29] However, Miller's involvement with it was short-lived and contingent upon his assessment of the implications of the war for advancing the possibilities of subject minorities in Europe and elsewhere.

The Survey – most likely, the editor, Kellogg – introduced Miller's article on 'The Bulwark of Freedom' to its readers with a description of its connection to the Carnegie project, writing that 'Professor Miller is one of the group brought together by Allen T. Burns in his survey of the problem of assimilation for the Carnegie Corporation. Through the cooperation of Professor Miller and Mr. Burns, readers of the Survey are getting the first fruits of their work in a series of articles' (Survey, 1918: 1). Miller's draft account of the period describes that in February he began his work on the Carnegie project, where his first task was to establish connections with the National Councils and influential individuals: 'The Carnegie Corporation gave me a free hand to proceed as I wished' (Miller, 1926, ch. II: 8). Each weekend, after teaching, he comments, 'I went to New York, Washington, or some army camp looking further into the situation among the soldiers' (Miller, 1926, ch. II: 8). In a letter in April to his brother-in-law, Paul Cravath, Miller wrote, 'you already know that I am helping in a national survey of Americanization under the Carnegie Corporation, and

---

29 The creation of the New School for Social Research by dissident Faculty from Columbia University is associated with the failure to give tenure to two pacifist faculty members in 1919. Horace Kallen was a faculty member for a number of decades, but the New School was rather late to issues of racial equality for Blacks in the US (Foulkes, 2017).

had been focusing on the Army side of it'.[30] For Miller, this involved making connections with all the immigrant groups associated with subject peoples – 'filling the gap' – and contributing to their formation into national organisations, with subsequent incorporation into the Mid-European Union, which was yet to be established.

Around this time, Burns was in a rather testy stand-off with the National Americanization Committee over its proposal, together with the Bureau of Education, to establish a 'Flag Day' and 'Loyalty Week'. The Carnegie Corporation had informed the Committee that it would no longer fund its work. The Committee had laid claim to the Carnegie Americanisation project as within its remit for promoting the war effort (as in Flag day), which Burns resisted firmly in correspondence with Henry Pritchett of the Carnegie Corporation, declaring the collaboration was instead aligned with the Committee on Information before concluding with the riposte, 'you are probably acquainted with the small opinion of leading educators regarding work done by the Board of Education … This general opinion ought to be given due weight in deciding about an appropriation to an activity of the Board of Education'.[31] By the time the war had ended the balance had shifted back in favour of the National Americanization Committee and it was the Carnegie project on Americanisation that was being sidelined.

30 Letter from Miller to Cravath, 29 April 1918. Masaryk papers, National Archive, London. Indeed, the March minutes of the Carnegie advisory committee describing the appointment of the heads of the ten divisions notes that Miller was a professor at Oberlin College and 'Military Adviser, Camp Sherman'. Americanization Studies, 1918–1945. Carnegie Corporation of New York Records. Rare Book and Manuscript Library. Columbia University Libraries. [Series III: Grants, 1911–1994., Subseries III.A., Box 41, Folder 4–6.]
31 Letter from Burns to Pritchett, 6 May 1918. The formal collaboration appears to have been with the Division of Work With the Foreign Born of the Committee on Public Information and continued until May 1919. Americanization Studies, 1918–1945. Carnegie Corporation of New York Records. Rare Book and Manuscript Library. Columbia University Libraries. [Series III: Grants, 1911–1994., Subseries III.A., Box 41, Folder 4–6.]

Raushenbush's later recollection of the peculiarities of the methodology adopted by Miller, then, is not so much incorrect as very partial. The methodology was possibly not that best suited to address immigrant heritages in normal times, but the times were not normal. Moreover, Miller's emphasis on the 'spirit of freedom' that motivated immigrant communities and its alignment with American interests at war represented a more profound and radical contribution to understanding 'Americanisation' than that of the other contributions to the Carnegie project. It is, however, a contribution that has been lost to the history of sociology. When Thomas came to write *Old World Traits*, he provided no discussion of the research undertaken by Miller and his different understanding of Americanisation organised in terms of immigrant heritages that expressed the aspirations of 'oppressed' peoples.[32] The Directors of the Divisions had permission to publish articles separately from the project reports and, in the case of Miller, this activity was of fundamental importance to the war effort and the aims of the Department of Information to which Burns reported. Miller published four articles derived from the Carnegie project during the period of the research (Miller, 1918a, 1918b, 1918c, 1919). Yet, when published, *Old World Traits* was but an addendum to the *Polish Peasant*, reinforced by the role of Znaniecki as field researcher in replacement of Ledbetter.

Thomas might have anticipated that his authorship would be recognised and would contribute to his rehabilitation, something that was blocked. However, Miller's authorship credit reflected his initial role in the work – fully half of the period of the field research – albeit that the substance of his contribution was left out. The puzzle is Park's authorship credit. Raushenbush does her best to justify it, but there is no evidence that he had any direct involvement at all.[33] As we have seen, the American government

---

32 The publication of the book was accompanied by a frontispiece map with the caption, 'The Peace Treaty is an attempt to make racial and political boundaries more nearly coincide', an echo of Miller's interests, but not otherwise addressed in the book.
33 The republication of the American Studies series of books in 1971 occurs with the author credit as 'William I. Thomas, together with Robert E. Park and Herbert A. Miller'.

wanted methods of Americanisation that would be aligned with the country's post-war foreign policy interests. This was something from which Miller had already indicated his divergence. Thomas delivered a manuscript that avoided the issue.

Conclusion

Frederick Keppel took over the presidency of the Carnegie Corporation from its acting President, Henry Pritchett, in 1923. Pritchett had served between 1921 and 1923, although he was the person at the Corporation with responsibility for the Americanisation studies from their inception (under the presidency of Elihu Root). Keppel set the foundation on a firm course in support of professional social science addressing pressing public issues, but he did so within the existing race-relations paradigm of the US. That the matter potentially appears differently is partly to do with his role in setting up the major Carnegie-funded study of race relations under the Swedish social scientist Gunnar Myrdal, which was published as *An American Dilemma* in 1944 (after Keppel's retirement in 1941 and death in 1943), and how that study has come to be interpreted as part of a 'liberal orthodoxy' (Jackson, 1990).

According to David Southern (1987), Keppel conceived the study in the mid-1930s and sought to commission someone to lead it from outside the US and someone who was not from one of the European imperial powers. Yet, Keppel and the Carnegie Corporation were not neutral on the matter of empire. As Tiffany Willoughby-Herard (2015) and Maribel Morey (2021) have shown, Keppel travelled to South Africa in 1927 and subsequently funded a study of 'poor whites' designed for their uplift and the maintenance of racial hierarchies. The new study of race relations was not conceived by Keppel outside this framework. Ellen Lagemann (1989: 6) describes Keppel's ambition as a 'mandate to define, develop and distribute knowledge' as part of a 'franchise' to govern indirectly. As Willoughby-Herard suggests, this included the governance of unequal race relations both locally and globally. According to Morey, this was Keppel's intention in funding the Myrdal study to provide a national (federal) focus on the management of race relations.

In fact, although the scale of the Myrdal study and its documentation of the disadvantages experienced by Black Americans was widely applauded, it was far from the only such study. In March 1925, a number of organisations active in race relations organised a national conference under the auspices of the Commission on the Church and Race Relations and the Commission on Interracial Cooperation in Cincinnati, Ohio.[34] The conference, which opened with a message from US President Calvin Coolidge, resolved to set up an Executive Committee under George E. Haynes (who was secretary of the Commission on the Church and Race Relations) which asked Charles S. Johnson (then director of research at the National Urban League) to organise a further series of studies of different aspects of the situation confronting Black Americans – migration, education, employment, housing, delinquency, citizenship rights, and so on – and another conference to discuss them.[35] The data from these studies were prepared at Fisk University (where Johnson had recently been appointed) for discussion at a later conference that took place in Washington in December 1928. The conference then disbanded, having charged Johnson with revising and publishing the findings in the light of its deliberations. This was published under the title, *The Negro in American Civilization: A Study of Negro Life and Race Relations in the Light of Social Research* (1931).[36]

34 The organisations included the Federal Council of Churches, the Commission on the Church and Race Relations (of which Haynes was also secretary), the Friends Service Commission, the Inquiry, the National Association for the Advancement of Colored People (NAACP), the National Federation of Settlements, the National Urban League – in fact, among around sixteen organisations in all, including many Black Church organisations such as the African Methodist Episcopal Church.
35 Also involved was Graham Taylor, who had been executive secretary of the inquiry organised by the Chicago Commission on Race Relations, with Charles Johnson as the associate executive secretary and the person doing the bulk of the work and writing.
36 In December 1929, Johnson was appointed to a commission set up by the League of Nations into the use of forced labour in the free colony of Liberia, the only African country to be a member of the League (Stanfield, 1987). The colony had been set up in the early nineteenth century under an

The methodology of the Conference had been to bring together researchers and practitioners from different interracial organisations to discuss the preliminary findings and their implications for racial cooperation. The volume amounted to 372 pages of findings and 100 pages of discussion around 5 topics. The latter included a section by Du Bois on The Negro Citizen and a section by Miller on Race Relations in America (the latter also participated in the 1925 Conference). The research process as well as the final conference was part-funded by the Social Science Research Council (SSRC), which would also go on to take a major role in organising the Myrdal study on behalf of the Carnegie Corporation (Morey, 2021). As Morey sets out, the SSRC made race relations a core focus of its activities and in 1925 had established an Advisory Committee on Interracial Relations with two subcommittees, all of which were disbanded in 1930.

Morey explains the shift in interest as deriving from changes at the philanthropic foundations that provided funding to the SSRC. The larger Rockefeller Foundation had subsumed the smaller Laura Spelman Rockefeller Memorial in 1929, whose director Beardsley Ruml had a keen interest in issues of race relations. The Rockefeller Foundation provided about 90 per cent of the SSRC's funding. One consequence of the SSRC disbanding of its committees on interracial relations was also withdrawal from Du Bois's proposed *Encyclopedia of the Negro*, which had been considered for funding by the SSRC, but was not supported by Rockefeller. The restructuring of Rockefeller coincided with that at the Carnegie Corporation and Keppel's rather different

alliance of slaveowners and formerly enslaved Africans from the US and the Caribbean which came to constitute a ruling elite involved in the oppression of the indigenous population. The colony did not allow White settlers and had been the focus of Marcus Garvey's Black nationalist movement and favourable comment from Du Bois. The claimed use of forced labour implicated plantations set up by the US Firestone Rubber Company and the transport of labour from Liberia to the Spanish colony of Fernando Po. The commission lasted for six months and concluded that de facto, labour conditions were akin to slavery, although Firestone were exonerated (Report, 1931). Johnson kept extensive notes and drafted a book on Liberia which remained unpublished until after his death (Johnson, 1987).

understanding of the problem of race as a challenge to a White global order.

If the moment was not right for the earlier Americanisation studies in the immediate aftermath of the First World War, the opposite was the case for Myrdal's study in the context of the Second World War and, to some extent, it created a federal mandate to govern directly beyond the intentions of those who had initiated it. Keppel settled on Myrdal, who began his work in spring 1938 with consultations with the major race-relations specialists associated with the Chicago school of sociology and Howard University, alongside individuals associated with the National Urban League and the NAACP. Initially included in the latter group was Du Bois, but Myrdal studiously avoided any idea of a 'global color line'. His study was firmly domestic. Nor did he refer to the earlier studies of Americanisation, despite adopting some of the themes of Chicago school sociology on assimilation and gradual processes of change undermining both caste-like social structures in the South and racial prejudice and de facto segregation in the North.[37] Myrdal's own position on race fell firmly within the second of the three positions described by Fallace, a position that emphasised the cultural superiority of north Europeans and represented enslavement as a process of 'de-racination' (Jackson, 1990).

The most comprehensive critique of the Chicago 'caste school of race relations', including what he called the 'mystical' approach of Myrdal, was provided by Oliver Cromwell Cox in his *Caste, Class, and Race* (1948). As with other criticisms, it was largely ignored by historians of the Chicago approach to race and ethnicity (Wacker, 1983; Persons, 1987).[38] Myrdal's study can be seen as

---

37 Myrdal and his wife Alva maintained friendly relations with William I. Thomas and Dorothy Swaine Thomas from an earlier fellowship visit to the US and reciprocal visit by the Thomases in the early 1930s (Jackson, 1990: 740–745). Dorothy Thomas was employed on the *American Dilemma* study for a brief period to provide statistical analyses.

38 Neither Persons nor Wacker refers to Cox. Wacker refers to a clash of paradigms between Park and Myrdal, but this largely devolves to taking issue with Myrdal characterising Park as 'pessimistic' (Wacker, 1983: 80). Chapoulie (2020) does not discuss Cox's criticism of the 'caste school' in his later account of Chicago sociology.

a variant of Americanisation, applied to White America (in the form of the incorporation of poor Whites into middle-class mores). Thus, Myrdal argued that 'the main thing happening to the South is that it is gradually becoming Americanized' (Myrdal, 1944: 466). This also involved arguments for gradual change, including the 'Americanisation' of African Americans, 'to begin allowing the higher strata of the Negro population to participate in the political process as soon as possible, and to push the movement down to the lowest groups gradually. The more urgent it is also to speed up the civic education of those masses who are bound to have votes in the future' (Myrdal, 1944: 519).

Miller, like Du Bois, as we have seen, was developing a global perspective on domination and oppression and he argued for a plural and multicultural America. On the face of it, Myrdal argued that the 'American creed' involved a 'unity of ideals and a diversity of culture' (Myrdal, 1944: 3), deriving from the Declaration of Independence. However, his version inverts what Miller had set out: 'American nationalism', Myrdal wrote, 'is permeated by the American Creed, and therefore becomes international in its essence' (Myrdal, 1944: 6). The unresolved dilemma of Myrdal's own approach is how to explain the occurrence of the 'problem', and its entrenched character, in the light of the Creed and its foundational character. Myrdal appeals to 'American nationalism' without addressing the problems of 100 per cent patriotism, as Miller had set out. Nonetheless, Myrdal's study set the new terms of debate and it would be some time before his 'dilemma' would be recognised as not only domestic – an 'American dilemma' – but global. Rightly, that would be the moment that Du Bois would be remembered. Miller would remain a forgotten figure.

5

Empire and international relations

In the preceding chapters we have shown how Herbert Adolphus Miller developed sociological positions that placed him at odds with those of mainstream (White) sociology. His arguments were distinctive, but they were grounded in common concerns. A conventional understanding would be that he was too entangled with issues of social reform and a progressive movement in politics which was in retreat after the First World War (Shapiro, 1971). As we have suggested, adaptation by withdrawal from those entanglements, as was characteristic of others in the professionalisation of social science that is otherwise described as taking place, would be no less political than one that engages the politics directly. For his part, Miller remained true to his commitment to sociology as a form of democratic knowledge that would facilitate public debate, but his commitment was also to 'science'. He held to science as the basis of action and he considered his political activities to be continuous with that science. The political climate may not have been propitious, but the science would provide for a different politics to come and, in an unfavourable present, a politics engaged with the issues of tomorrow remained necessary.

On the surface, his experiences of the First World War – the Carnegie project, and the formation of the Mid-European Union – may appear to be a shift from 'science' to 'action', but, in truth, his actions were based on a sociological understanding that was always developing and being reformulated in the light of his new experiences. For example, *Races, Nations and Classes* (1924) was based upon his work on the Carnegie research project and his experiences with the Mid-European Union, but he had also become involved in other anti-colonial movements in Korea, China and India, which were represented in that book and a sequel to it, published in 1933, *The Beginnings of To-morrow*.

Miller's activities in the 1920s and 1930s were formidable, sustained and deeply engaged with international relations. They involved his role as director of the Mid-European Union between 1918 and 1919 (when he also was involved in drafting the Czechoslovakian Declaration of Independence, as we shall see) and a later role as vice-president of the League of Friends of Korea (as well as a member of the National Committee of the Korean-American Council that organised a Liberty Conference in Washington in February/March 1942). He published widely in academic venues, but also in *The Survey* magazine, which, as we have seen, for some historians of sociology was increasingly a mark of marginality to the direction otherwise being taken by the discipline and its professionalisation (Bulmer, 1996).

Notwithstanding this claim, as we shall show, Miller's arguments were more advanced – sociologically as well as politically – than his mainstream colleagues. Just as W. E. B. Du Bois drew a global 'color line' connecting the experiences of African Americans with those of peoples subordinated to the operation of European empires in Africa and elsewhere (King, 2022), so, too, Miller connected race relations in the US to European and American imperialism and the domination of subject peoples.

In 1930, the sociologists Luther and Jessie Bernard were asked by the Social Science Research Council in New York to write a short report on sociological contributions to the field of international relations. An expanded version was published a few years later, reviewing contributions from the late nineteenth century onwards (Bernard and Bernard, 1934). Their organisation of topics might seem idiosyncratic today, but it was soundly based in a review of articles in the *American Journal of Sociology* and textbooks in sociology and social psychology. It also threw its net wide to include comparative studies and evolutionary accounts of types of society, as well as studies of individual countries other than the US.

Three topics dominated: race and culture; immigration and assimilation (what, in the US context, as we have seen, was called 'Americanisation'); and war and peace. The approaches to these topics typically involved assumptions of Western cultural superiority (frequently grounded in racist arguments derived from eugenics) and of the developmental benefits of empire. Indeed, sociology was also recommended by the Bernards to provide local knowledge to facilitate the governance of colonial subjects. Nationalism received scant mention except in the motivation of European empires as an expression of their 'superior cultures'. There was no discussion of anti-colonial movements, whether in Ireland, India, Africa or the Middle and Far East.[1] The rise of fascism was not mentioned, nor were the problems of endemic anti-Semitism and its relation to ethno-nationalism and the end of empires in Europe.

The First World War had ended barely a decade earlier and yet, despite a wider interest in war and peace, it was not a major topic for sociologists; rather, they tended to operate on a broad canvas and to understand conflict as a natural expression of relations among human groups across history and types of society.[2] Moreover, if the Second World War is now understood to be prefigured in failures of the peace process in Paris after 1919, any looming issues were safely under the Bernards' radar (and that of most other sociologists at the time, as well). The American Sociological Society had set up a Committee on International Relations (of which Miller was a member) shortly after the First World War, as they note, but not the circumstances that led to this initiative. These included the failure of the US to join the newly formed League of Nations, despite President Woodrow Wilson's urging (Manela, 2007) and the continuing problems the League confronted. However, these failures would emerge more generally into the sociological consciousness only after the onset of the Second World War. Few sociologists were alert to the issues at the time. Yet the First World War had put European empires on notice, whether that was fully recognised or not.

---

[1] There was no place in the Bernards' survey for Du Bois, or other African American pioneers of sociology such as Charles S. Johnson or E. Franklin Frazer.
[2] In fact, Luther Bernard (1944) published a book of just this character on war as a social institution.

Miller's contributions are discussed by the Bernards, but without a full appreciation of their significance.[3] He made distinctive contributions to the three central topics delineated by the Bernards and he did so not by treating them as discrete topics, but as mutually implicated fields of inquiry. Miller also discussed topics absent from the Bernards' account, especially that of nationalism, a topic that Anthony Smith (1983) has argued was absent from sociological discussions in the inter-war years, with the exception of Park, Thomas and Znaniecki. Smith comments that, 'on the whole, the inter-War years and the immediate aftermath of World War II, evinced a curious lack of interest in nationalism, despite some concern with fascism in Parsons' essays during the War ... Park, of course, like Thomas and Znaniecki, studied intensively processes of immigration and cultural assimilation, subjects adjacent to nationalism; but only Louis Wirth spared any time to consider the forms of nationalist movements and the nature of nations' (Smith, 1983: 24). Despite identifying the contributions of Chicago sociologists, Smith misses Miller. Significantly, the cited article by Wirth published in 1936 is written from within the Chicago milieu on 'types of nationalism' in Europe, covering nationalism in central Europe, yet neglecting entirely the work of Miller (Wirth's sources are nearly all German).

We shall also see that Miller's contributions are theoretically distinctive when compared with those of other sociologists. This is so with regard to each of the topics taken separately, as well as in the relations he drew between them. In fact, it is precisely the articulation of those relationships that represents the distinctiveness of his approach, an approach we will set out more formally in Chapter 7, when we will discuss Wirth's typology of nationalism further.

---

3 As the Bernards (1934: 21) also note, Miller chaired two reports on behalf of the ASS in 1923 and 1924 on news and international public opinion. Actions recommended from these reports were to be taken up by the Social Science Research Council (SSRC), as indicated in a meeting of that body in 1924, but not pursued until the Bernards were asked to submit their survey in 1930. The archive of the SSRC is sparse for its early years and does not have material pertaining to this episode. The successor organisation to the ASS, the American Sociological Association, did not maintain an archive for its early years (see Sun, 2020).

Empires, immigration and subject peoples

As we saw in the last chapter, Miller left the Carnegie project mid-way through the time allotted to research in November 1918 after taking up the role of director of the Mid-European Union, a body devoted to the interests of subject peoples in Europe. The contribution of immigrants to the US was a major part of Miller's research for the project. This had involved addressing the 'spirit of freedom' as it motivated immigrants to the US from those parts of central Europe under rule by the German and Austro-Hungarian Empires. Miller criticised ideas of assimilation and developed a critique of 'Americanisation' as it was understood by other sociologists at the time, such as William I. Thomas. He argued that immigration could pluralise and 'cosmopolitanise' American political culture, something rejected by those promoting assimilation, including Thomas. We will see that he also sought to pluralise 'cosmopolitanism' itself in order to recognise the necessary contribution of the ethical content of 'civilisations' and religions other than those of the (Christian and capitalist) West (Miller, 1933).

Miller had hoped that the Mid-European Union might be a vehicle for the expression of minority rights and be incorporated as part of the new League of Nations promoted by US President Woodrow Wilson. However, it collapsed within a year of its formation, in part because the war had ended and the settlement of disputed territories was determined among the victorious powers, but also because of internal conflicts over the territorial claims of its members. In one of the few studies of the Mid-European Union, Arthur May concludes with an epitaph from Miller: 'The story of the Mid-European Union reveals the fact that the New Europe ... refused to be born' (May, 1957: 488). Miller, May suggests, returned to 'the tranquillity of Oberlin'.

In fact, Miller returned to a period of intense writing based on his experiences of the Carnegie project and the Mid-European Union and engagement with the new movement for Korean independence, as well as a programme of extensive travels to global sites of interest to his concern with the rights of subject minorities. We will return to a discussion of his experience with the Mid-European Union and how it prefigured the fate of the League of Nations. Our purpose in this chapter is to consider how Miller's experience of war and peace associated with the founding and (rapid) dissolution of the Mid-European Union contributed to the development of his critique of empires, both the global, overseas empires of European powers and the newer empire of Japan.

The issue for Miller became not just a new order in Europe, but also a new order globally *where the obstacle was Europe itself*. This was bound up with what Miller called nationalist revolutions. In *The Beginnings of To-morrow*, he proposed that the problems at hand began with Europe and must run their course. He wrote about the 'nationalistic epidemic, induced by the reaction in Asia to European imperialism … In Europe it is the boomerang sent out by imperialism, returning to strike a deadlier blow at the sender' (Miller, 1933: 9). Further, 'nationalism, which began about a century ago, has swept the world until all imperialism seems doomed. Closely related to nationalism is the growing resentment of the colored races to white control' (Miller, 1933: 21).

The latter observation was a theme that can be traced back to his earliest interests. In a letter to Du Bois written in 1924, Miller explained that 'for a good many years I have been devoting myself to the study of minority peoples in Europe. My interest in them, however, originated from an effort to get perspective for the study of the race problems.'[4] This association of ideas is indicative of his

---

4 Letter from Miller to Du Bois, 16 December 1924, W. E. B. Du Bois Papers (MS 312), Special Collections and University Archives, University of Massachusetts Amherst Libraries. Miller's connections with Du Bois were extensive. His first appointment in sociology was between 1899 and 1902 at Fisk University, Du Bois's *alma mater*. While he left to study for a PhD at Harvard (as had Du Bois), he retained a connection with Fisk. As we saw, while at Fisk, Miller had met and married the daughter of the founding President Erastus Milo Cravath. Miller's brother-in-law, Paul D. Cravath, was a prominent New York corporate lawyer and active in foreign affairs at the same time as Miller. According to Priscilla Roberts (2005), Cravath was part of group committed to an 'Anglo-American new order' of international relations. He 'displayed a distinct prejudice in favour of efficient and stable European imperial rule and a near complete failure to appreciate the strength of nationalist sentiment' (Roberts, 2005: 204). Miller's views were

interest in subject *peoples*, as distinct from subject *nationalities*; national self-determination, for Miller, could also produce a new oppression of minorities (Miller, 1924a).

The end of empire/empire redux?

In order to appreciate the distinctiveness of Miller's position, we need to address the wider context of international relations before the First World War that was broadly accepted by academics and wider publics alike. International relations were dominated by the relations among global imperial powers and their alliances. They were expressed in conflicts between European powers *within* Europe (as in the annexation of Alsace-Lorraine in 1871 as part of German unification under Prussia and the wider project of German imperial expansion), as well as conflicts associated with European powers and their territorial ambitions *beyond* Europe (for example, as in the 'scramble for Africa' of European powers after the Berlin Conference of 1884).

The reach of European empires was not only an issue of the conflicts between them. It also involved confrontation with the Ottoman empire in the Middle East and North Africa, and including areas of eastern Europe (for example, Bosnia Herzegovina).[5] Ironically, as the European empires were determining their domination over African peoples, they were requiring the Ottoman empire to accept peace treaties in which minority rights were recognised (Macartney, 1934; Minawi, 2016). While the Ottoman empire

   diametrically opposed, but they would appear to have maintained cordial relations. In fact, when Miller was appointed to a junior position at Bryn Mawr after his dismissal from Ohio State University, Paul Cravath provided an annual subvention to the college to increase Miller's salary and requested that he not be told of the donation. Letter from administrator Park to Cravath, 5 May 1938, Herbert Adolphus Miller Papers, Bryn Mawr College Special Collections.
5 See Minawi (2016) for discussion of Ottoman participation in the Berlin Conference and the retrenchment of its North African possessions and consolidation in the Eastern Sahara, and Greble (2021) for discussion of Bosnia-Herzegovina.

was in decline, European empires globally were also facing the rise of Japan as an imperial power with claims over Korea and China and wider interests in Indo-China. Japan had signed a treaty with Korea in 1904 to provide transit for troops through Korea to Manchuria and Siberia as part of the prosecution of the Russo-Japanese war, but instead of demobilising its troops, Japan annexed Korea and incorporated its population under an aggressive regime of 'Japanisation'.[6]

Put simply, the First World War represented both a culmination of European imperial conflicts and the beginning of the end of empire *in* Europe (it would re-emerge as a project of Nazi Germany). The triple entente of Britain (and its empire and dominions), France (and its empire) and Russia was joined by Serbia, Montenegro and Belgium (and by Japan and Italy after May 1915, and the US in April 1917) in an alliance to defeat the German, Austro-Hungarian and Ottoman empires. These defeats – together with the revolutionary overthrow of the Russian tsarist regime in 1917 – set the conditions for the redrawing of boundaries and the creation of new nation states in central Europe. This extended from Finland and the east Baltic in the North, through Poland and Ukraine to the Black Sea, and down to Romania, Serbia and Albania in the south.

However, the treaties enacted at the end of the war left Britain and France with their global empires not only intact, but also extended by the incorporation of the Middle East under new imperial 'mandates', as well as the redistribution of Germany's African and Pacific colonies between France and Britain and its Dominions (under separate mandates). The US was even offered a mandate in Istanbul over 'European' Turkey, something it turned

---

6 The circumstances were particularly significant in US politics and public opinion. The US had signed a treaty of mutual protection with Korea in 1882, but had given support to Japan in its prosecution of war with Russia. The Treaty of Portsmouth in 1905 that settled the war was brokered by US President Theodore Roosevelt and provided tacit support for the annexation of Korea. Following the earlier treaty, however, US Christian missionaries had entered Korea and enjoyed very considerable success, such that 'Christianity' provided a point of resistance to 'Japanisation' and a powerful constituency in the US among Protestant churches (see Fields, 2019).

down (Manela, 2007). However, it had taken possession of Guam and the Philippines (as well as Puerto Rico) in 1892, and annexed Hawaii in 1898. The latter was important because it was a conduit for Korean immigration and publicity in the US for Korean independence, a situation rendered more complex by the role of Japan as one of the Allied powers in the war.

The Mandate System has been argued to be a first step in the transition from global empire to a system of international law (Anghie, 2004), but, as Susan Pedersen (2006, 2015) argues, it operated in a similar fashion to annexations, albeit providing some obligation for the development and protection of the peoples under a mandate. Even here access was to be provided to raw materials and resources for companies operating under the protection of the European powers (Pedersen, 2006), as part of what was called the 'strenuous conditions of the modern world'.[7] Nor would that 'protection' include the labour and other standards elaborated as part of the League protocols through the nascent International Labour Organisation.[8] These international standards were not to apply within colonies or territories under the Mandate System (Maul, 2012).

The economic issues were not peripheral to Miller's concerns. Not only were European empires based on political oppression and exploitation externally, they failed to provide just distribution within their national territories, too (Miller, 1933). Indeed, while not endorsing communism as the solution, Miller believed

---

[7] Article 22 of the Covenant of the League of Nations is clear: 'To those colonies and territories which as a consequence of the late war have ceased to be under the sovereignty of the States which formerly governed them and which are inhabited by peoples not yet able to stand by themselves under the strenuous conditions of the modern world, there should be applied the principle that the well-being and development of such peoples form a sacred trust of civilisation and that securities for the performance of this trust should be embodied in this Covenant. The best method of giving practical effect to this principle is that the tutelage of such peoples should be entrusted to advanced nations who by reason of their resources, their experience or their geographical position can best undertake this responsibility' (Covenant of the League of Nations, 1920).

[8] It also set out model tax treaties in 1928 that protected 'overseas' income derived from newly constituted states (Jogarajan, 2018).

that Western capitalist 'civilisation' had shown itself incapable of resolving issues of poverty and inequality and solutions might be found in other traditions from the 'East' (in which he included Russia, as well as India and China).

The League of Nations, then, was firmly directed towards a European international order, purporting to settle the problem of empire within Europe, but reinforcing and even extending the empires of the victorious European powers beyond Europe. Sociologically, this involved addressing the growing 'ethno-nationalisms' associated with claims within defeated European powers for national self-determination based upon common language or religion. This had already been a feature of the Russian and German empires in their policies of 'Russification' and 'Germanification' in lands associated with the earlier Commonwealth of Lithuania and Poland. This, in turn, was also directed at other 'foreign' minorities, such as Jews, involving pogroms directed against them as the new nations of Ukraine, Lithuania and Poland were being formed and as conflict continued after the formal peace settlement in 1919.

If the 'Jewish question' in Europe was intensifying, so, too, was a new 'Muslim question' being created by the retreat of the Ottoman empire to Turkey. This created new Muslim minorities in southeastern Europe and nationalist calls for their expulsion. This was to be the form of a new 'Muslim question' in Europe (Greble, 2021). It would later be accentuated by the Muslim populations that were part of European empires *beyond* Europe, whether of France in North Africa and the Middle East, or Britain in India, the Middle and Far East, and their migration to Europe after the Second World War.

Enter the US

The US entered the First World War in April 1917 under President Wilson, who also made far-reaching arrangements to plan for an ensuing peace. To this end he established a substantial body of expert advisers – mainly academics and numbering around 150 individuals – under the direction of his close adviser, Colonel Edward House (Gelfand, 1963). Called 'The Inquiry', they were assembled in September 1917, covered all global regions, and would continue to play a role through to January 1919 (with experts on Europe increasingly to the fore). Members of the Inquiry with special expertise associated with the conflicts to be resolved at the Paris Peace Conference continued in separate advisory roles.

As Lawrence Gelfand notes, Wilson had already indicated that part of the planning for peace should be the formation of a global organisation to serve the maintenance of peace, and he was involved in the formation of 'The League to Enforce Peace' in June 1915. In January 1918, Wilson set out 'Fourteen Points' that should determine the contours of peace. These included the formation of a League of Nations, and also articulated principles of 'self-determination'. This was a propitious moment for other organisations, such as the League of Free Nations, set up in April 1918 by Paul Kellogg, as we saw in the last chapter. Miller's own involvement in the Mid-European Union, however, did not begin until later with its formation in September 1918, although he had hopes that it would be incorporated within the League of Nations.

Issues of empire outside Europe would come to be displaced from the Paris Peace talks with representations from the Pan-African Congress (in which Du Bois was involved) marginalised (Contee, 1972). The participation of the Syrian Congress, which declared Independence for Greater Syria in March 1920, was also rejected as the peace settlement set about dividing the region (including Palestine) between British and French mandates (Thompson, 2020). India might seem to be a separate case, except that Pan-India was the direction which various movements against British rule were taking. As Nazmul Sultan (2022a) has argued, this took the form of arguing for a federal system that represented different groups and did so in direct criticism of the European idea of the 'national state' and stadial understandings of institutional development. A leading intellectual figure in making this argument, Brajendra Nath Seal gave the first paper at the Universal Races Congress in London in 1911. His presentation followed Du Bois's recitation of 'A Hymn to the Peoples' (Sultan, 2002a).[9]

---

9 The conference was attended by John Dewey, Jane Addams and Mary White Ovington from the NAACP, and, from South Africa, Mohandas Gandhi. Du Bois's poem invoked a new humanity: 'Save us, World Spirit,

In his manuscript on the Mid-European Union, Miller suggested that one model was the Pan-American Union which had been established in 1889 (Miller, 1926). Otherwise, it seemed to represent a Pan-European moment, albeit one led from the US, and, therefore, not generally understood to be a precursor to later developments towards a European union (Hansen and Jonsson, 2014). As Katherine Sorrels (2016) suggests, a Pan-European Union that would bring Austria, Germany and other nations of Europe together had been advocated by the Austrian aristocrat Richard Coudenhove-Kalergi in 1922. It was one of the possible reconfigurations of Austria and Germany in the aftermath of the First World War. This was undermined by Czechoslovakia's successful bid for independence outside such a federation, an event that was intertwined with the formation of the Mid-European Union, as we shall see. In contrast to Miller's vision for the Mid-European Union, Coudenhove-Kalergi's proposals represented a sublimated nationalism that endorsed European domination elsewhere. In fact, as Peo Hansen and Stefan Jonsson (2014) have shown, ideas of Pan-Europe within Europe were associated with arguments for a federated Europe that would guarantee peace within Europe, at the same time as benefiting from the exploitation of colonies in Africa and elsewhere.

As we shall see, the Mid-European Union broke up as it was overtaken by internal differences and ethno-nationalist conflicts. However, Miller was clear that the issue at hand was the representation of subject minorities and their rights, rather than the self-determination of (European) ethno-nations which came to be the focus of the peace settlement and had already become foreshadowed within the Mid-European Union. Indeed, in an article on what Woodrow Wilson and America meant for Czechoslovakia, Miller later reflected that by 1918, 'the principle of self-determination of nations had been formulated by President

---

from our lesser selves! / Grant us that war and hatred cease, / Reveal our souls in every race and hue! / Help us, O Human God, in this Thy Truce / To make Humanity divine!' The poem was published in a special issue of *The Crisis* that had the Races Congress as its main feature. *The Crisis*, 2 September 1911, p. 209.

Wilson early in the year, without, however, his envisioning the dissolution of the Austro-Hungarian Empire. This was an outcome that he was slow to accept. The subject nations immediately seized upon self-determination' (Miller, 1940: 75).

Wilson had anticipated that the young Emperor Charles who had acceded to the thrones of Austria and Hungary in November 1916 would be amenable to a solution within a new Austrian federation (Unterberger, 1989; see also Gelfand, 1963; Fink, 2004). This was something for which the Emperor petitioned shortly before the Czechoslovakian declaration of independence in October 1918 precipitated its dissolution.

Recent scholarship has suggested that the shift from the self-determination of minorities to the self-determination of nations was something unintended by President Wilson. Trygve Throntveit (2011: 460), for example, cites his 'civic nationalist' commitments deriving from progressive politics and pragmatist philosophy (affiliations that were shared by Miller). Nonetheless, that commitment was not immune from ideas of a hierarchy of cultures (which, were central to Woodrow Wilson's Inquiry team and, as we have seen, would come to be incorporated in the Covenant of the League of Nations) and he had an antipathy to the full inclusion of African Americans within the US political community, something shared with Colonel House. These were both positions that were antithetical to those expressed by Miller and developed through his work with the Mid-European Union, as a precursor of a possible world free of empires and of his analysis of the European (and US) obstacles to the realisation of such a world.

The Mid-European Union

As part of his work on the Carnegie project, Miller describes organising talks with men of different nationalities – Poles, Czechoslovaks, Roumanians and Jugoslavs. In an article, 'America's Lost Division', published in *The Survey*, he wrote that 'when it was explained to those men that America's fight for freedom was the same as their own long struggle for freedom, the result was nothing short of amazing' (Miller, 1918a: 307). Miller developed contacts with different organisations representing the different subject peoples of Europe. He conceived this in ethno-geographical terms establishing connections with representatives of different groups across eastern and central Europe. By June 1918, he wrote, 'if, as is hoped, the Ruthenians and Ukrainians can be brought together in a similar way, the line from the Adriatic to the Baltic will be complete, and the task will then be to secure action as far as possible simultaneously the whole length of the line' (Miller, 1918b: 292). By September 1918, he was describing this line as a 'Bulwark of Freedom' (Miller, 1918c).

On the surface, it may appear that Miller was advocating for nationalism, just as the domestic US policy towards immigration was one of assimilation. However, he was clear in his own mind that the objective was *internationalism*, not nationalism. His approach stressed freedom from oppression and its association with underlying and unrealised (American) values of freedom, not patriotism as such. They were unrealised because of the exclusion of African Americans. Miller argued against the 'pathologies' of nationalism, advocating for an internationalism reconciled with a 'proportional patriotism': 'It is my claim that already more than half of the values that give reality to our lives are internationally in existence and that the possibilities of pluralistic sovereignty make it entirely possible to be loyal to them. Most specific patriotic claims are anachronous' (Miller, 1921a: 143).

This was an argument he applied both to domestic policies of 'Americanisation' and ethno-nationalist claims of new states in his search for plural sovereignty. In so far as Miller's arguments are discussed in the context of Chicago sociology, they are frequently either elided with those of Park and Thomas, or seriously misrepresented. Fred Wacker (1983), for example, suggests that Miller harboured 'nationalist' sympathies up to the end of the First World War, but subsequently allied national consciousness with racial and class consciousness and saw them all as equally 'pathological'. According to Wacker (1983: 26), Miller's position evolved to be a more conservative position than that of Park and he argues that he became concerned with threats to stability and order (see also Švec, 2007).

Robert E. Park (1926) had, in fact, also criticised Miller's treatment of 'pathologies of domination', albeit without understanding the argument. His own view was that there was steady progress towards assimilation, an outcome that Miller criticised since it lacked an appreciation of the possibility of a positive transformation brought about by the immigrant group. Park also lacked Miller's sense of urgency of the need to address racial equality. It was Miller, not Park, who understood that the world was moving towards another world war and that 'pathologies of domination' were part of the explanation. The Bernards, for their part, although offering only a capsule description, capture the subtlety of Miller's position, that nationalism 'is essentially a revolt against political and cultural imperialism. It flourishes to best advantage under repression, and as a consequence it develops an oppression psychosis. He believes it to be a disease, but thinks it must run its course and, ... that its cure will be the disappearance of imperialism' (Bernard and Bernard, 1934: 63–64). Miller (1933) argued that revolution against imperial powers was necessary, but that the 'consciousness' necessary for revolution did not provide the basis for a peace that respected the rights of minorities.

Having 'filled the gap' in the bringing together of representative organisations in the unbroken line from the Baltic to the Adriatic via the Black Sea,[10] Miller proposed the formation of the Mid-European Union. This was after a preliminary meeting of interested parties over a luncheon in Washington on 3 October 1918 where the participants were provided with two articles by Miller from *The Survey* – 'The Bulwark of Freedom' and 'The Emergent Democracies' – as well as a map of European subject nationalities located in the territories of the Central Powers.[11] Tomáš Garrigue Masaryk assumed the role of President of the Union, with Miller as its Director.

10 This involved contacting churches serving immigrant populations and benevolent societies, as part of the job of 'filling the gap' between Czechs and Jugoslavs by contacting Roumanian and Greek organisations (Miller, 1926, ch. III: 3).
11 It had been preceded on 15 September by a mass meeting at Carnegie Hall organised by the Committee on Public Information on the topic of 'The Will of the Peoples of Austria-Hungary. Victory Meeting for the Oppressed Nationalities of Central Europe'. Miller prepared the resolutions for the meeting (Miller, 1940).

The formation of the Mid-European Union was not an entirely happy one. Whereas President Wilson had been content to receive deputations from Masaryk (representing Czechoslovakia) and Paderewski (representing Poland), which Miller facilitated, there were complaints from the Italian ambassador that Miller was involving nationalities with claims upon each other's territories (for example, Jugoslavia and territory claimed by Italy). Miller was told that he should cease his activities with the Union. However, he was also told by a secretary within the State Department that he should ignore that advice, that 'I ought to forget my future and do what I could' (Miller, 1926, ch. IV: 7).

Miller resolved to press on with gathering more representatives of oppressed peoples and nationalities within his idea for an organisation that could contribute to a post-Imperial peace, despite being told by the State Department to desist. Indeed, as we have seen, there is evidence (Miller, 1940; Gelfand, 1963; Fink, 2004) that, notwithstanding Woodrow Wilson's pre-war commitments to self-determination, US policy towards peace prior to entry in the war favoured an Austrian federation rather than independence for small nations. Miller writes, 'from that time on I was very much under official disapproval' (Miller, 1926, ch. IV: 10).

Miller (together with a small group) was responsible for the redrafting of the Czechoslovakian Declaration of Independence in a form designed to garner US support. It was delivered by Masaryk (with Miller attending) to President Wilson, who ratified his support, and it was announced in the press on 19 October 1918 to coincide with its launch by Edvard Beneš in Paris. Around a week later, on 26 October, at the Independence Hall in Philadelphia, following a three-day conference, the Mid-European Union made its own Declaration of Common Aims, along with the ringing of a replica Liberty Bell.[12] Miller had a talent for publicity. A replica Liberty Bell was struck for each of the signatories and a large display of his map of the 'Bulwark of Freedom' was set up

12 The bells were not quite replicas. The proclamation on the original – 'Proclaim Liberty throughout all the land unto all the inhabitants thereof' – was replaced with the statement, 'Proclaim liberty throughout the world unto all the inhabitants thereof'.

in New York outside the public library on Fifth Avenue, as well as displays in shop windows organised by the Committee on Public Information (Miller, 1926).

As reported in *The Survey* (1918a: 115), the Declaration of Common Aims included 'the possibility of an economic as well as political alliance of the oppressed nationalities of Central Europe'. This was separately announced in *The Survey* (1918b: ix) in glowing terms as something that 'might live in the text books of history after the week's "exits and alarums" of military happenings had been relegated into the undated generalized background of the war'.[13] The declaration set out six principles, of which the last two were: '5. That we believe our peoples, have kindred ideals and purposes, should coordinate their efforts to insure the liberties of their individual nations for the furtherance of their common welfare, provided such a union contributes to the peace and welfare of the world. 6. That there should be formed a league of the nations of the world in a common and binding agreement for genuine and practical cooperation to secure justice and therefore peace among nations.'[14] There were twelve signatories on behalf of their subject peoples: Czechoslovakia, Poland, Jugoslavia, Ukraine, Uhro-Rusine, Lithuania, Roumania, Italian

---

13 They also referred to an earlier body set up in 1917, the League for Small and Subject Nationalities. This was chaired by Cleveland Senator Frederic C. Howe, and had been subject to press vilification for being pro-German, which was part of the context to Miller's trip to Camp Sherman.

14 The other four principles were: 'We accept and subscribe to the following as basic principles for all free peoples: 1. That all governments derive their just power from the consent of the governed. 2. That it is the inalienable right of every people to organize their own government on such principles and in such form as they believe will best promote their welfare, safety and happiness. 3. That the free and natural development of the ideals of any state should be allowed to pursue their normal and unhindered course unless such course harms or threatens the common interest of all. 4. That there should be no secret diplomacy, and all proposed treaties and agreements between nations should be made public — prior to their adoption and ratification.' See Declaration of Common Aims of the Independent Mid-European Nations', Herbert A. Miller Papers, Oberlin College Archives, RG 30/23, series 6, Box 1, 1918.

Irridentists, Unredeemed Greeks, Albania, Zionists and Armenia. Space was left for other signatories.

The objectives of the Union were described as designed to aid oppressed nationalities in central Europe and Asia Minor in winning their freedom; to disseminate information on the just demands of these nationalities, to exert pressure at the peace conference to realise these ends and to ensure mutual cooperation in the tasks of reconstruction (May, 1957: 488). Although it was formed as a body advocating for the rights of oppressed peoples, Miller had hopes that it would break ground in understanding the rights of minorities in the context of colonialism and empire.

To outside observers, the Mid-European Union was a success, if short-lived and quickly superseded. It represented 'a solid front of free, united nations, ranged in mutually protective formation in a long sentry-line from the Baltic to the Adriatic. It means the basis of a rational and enduring peace' (Miller, 1918c: 10). However, the combination of patriotism, nationalism and territorial claims threatened to dominate the negotiations. What, it was asked, would prevent the Union from becoming another Austria? Miller answered, 'No, we would have voluntary relationships' (Miller, 1926, ch. VII: 8). The other question was in what name the delegates acted? As the Jugoslav representative, Hinko Hinković, put it, 'we have no right to settle these questions. First because we are here in America where we represent American organizations – that is our respective colonies. We are not today representatives of our peoples in our respective countries' (Miller, 1926, ch. VII: 8).[15]

---

15 This discussion is mirrored in an exchange over the Czechoslovakian flag between Miller and Masaryk's daughter, Olga Masaryk. Miller preferred a new flag involving the colours blue, red and white and four stars, which was used to recruit Czechoslovakian immigrants to the US army (we have used it as our cover illustration). Otherwise the Czechoslovakian flag was the same as that of Poland and strongly associated with Bohemia. Masaryk replied, 'as to the flag, I must tell you, that no one in exile or emigrated has any right to introduce a brand new flag without the sanction of the whole nation. We prefer our old simple flag to any local innovations ... and "we are all just the servants on the inherited soil of our nation", as one of our poems says.' See Brožek (2011: 78–79).

Much to Miller's regret, the Union ceased to be a political platform for addressing minority rights almost immediately after the end of the war. Its broad basis fragmented into competing alliances of national states. In October 1921, the Allied powers proposed a 'Danubian Union', bringing together Austria, Hungary, Italy, Czechoslovakia, Roumania and Yugoslavia, to be discussed at a conference of the successor states to the Austro-Hungarian Empire in Porto Rose (in the Slovenian region of the new Kingdom of Serbs, Croats and Slovenes). As Donald Hempson (2013) suggests, England and France were most interested in an alliance of Austria, Hungary and Czechoslovakia.[16] Foreign minister Edvard Beneš, representing the latter and not involved in the Mid-European Union, was sceptical of the motivations of Hungary and Austria. He sought to promote the interests of Czechoslovakia as the former industrial heartland of the old Austro-Hungary. He proposed, instead, a 'little Entente' of Czechoslovakia, Romania and the Kingdom of Serbs, Croats and Slovenes against the revanchist ambitions of Hungary. Hempson (2013) sees the Mid-European Union as the precursor to the idea of a Danubian Union, but, of course, the former was a wider grouping of subject nations which expressed opposition both to the German empire and that of Austro-Hungary. Miller had wanted the Mid-European Union to expand beyond Europe and certainly not to become the cockpit in which the 'pathologies of nationalism' would be fought out.

Miller was still expressing hopes that the situation might be different, following travels in central Europe in summer 1920. He reflected on the fact that in Bulgaria its representatives had a surer grasp of different possible futures: 'to Balkanize may yet come to mean to federate and to cooperate; at least, this is the inner impulse,

---

16 See also Géza Jeszenszky (1988), who traces the idea of the Danubian Federation back to the 'Inquiry'. For him, the problem of the Mid-European Union was that it did not also represent the defeated powers of Austria and Hungary, though that judgement misses the intention of its incorporation into the League of Nations, where such issues might have been addressed alongside a robust representation of previously subject nations. Indeed, Miller made precisely Jeszenszky's point in his discussion of the relations between Korea and Japan should independence succeed, as we shall see.

and the rest of the world should try to help it rather than to sit back and say it is impossible, or to follow the historic precedent of stimulating antagonisms in order that the great powers may reap the benefit' (Miller, 1921d: 563). He wrote further, that 'the old empire had gone in seven different directions, and no one can tell whether we are now on the verge of chaos or cosmos'.

Beyond Europe

The founding and (rapid) dissolution of the Mid-European Union was a formative experience for Miller. Many of the reasons behind its dissolution pertained to nationalist exclusions of minority rights within the proposed new nations and their identity as 'ethno-nations'. This was similar, he thought, to the calls for the assimilation of immigrants in the US. Assimilation, if it was to have a meaning other than the domination of one group over another, required the mutual recognition of difference (difference that would itself become less pertinent because identities would not be formed in mutual opposition). Thus, he wrote, 'self-determination of nations does not mean race segregation but an opportunity to develop normally; in other words, so that the group may survive without the use of defensive antipathies. Not until groups are normal is assimilation possible' (Miller, 1919b: 205). This is the argument he would develop in *Races, Nations and Classes* (Miller, 1924a) and further in a global context in *The Beginnings of To-morrow* (Miller, 1933). Each book would include a sharp analysis of the role of religion as both a vehicle of group identity and as a possible pathology. However, he did not pose science against religion; there were pathological forms of science, too, such as eugenics (Miller, 1925).

Contrary to Arthur May's (1957: 488) suggestion that after a short political engagement, Miller returned to 'the tranquillity of Oberlin', he put his efforts into the development of a sociological framework to understand the reasons for the demise of the Mid-European Union. He also substantially extended his critique of empires, both the global empires of European powers and the newer empire of Japan.

The opportunity to engage with other anti-colonial movements came very quickly. In spring 1919, still as director of the Mid-European Union, Miller addressed the Korean Congress held in Philadelphia (also at Independence Hall) as a response to the Japanese suppression of the Korean independence movement.[17] The Congress issued a declaration that was proclaimed in Independence Hall, much in the manner of the action of the Mid-European Union a few months earlier. Impressed by 'their Christian attitude and singleness of purpose' (Miller, 1921c: 10), he established close links with the Korean immigrant leaders, such as Philip Jaisohn and Syngman Rhee, and with the Korean question as such.

For Miller (1929: 5), Korea was 'part and parcel of the problem of Ireland and Central Europe'. As he put it in his address to the Congress, 'the problems of the world now are the problems of society. The great fundamental problem of the world is that of living together. We have a part to play in the world's history in the maintaining of this principle, and men and women must play their part, and Korean men must work with the Korean women not only for the realization of the Korean idea of independence but for the realization of the democracy of the world' (Miller, 2018: 21).

Unlike his engagements with the countries of central Europe that were rather short-lived in terms of practical politics, Miller's connections to Korea embodied an ongoing political commitment, spanning over three decades. Miller became the vice-president of the League of the Friends of Korea (created in Philadelphia on 16 June 1919) and was instrumental in promoting its main goals: raising awareness of Korea's oppression under Japanese imperial rule and generating American support for democracy and religious

---

17 His explanation is characteristically modest, even blasé – he happened to be walking past Independence Hall and noticed a meeting was taking place, entered, and happened to be invited onto the platform to give a speech (Miller, 1929: 5). It may be significant that one of the other main speakers at the conference was Nodie Dora Kim (Nodie Kimhaekim Sohn), a student at Oberlin. Miller had moved from Olivet College to Oberlin in 1914 and prior to going to Ohio State University in 1924.

liberty for Korean Christians in East Asia.[18] Indeed, this was a practical illustration of Miller's view that immigration provided a plural and cosmopolitan sensibility to the host society, by lifting its eyes to what can be learned from the experiences of others and providing an influence over domestic foreign policy – what we might call making 'internationalism national' as part of a 'proportionate patriotism' (Miller, 1924).

This engagement enlarged Miller's perspective on international relations and brought forth new ways to challenge the relationships between race and domination, particularly in his account of religious aspects in anticolonial ethno-nationalisms. The Korean situation exemplified 'imperialistic aggrandizement of the ruling power' (Miller, 1921b: 10), as well as the reality of the new international order for non-Europeans and non-whites. In his understanding, the spirit of freedom, democracy and equality was in contradiction to any hierarchy of race and civilisation, and was superior to the right of self-determination. Moreover, self-determination as a political principle of legitimacy reinforced the nationalist spirit and put issues of race and minority rights to the side.[19]

What Erez Manela (2007: 62) has called the 'internationalization of nationalism' in the context of postwar Egypt, India, China and Korea had been, for Miller, a crucial (and probably inevitable

---

18 By June 1920, it was reported that 18 branches of the League of the Friends of Korea had been established from Boston to San Francisco, with a total membership of 10,000, in part because of its links to the Protestant churches that had supported African American emancipation: 'with strong links to American Protestant missionaries in Korea, the League declared in its founding statement that the United States had a moral obligation to uphold its principles of justice, equality, and freedom throughout the world' (Kim, 2011: 61).
19 As Manela (2007: 62) puts it: 'Taking the right of self-determination as now an established principle of international relations, colonial nationalists moved to leverage Wilson's rhetoric, his perceived power in the international arena, and the opportunities for international action presented by the peace conference to launch international campaigns for the recognition of their own right to national independence and sovereignty. In so doing, they brought the practice as well as the principle of anticolonial nationalism into the arena of international relations.'

aspect) of anti-colonialism. As we have seen, he called it an 'epidemic' brought about as a reaction to European imperialism.[20] His strictures applied also to the Japanese project of imperial expansion. No reference to the duty of an advanced nation was acceptable as the rationale for the imperial conquest. Japan's decision to enlarge her empire by the annexation of Korea was an imitation of Europe, as well as a bid to 'assimilate people by methods similar to those practiced by European powers' (Miller, 1924a: 57).[21] In psychological terms, 'Japan suffers from being the last of the predatory nations' (Miller, 1924a: 127). This was to be an optimistic judgement, given that Nazi Germany would subsequently embark upon a predatory programme of imperial conquest, involving the imposition of a racial order of rule against Slavs and the elimination of Jews (Connelly, 1999). Miller, was, however, sensitive to anti-Semitism in Europe and the threat posed by fascist ethno-nationalism.

Although Miller was clearly on the Korean side, his position laid stress on the rights of minorities, including any 'new' minorities constituted out of the former dominant power. Thus, in his address to the Korean Congress, he affirmed that, 'your cause is the cause of democracy. There is one other thing, however, which we must never forget as being one of the essentials of world democracy; that is, after the group gets free it should cooperate with other groups. In other words, Koreans, Chinese, Japanese, Russians must live together in the same general part of the world' (Miller, 2018: 20).[22]

Miller was also sympathetic to Japan's attempt to insert the clause on racial equality into the Covenant of the League of Nations.

---

20 Miller (1933: 9) wrote, 'when the struggle for freedom in Ireland and in Central Europe reverberated around the world, victims of domination in Asia rose to the call and started a movement that has become a panic'.
21 As he put it elsewhere: 'One wonders how a nation which is such an apt pupil of modern life as Japan can have been so blind to the horrible and inevitable consequences, of which Ireland and the fallen monarchies of Central Europe are such glaring examples' (Miller, 1921b: 10).
22 Miller (1921b) also claimed that 'there can be no peace in the Pacific without settling justly the question of the independence of Korea and the protection of Japan'.

In Asia, the principle of racial equality started to have an effect as one of the only shared ideas of Pan-Asianism. Taken together, Asia was 'one in its humiliation' (Takeuchi, 2004: 319). Japan participated in the Paris Peace Conference as one of the five victorious states. However, the attempt to include racial equality in the Versailles Peace System alongside the principle of national self-determination was dismissed due to Wilson's opposition to it.[23] This was at odds with Miller's understanding that the reaction in Asia to European imperialism would be the end of the project of European empires justified as an expression of their 'superior cultures'.

Conclusion

We began with the idea that Miller directed his science beyond an unfavourable political present to a future that might be coming into being. Events undermined those beginnings, even during Miller's lifetime, from the Nazi invasion and dismemberment of Czechoslovakia in 1939 to the partition of India and Pakistan in 1947, and the deformation of anti-colonial movements into ethno-nationalisms elsewhere. Is there, then, little to learn from the sociology and politics of Herbert Adolphus Miller? Paradoxically, despite his hopes being unrealised they remain relevant to our times, too, which have returned us to problems familiar at the end of the First World War.

23 The Japanese proposal was initially sustained (11 in favour: France, Italy, Japan (2 each), China, Yugoslavia, Greece, Portugal, Czechoslovakia (1 each). 5 against: Great Britain, United States, Poland, Romania, Brazil (1 each)) but then a unanimous vote was introduced as a requirement. Only equality among the members of the League of Nations was prescribed in the Covenant, although Wilson's second draft and the Paris supplemental rules on the draft of Article 6 presented on 10 January 1919 included the following: 'The League of Nations shall require all new States to bind themselves as a condition precedent to their recognition as independent or autonomous States, to accord to all racial or national minorities within their several jurisdictions exactly the same treatment and security, both in law and in fact, that is accorded the racial or national majority of their people' (Miller, 1928: 65).

6

From Fisk to dismissal

Herbert Adolphus Miller had left Oberlin to join Ohio State University in 1924 with the intention of developing his arguments for a global cosmopolitan sociology through study trips abroad. Between 1925 and 1931, these involved visits to the Soviet Union and Baltic States, central Europe, the Middle East, East Asia and India. In all of these contexts, he was interested in the dialectic of oppression and freedom and revolutions against domination, especially where these involved one racialised group claiming superiority over another. The trips, as we shall see, would get him into trouble with Ohio State University. They would reinforce misgivings within the university associated with his commitment to equality among the races and his pedagogic practices.

We have seen in earlier chapters that Miller had a long-standing connection with Fisk following his first teaching appointment there between 1899 and 1902. He had married the daughter of the founding President, Erastus Milo Cravath, and they continued to visit, with Miller offering lectures on what was virtually an annual basis. He also developed close connections with local Black colleges when he was at Olivet and Oberlin, for example, with Wilberforce University in Ohio. He had also taken over as Chair of the Columbus branch of the National Urban League when he joined Ohio State University.

Unfortunately, we have been unable to locate any archival records of the branch and there is nothing in the standard history of the League about the branch during his tenure (Parris and Brooks, 1971). Knowing Miller's character and commitments, it would not have been a sinecure and nor would he have accommodated to its moderate White membership (the League brought Black and White leaders, business people and community organisations together, and so was subject to the trends otherwise described for municipal bodies and Black colleges). Indeed, one of the trustees at Fisk, the Quaker social reformer Levi Hollingsworth Wood, was instrumental in setting up the National Urban League, as was his brother-in-law, Paul Cravath. Robert E. Park was chair for two years of the newly formed Chicago branch in 1918 and helped to push for a 'moderate' response to the Chicago race riots of 1919 through the branch discouraging migration north (Strickland, 1966).

In 1924–25 Miller was drawn into a dispute at Fisk University when he was appointed as chair of a committee to resolve the future of the university after student protests had forced the resignation of its president, Fayette McKenzie. Having been drafted in to resolve the situation at Fisk, he would be subject to dismissal proceedings by his own university. In this section, we will discuss the relation between these two events and his investigative trips abroad. In a deposition to the American Association of University Professors which investigated the circumstances of his dismissal, he described the president at Ohio State University investigating various allegations made against him: '(1) My activities in India; (2) that I had been on the point of being dismissed from Oberlin when I came to Ohio State University in 1924; and (3) that my attitude on matters of Race were [sic] unsound' (Sabine, 1931: 467).

The Fisk University Strike

In previous chapters we discussed the racial tensions associated with the professionalisation of higher education (including research) and city governance. The need for civil rights activists to adjust the aspiration for equality to pleas for caution made by White liberals and business interests, for example, chafed upon Black citizens. This was especially so in the context of the great migration north that had begun in the decade prior to the First World War. Organisations like the Urban League and the NAACP were set up as coalitions of White and Black interests, while the historically Black colleges depended on White philanthropy and were run by White presidents and White chairs of their boards of trustees (the Tuskegee Institute was an exception, with Booker T. Washington as President). W. E. B. Du Bois's hopes that African American participation in the First World War would lead to greater equality were dashed and 1919 saw a series of race riots across American cities, with those in Chicago being particularly violent. Violence against Black Americans was not new, but as Arthur Waskow (1966) has argued, these riots represented a new confidence in fighting back against suppression and they gave birth to a more assertive position associated with what came to be called the 'new Negro' (Locke, 1925; Baldwin, 2003). The Chicago Urban League was persuaded that the problem lay in the rapid movement of the rural poor from the South into a new urban environment and became engaged in programmes to persuade prospective migrants to stay. In contrast, the activists in the NAACP pressed for a more radical response.

The tensions were not new, but they were becoming more acute. They came to a head at the historically Black colleges, for example at Howard and, especially, Fisk University, and in their local communities. Du Bois began to address these concerns through the pages of *The Crisis* following the formation of the Niagara Movement in 1905, which had called for a 'torrent' of activism (Jones, 2011). Problems of inadequate college education were of long standing but became acute in the period following the First World War. For example, there had been concerns at Fisk under the regime of President George Augustus Gates during his short term in office between 1909 and the end of 1912 (following his death in a train accident that damaged his health there was a brief hiatus before the appointment of a new president, Fayette McKenzie, in 1915). Gates was criticised by the local Black community in Nashville for sacking Black faculty and replacing them with White teachers (Lamon, 1974). A hardening of race relations in Nashville was also evident in new Jim Crow laws segregating streetcars in 1906 and protest against it by newspapers serving the Black community, such as the Nashville *Globe* (Meier and Rudwick, 1969). The university was seen as bending towards the White community, a process reinforced in the actions of its new president, the dour McKenzie.

President McKenzie pursued a conservative line towards student expression, both socially and politically. He enforced a rigid dress code, banned student fraternities and sororities, and in 1915 closed the student newspaper, the *Fisk Bulletin*, merging it with the university's *Fisk University News*. This was particularly irksome to the student body after 1919. Many of the male students had been in the armed services, including as officers in segregated regiments, and they resented the restrictions placed upon them and the paternalism of the president. McKenzie resisted calls to appoint Black Heads of Department, or to appoint Black office staff (Lamon, 1974). Instead, he demanded loyalty from faculty and, in the course of the dispute that would come to envelop the university late in 1924, he stated that students and staff alike who would not toe his line should leave. Those that continued to oppose him were suspended.

The conditions for a challenge to President McKenzie's authority were set, but the precipitating cause was a speech by Du Bois, one of Fisk's most illustrious alumni, given at the commencement ceremony in June 1924. He was due to attend for the graduation of his daughter, Yolande, and the university had taken the opportunity to invite him to give the address to the graduating class. With faculty and dignitaries on the platform behind him, Du Bois delivered a blistering attack on the regime of President McKenzie, who was also sitting among the other dignitaries. Fisk University had just concluded a successful campaign for a $1 million endowment fund, but Du Bois lamented its loss of the ideals of its founders and their commitment to racial equality. His speech – entitled '*Diuturni silenti*' (Du Bois 1924a) – invoked Cicero and began with a Latin epigram from Cicero.[1] This was intended to call up the lost ideals of racial equality in education as well as to be a *mea culpa* by Du Bois for his silence hitherto over the decline. More specifically, it was a call to action to the alumni to recover their college. His intervention had been prefigured by

1 '*Diuturni silenti, patres conscripti, quo eram his temporibus usus, non timore aliquo, sed partim dolore, partim verecundia, finem hodiernus dies attulit, idemque initium quae vellem quaeque sentirem meo pristino more dicendi.*' [Today has ended my lasting silence, senate elders, not on account of any particular fear, but because I have been sad and dumb for long enough, and this speech marks the resumption of my former custom of saying what I will and what I think.]

other articles on race, education and equality in the *Mercury* and *The Crisis* which continued through into 1925 with regular exposés of the situation at Fisk (Du Bois, 1924b, 1925a, 1925b). He also re-established the *Fisk Bulletin* and published it from the New York Fisk Alumni Club. It printed his speech (Du Bois, 1924a) and other attacks upon President McKenzie and other analyses of the situation confronting Black Americans. Essentially, Du Bois argued that McKenzie had accommodated the views of the White South, which were hardening against the dismantling of any of the bi-racial institutions and practices which sustained their domination.

Stung by Du Bois's rebukes, President McKenzie demanded endorsement of his policies from the Board of Trustees, which was forthcoming in October 1924, alongside a number of further statements from Du Bois (1924b, 1924c) and 'A statement of grievances against Fayette A. McKenzie as President of Fisk University'.[2] Paul Cravath was Chair of the Board of Trustees and it was resolved to announce a committee of alumni to inquire into the grievances and broker a way forward. The appointees were largely favourable to compromise and support for McKenzie (they included Margaret Murray Washington, wife of Booker T. Washington). This was announced, together with speeches, at Jubilee Day in November 1924, where Miller also made a speech arguing that there was a global problem of suppressed and oppressed peoples, of which African Americans were one, and that there was a need to look beyond the situation of oppression to a wider equality for all (Miller, 1924b).

In all the discussion of the events at Fisk and his role within it, there is no mention of Miller's close connection to Fisk, though his family connections and sympathies were known to Du Bois

---

2   A number of copies of the latter document are in the Fisk archives, but its authorship is not clear even in the Trustees' response to it. The suggestion is that it was written by Du Bois as a summary from notes of his commencement speech in response to a request from the Trustees for a copy of the speech. By the time the Trustees met in October the speech was published in its full form. Statement of Grievances against Fayette A. McKenzie as President of Fisk University, Executive Committee Minutes of the Board of Fisk University, 22 October 1924.

and to Mary Spence, the first white female graduate of Fisk and professor there (she was the daughter of Adam Spence, academic Dean under Erastus Cravath's regime and someone regarded in the highest estimation by Du Bois), as well as to other members of the alumni group. According to Alrutheus Taylor (1952), this group were aware of the humiliations visited upon the students by President McKenzie and were determined to draw a conciliatory tone.[3] Paul Cravath also arranged for a delegation of seven students to meet with the President and Trustees to present their grievances, including concerns about the 'spirit of distrust', the 'spirit of oppression' and the 'race element'.[4]

In a letter to Du Bois in December, Miller describes being appointed to the group as 'educational expert', along with Georgia Laura White, Dean of Women at Cornell. He goes on, 'I may say that we gave a good deal of advice, and the trustees are now fully aware of the situation.' It is also evident that he was in contact with the student committee.[5] However, it seems that President McKenzie had little intention of listening either to the alumni or students. Miller later described that his role as adviser was largely redundant, writing to George Streator in March 1925 that 'although I have talked with a number of people and read what has been printed I have had little direct communication about the situation at Fisk'.[6] Streator was a talented communicator and had joined Du Bois as editor of the new *Fisk Bulletin* and would go on to be business manager of *The Crisis*.

The student body's longstanding grievances with President McKenzie developed into regular and noisy protests at the dormitories from October 1924 onwards. On 4 February 1925 students staged a demonstration and McKenzie called police onto campus.

---

3 These humiliations included holding a concert in the town following its tradition of segregated audiences.
4 Board of Trustees Minutes, 17 November 1924.
5 Letter from Miller to Du Bois, 16 December 1924. Temple University, Samuel Paley Library, Conwellana-Templana Collection.
6 Letter from Miller to George Streator, 11 March 1925. Temple University, Samuel Paley Library, Conwellana-Templana Collection. Significantly, letters by Du Bois and Streator are addressed to both Miller and Mrs Miller. Streator addresses them, 'My dear friends'.

This was a deeply provocative gesture given that this was a White police force and over seventy officers were involved. In addition, it had followed a year of violence against the Black community in Nashville, including a lynching. He also brought felony riot charges against five of the students who had presented their grievances in November. They were imprisoned because bail was not available for such a serious charge. However, the charges collapsed when it transpired that they had not been on campus at the time. The students responded by calling a strike and boycott led by Streator, one of the five arrested, which was the occasion of his letter to Miller in March.

Still McKenzie held out, with the support of the Board of Trustees, although Paul Cravath was away. However, despite trying to support McKenzie, the Board was beginning to fracture because of his intransigence. Some of the Black members of the Board blamed the agitation of Du Bois, but it was clear that the local Black community was coming around to his way of thinking, in part mobilised by Streator who, on 9 February, called a mass meeting of 3,000 at the Negro Board of Trade. The meeting demanded, among other resolutions, an impartial investigation of student demands and the removal of President McKenzie. Obdurate to the end, McKenzie continued in office until, on 16 April 1925, he ungraciously resigned, which the Board of Trustees allowed with immediate effect.

As Lester Lamon puts it, 'the Board of Trustees had the delicate task of replacing McKenzie with a man who could regain Negro confidence without antagonizing Nashville whites' (1974: 243). A Committee on Administration was set up by the trustees, headed by Miller, and comprising four Black members of faculty, Professor Augustus F. Shaw, Professor Thomas W. Brumfield, Mrs Minnie Scott Crosthwait and Miss L. Elizabeth Collinge, and one trustee, L. Hollingsworth Wood. According to Taylor (1952: 468), Miller had agreed to be seconded from Ohio State University to Fisk for several days a week until the end of the academic year. The task was to find a new president and resolve the difficulties that had led to the resignation of President McKenzie, as well as to secure the endowment fund and the support of White philanthropy.

There was no expectation that Fisk would appoint a Black president and, indeed, Du Bois had not made it part of the demands for reform, although the events at Fisk would presage a pronounced shift in that direction. In the meantime, however, *The Crisis* referred to Miller as 'acting president', while Du Bois sought to persuade Miller to take on the role on a permanent basis and others, including Mary Spence, lobbied the trustees to that effect. There is no correspondence to indicate why Miller was unwilling to do so. In the end a sociologist from Columbia, Thomas Elsa Jones, was recommended by the Committee. He took up the position in February 1926 and was widely regarded to be a successful appointment. He was succeeded in 1946 by Charles Johnson, who had come to Fisk in 1926 after the reforms initiated under Miller's direction.

There are few surviving records to describe the actions of the Committee on Administration. Early in its tenure, Miller made reports to the alumni via the *Fisk University News* in April and May 1925. Taylor (1952: 434–471) quotes liberally from them, but we have found no copies in any archive and the Hathi Trust digital catalogue lists no location for extant copies. Nor do there seem to be minutes of the Committee in the Fisk archive. We have to rely on the reported outcomes of its interventions and their celebration in the pages of *The Crisis*. Taylor, however, does report a statement by Miller at the start of the process, which is characteristic both of his forthright style and his diplomacy. It is reminiscent of the character shown in his time with the Mid-European Union: 'I know of nothing more significant for the future than the awakening self-consciousness of the group which Fisk represents to its possibilities of cultural development. The stimulus of its difficulties will both accelerate it and multiply its values' (Taylor, 1952: 469).

The actions of the Committee on Administration were both direct and comprehensive. All suspended staff and students were reinstated, representative committees were set up in halls, along with a student council and a new student paper supported by a $500 grant. A sorority and fraternity were put in place alongside a new athletic association. Black faculty members were appointed to head all departments and Professor Shaw made Dean. At the same time measures were taken to make new appointments of Black faculty. Remarkably, this was all done while securing the endowment fund which had precipitated Du Bois's critique and a crisis from which Fisk now appeared to emerge restored. As Lamon describes the graduating class of 1926 – the strikers of 1925 – they showed their 'pleasure' at the changes made under Miller and Thomas Elsa Jones. During the 1926 commencement they 'had their lives insured in a colored insurance company, the Supreme Life and Casualty Company of Columbus, Ohio, in favour of the university' (Lamon, 1974: 244).[7]

Earl Wright II calls the development of sociology at Fisk after 1926 its 'golden age', with the appointment of Charles S. Johnson as the Chair of Department. Johnson, as we have seen, was strongly associated with Chicago sociology and other appointments had a similar connection. Johnson was also responsible for inviting Park to a part-time appointment at Fisk following his retirement from Chicago in 1934. Although Miller is now a largely forgotten figure, his trajectory from the Carnegie project on Americanisation through his engagement with the Mid-European Union and on to his brief return to Fisk involved decisive interventions formed around his sociological commitments to racial equality and the self-determination of oppressed groups. He created the conditions for the incorporation of Fisk into the Chicago school circle (Chapoulie, 2020), even as his own role was effaced.

The future moves East

Paul Cravath had responded to Mary Spence's urging of Miller's appointment as President in September 1925 with the comment that Miller was preparing for a trip abroad. We have already indicated that these trips were an integral part of his pedagogic practice. His first trip abroad was to Czechoslovakia in 1912, a trip which concluded with a visit to Vienna and Moscow. In 1920, following the demise of the Mid-European Union, he visited Czechoslovakia, Hungary and Bulgaria. After the publication of *Races, Nations and Classes* in 1924 and his move from Oberlin to Ohio State University, these travels took on a new, global significance. He negotiated periods of leave from Ohio State in order to develop his arguments for a global cosmopolitan sociology through study trips further afield. They incorporated visits to sites of social reform (hospitals,

---

7 Lamon is citing a report in *The Crisis* XXXII (July 1926).

leper colonies, reformatories, and so on) within the countries visited, lectures and meetings with key figures, both political and academic). In autumn and spring 1925/26 he undertook a trip from Czechoslovakia to Russia and the Baltic states, and, thence on to Greece, Turkey, Syria, Lebanon and Palestine. This trip was undertaken without his wife Bessy. Finally, in 1929/30, he made an extensive trip, together with Bessy, for the academic year taking in Japan, Korea, and spending a lengthy period in China, including Manchuria, before travelling through Indo-China (Vietnam, Laos, Cambodia, Burma and Thailand) and on to India, Iraq, Palestine, Syria and Turkey. For the first of these trips, he wrote a regular correspondence with Bessy, of which the letters from the Soviet Russian leg remain. For the second trip he wrote a 'log' of each leg of the trip, which he sent to a number of colleagues, including at Ohio State University, as well as Tomáš Masaryk. Edited versions were also published in instalments in the Ba'hai magazine *World Unity* and in the *Ohio Sociologist*.

Miller had a capacious definition of what constituted the 'East', which is perhaps best understood in terms of his map of the 'Bulwark of Freedom' (reproduced here as Figure 4.1). Essentially, it meant going forth into the hinterlands of that line from the Baltic to the Adriatic via the Black Sea. In this sense, Russia is 'Eastern', as much as India and China. His pragmatic orientation was towards what can be learned from others, which involved placing Western 'civilisation' into question. He repudiated the idea of a linear development which divided the 'West' from the 'rest' and has them playing 'catch-up' under imperial tutelage. The 'rest' were civilisations – ethical systems and political practices – of great longevity and maturity. They are expressed in religious beliefs and political philosophies of world-historical significance. These are part of the past and present, but also form new possibilities for the future.

Miller's approach was symmetrical; just as the West can learn from others, so, too, can others learn from Christianity and science represented by the West. Miller reports seeing a bible on a side table on a visit to Gandhi's ashram and asking him about the significance of Christianity in India, to which the Mahatma had replied: 'In their efforts to convert the Hindus they had pointed out many of the bad practices of the Hindu religion. The important result has been to send the Hindus back to their own Scriptures to see whether objectionable ideas like that of caste are inherent in the original teachings. They found that they are not. The result has been reform revival throughout Hinduism.'[8]

However, according to Miller, reciprocal learning cannot take place in circumstances of domination. Domination creates mutual and reciprocal 'pathologies', of which ethno-nationalism is one, which in turn can create the oppression of subject minorities (Miller, 1924a). Empires, according to Miller, also frequently secure their domination through a tactic of divide and rule, which exacerbates relations among groups in the context of anti-colonial struggles. This is something that he sees as a particular feature of British rule in India (Miller, 1933). It is also something that gives rise to attempts to fix new national boundaries through population movement and exchange (whether voluntary or coerced) which accentuates nationalist sentiments and makes remaining minority populations more vulnerable.

We have already seen that, from his experiences with the Mid-European Union, Miller developed an interest in what we can term postcolonial, 'un-national' political arrangements associated with unions and federations in which there would be mutual protection of minorities and self-determination in relation to language and religion. He believed that capitalism had shown itself incapable of reform to address poverty and inequality and that it was entangled with imperialism, but he did not believe that communism represented the answer to its ills. His pragmatism opposed the idea of 'social theory' or 'laws' as 'the exclusive explanation of all the forces and problems in society. Witness the Eugenists and Economic Determinists' (Miller, 1924a: xi).

In fact, Miller came to understand that Gandhi's movement might pose significant new ways of thinking about the economy: 'I never quite understood the principle underlying Gandhi's economic theory. It seemed to be flying in the face of what the world has

---

8 H. A. Miller, 'Round the World Log of a Sociologist: Bombay, India, March 13, 1930', Archive of the T. G. Masaryk Institute, Prague, R–46-29/c, Box 509, 1930, p. 4.

accepted as the inevitable economic process. I am not so sure now. We have accepted that the right thing is more production and more consumption; our system is based on the principle that people must be made dissatisfied with what they have in order to make them buy a new model. We have carried this almost to fanaticism. It may be another of India's contributions to show that there is something wrong with us.'[9]

In contrast, Miller's interest in Russia was in the way in which minority rights were addressed and the 'internationalism' it represented. The Soviet Union's structure of separate republics and the principle of the equality of nationalities – through the Commissariat of Nationalities – was real in its consequences, albeit that it derived from a political necessity of maintaining a united front against threats from the Western powers. Even if its ideological framework repudiated bourgeois rights of individuals, the Soviet counter-principle of (proletarian) 'internationalism' was set against ethno-national claims while accommodating minority rights. However, according to Miller, communism was also functioning as a religion and its zeal would soon fade, leaving a crisis of legitimacy in its wake, a crisis that would most likely involve repression by the secret police.[10] This might be the occasion for the rise of ethno-nationalist claims.

Miller was more convinced by the prospects of pluralism in India and in China as each negotiated the problems created by imperialism. In China, he supported the revolution of 1911 and Sun Yat-sen's Kuomintang government. However, he also found deep poverty and conflicts between war lords, among whom he regarded Chang Kai-shek as pre-eminent (albeit that he was successor of Sun Yat-sen as leader of the Kuomintang). Characteristically, Miller was drawn to Sun Yat-sen through the latter's conversion to Christianity, and his negotiation of its principles alongside Confucian values as indicating a promising future way forward.

---

9 H. A. Miller, 'Round the World Log of a Sociologist: Bombay, India, March 13, 1930', Archive of the T. G. Masaryk Institute, Prague, R–46–29/c, Box 509, 1930, p. 5.
10 See H. A. Miller, 'Personal notes on Russia and the Baltic States', Archive of the T. G. Masaryk Institute, Prague, R–46–89/i, Box 522, 1925.

Significantly, the combination of Christianity and traditional values had proven potent in the case of Korea and, on his visit to Japan, he had found a similarly inspiring combination in the person and practice of the social reformer Toyohiko Kagawa.[11]

While it might appear that Miller was advocating learning from the West, he was clear that learning should be symmetrical and the East had answers to a deep crisis in the West. His real interest was in a productive plurality of influences; that is, in a plural cosmopolitanism. Japan, Korea and China all manifested pathological forms of nationalism to a greater or lesser degree, and it was in India that Miller saw the most complete realisation of the possibility of a plural global order, embodied in the teachings and practices of Gandhi. It is likely that Miller's interest in India was developed and refined by his student Jayaprakash Narayan, who enrolled in the MA programme in sociology at Ohio State University in 1928 and was taught by Miller. Narayan imbibed Marxism and communist politics in the USA and went on to direct the radical wing of the Indian Congress Party before and after independence. Pranav Jani (2013) reports a long interview provided by Narayan in Hindi to the Nehru Memorial Museum and Library in Delhi in 1972 where he credits Miller with developing the connections between anti-colonial struggles and struggles for racial equality in the US. By the time that the Millers travelled to India, Narayan had also returned there and it was he who facilitated their meeting with Gandhi.

As Nazmul Sultan (2022b) has suggested, any 'global' appropriation of Gandhi is paradoxical because he was firmly grounded in the 'local' and indifferent to universalising claims, including those of anti-imperialism. But, while Miller was concerned with imperialism and resistance to it as global phenomena, his view was that what

---

11 Kagawa's last book *Cosmic Purpose* set out a religiously infused humanism very much attuned with Miller's idea of a 'cosmic' cosmopolitanism. While this may seem out of step with contemporary social-scientific sensibilities, it was very much the language of the First Universal Races Congress in London in 1911. This was organised by the Ethical Society (forerunner of Humanists UK), but in a context where humanism was aligned with a plurality of religiously-derived ethical systems (see Hisakazu, 2016). See also H. A. Miller, 'A New Prophet in Asia', Archive of the T. G. Masaryk Institute, Prague, R–46–35/f, Box 511, 1929.

followed would be a plural cosmopolitanism, reflecting different local traditions and ways of living together.[12] Sultan locates Gandhi in the federalist and pluralist way of thinking set out by Brajendra Nath Seal and this was part of the milieu in which Miller was moving in India. The Millers travelled to Lucknow in February 1930 and met with Professor Radhakamal Mukerjee, who, as Sultan (2022a) argues, was the most important developer of Seal's ideas.

The impact on Miller of his meeting with Gandhi was profound. It followed meetings with other leaders of Indian independence, such as Nehru, Muhammed Ali Jinnah and Sardar Patel, where he discussed issues of religious representation (especially that of Muslims, in the context of Jinna's leaning towards separatism) as well as the role of violence in the struggle for independence. These meetings had been overshadowed by the forthcoming London Round Table Conference set up by then Labour party Prime Minister Ramsay MacDonald. The conference would offer neither independence, nor Dominion status (such as enjoyed by White-settler colonies, such as Canada, Australia and New Zealand, among others, which would shortly thereafter become equal members of the British Commonwealth of Nations in 1931). The civil disobedience campaign by the Indian National Congress, inspired by Gandhi, was being vigorously suppressed so Congress party members would not initially be part of the conference.[13]

Miller describes *Satyāgraha* (Gandhi's popular 'movement of truth') as overcoming an otherwise elite-dominated independence movement by developing consciousness among the peasant masses to overcome an 'oppression psychosis' whereby those who were dominated internalised the negative judgements of their oppressors,

---

12 Miller comments in his 'log' that 'Gandhi is not an internationalist, nor a statesman. He is a saint.' and that he is 'a man with a modern education who is dominated by the spiritual technic of India with which he is attacking problems of modern government and industrial reorganization'. H. A. Miller, 'Around the World Log of a Sociologist: Delhi, India, February 27', Archive of the T. G. Masaryk Institute, Prague, R–46–29/c, Box 509, 1930, pp. 10, 6.

13 As the crisis deepened, they would be released to attend subsequent conferences.

or released their feelings in revenge. The timing of Miller's visit to Gandhi's ashram near Ahmedabad was propitious. It was just as the march in protest at the salt tax was being prepared.[14] In his log for 13 March 1930 written in Bombay, he records that 'I have told the students at various universities that it was impossible to judge just what the nationalist situation is in India because I do not know how insane they are. I think they are now in a way to increase their insanity greatly in the near future.'[15] It is clear that he holds this 'insanity' in the highest regard as the revolutionary spirit that will sweep the British from India. It is this sentiment that underpinned his speech reported in the Indian press that would be a factor in his dismissal from Ohio State University.

Dismissal

In a cause célèbre of the American Association of University Professors (AAUP), action for dismissal was brought against Miller by Ohio State University in 1931 for speeches in India deemed to be 'anti-British' and offensive to the trustees of the university. In the AAUP's deposition (Sabine, 1931), it identified that he had also been subject to complaints by parents of students for his liberal attitudes toward race relations, as well as his stances on domestic politics.[16]

The evidence shows that the case against Miller had its roots in a long-term disgruntlement on the side of the Board of Trustees and its dominant figure, an industrialist and banker Julius Stone, with what was perceived as liberal radicalism. Complaints against Miller

14 The Millers' guide, Jayaprakash Narayan, was jailed for civil disobedience in 1932.
15 H. A. Miller, 'Around the World Log of a Sociologist: Delhi, India, March 1', Archive of the T. G. Masaryk Institute, Prague, R–46–29/c, Box 509, 1930, p. 3.
16 The Board of Trustees gave three reasons for the decision not to re-engage Miller: the incident in Korea where Miller's public speech was interrupted by Japanese police after Miller had mentioned a forbidden word 'republic' in a reference to the situation in Czechoslovakia, the Bombay speech, and recurring complaints from parents (Sabine, 1931: 450).

stretched back a number of years and, although action was taken on the basis of the speech in Bombay, it dragged out and the latter did not seem to be decisive. The AAUP's deposition – as well as reports in the local newspaper – suggest that the tipping factor might have been his supportive speech to a student meeting protesting compulsory military drill for male students.[17] This took place just before the state legislature was meeting to discuss possible cuts to the university's grant. It is also clear that the decision of the Board was not based on faculty advice. Both the Dean of the College, Walter C. Weidler, and the head of the sociology department, James E. Hagerty, stood up strongly for Miller, seeing the case as an ad hoc fabrication and an outrageous interference of the Board in university matters.[18] The fact that Miller was by far the most internationally recognised social scientist at Ohio State made him a target for the Board's determination to escalate the actions against members of the liberal group.

Although the whole report of the AAUP revolved around academic freedom and the definition of tenure, the response of engaged publics threw a spotlight on the business interests involved. Clearly, the Board's disrespect for the faculty, its

17 Letter from Coble to Tyler, 23 June 1931. 'The debate on compulsory military drill appears to have had no direct connection with the Miller case, although it has importance in connection with the present status of freedom of speech at Ohio State University', Special Collections Research Center, George Washington University, AAUP Records, Committee A on Academic Freedom and Tenure, Box 106, Folder 2: Series 6, Subseries 1, p. 30.

18 The ASS issued a resolution in support of Hagerty, the head of the department of sociology, for 'his recent courageous stand for academic freedom at Ohio State University in the situation there'. Letter from Wirth to Tyler, 15 February 1932, Special Collections Research Center, George Washington University, AAUP Records, Committee A on Academic Freedom and Tenure, Box 106, Folder 2: Series 6, Subseries 1, p. 182. Louis Wirth was Secretary to the ASS and a note indicates a copy was sent to Hagerty and Miller. The letter makes no mention of Miller by name, referring instead to its disapproval of the situation at the university 'along the lines of the report' of the AAUP. Significantly, Miller was listed on the ASS headed notepaper as a member of the Executive Committee, and as being at Oberlin (where he had a house to which he and Bessy had moved following his dismissal).

refusal to engage in any further discussion and the weak position of the administration indicated the disproportionate power of the trustees. 153 members of the Ohio State faculty signed a protest against the actions of the Board and the president. Straight after the final letter of dismissal, 3,000 students signed a petition for Miller's reinstatement. An article in *The Nation* by Norman Thomas, presidential candidate for the Socialist party, commented that 'not for many years there has been so clear a demonstration that a board of trustees, dominated by the usual business ideas, expects its students to be docile Babbitts in embryo, its university president to be a high-grade office manager, and its faculty to conform or get out'.[19]

In many respects, Miller's case was emblematic of the situation in many American universities, whether public or private. It epitomised rising tensions among university boards and faculties in the difficult circumstances of the Great Depression. The Board at Ohio State did not care much to build up a credible case against Miller.[20] Presumably, its main motivation, besides demonstrating its own power, was that of establishing that there were restrictions on academic freedom when it came to issues of activism.[21] The AAUP, for its part, knew that they had been holding all the (symbolic) aces

---

19 'Hire Learning' at Ohio State, Norman Thomas, *The Nation* 1132(3441), 7 June 1931, pp. 652–656.
20 The formal position at the university was that academics were employed on an annual rolling contract, although the expectation was that contracts would be renewed. When Miller was advised that his contract would end, he was also informed that, although his dismissal was with effect from the start of the 1931/32 academic year, because of earlier leave he would be required to teach out two semesters beginning in autumn 1931. News items on his dismissal and the failure of the university to reinstate him after the AAUP report are frequently accompanied by him teaching classes at Ohio State.
21 Miller's views came under scrutiny in the course of the investigation. The outcome was that the views expressed in his 'writings and teaching were more moderate than those held by other distinguished workers (sociologists and anthropologists) in the field' (Sabine, 1931: 459). This was largely because Miller could not be enrolled under a 'red scare' since his main focus was the rights of suppressed peoples, rather than economic exploitation.

and had been able to press Miller's case towards a message about the academic profession in a situation when economic constraints increasingly legitimised actions against the faculty.[22] It was not sufficient to stay the execution of Miller's dismissal. Miller's own understanding of his position in the midst of the excitement was largely stoic. This is probably best captured in Miller's comments for the *New York Times* which he made right after his exoneration by the AAUP: 'In this controversy I am only an incident. The real issue is Ohio State University and its standing among the universities of the world.'[23] Both his public comments and private considerations indicated that he became embroiled in the conflict rather than sought it out. Indeed, it is ironic that his one failure at diplomacy was in his own interest.

Interestingly, the Bombay speech – a public outdoor gathering on the eve of Gandhi's Salt March – that sparked the whole affair reckoned on a pragmatist embrace of problem-solving as the way forward. 'I feel that it is not right that an American should be asked to speak at this meeting. But I am a professor who is interested in the way human beings are trying to solve their problems ... The thing that you are trying to do now is to bring religion to the solution of the two great problems ..., namely, the problem of settling your differences in a genuine religious spirit and the problem of applying religion to the solution of practical problems.'[24]

The seemingly inoffensive nature of the Bombay speech gives credibility to other sources of the Board's animosity towards Miller, namely his views on racial issues. Of course, these were connected in that he viewed the issues to be those of 'colored peoples everywhere'. In a letter to the president of the Ohio State University, George W. Rightmire, Miller explicitly stated, 'it is my

---

22 The response of the AAUP was prompt. It took only four months from the first meeting of the investigating committee to the publication of the overall report. The number of requests for defence against various forms of maltreatment of faculty members skyrocketed in 1931. The AAUP mentions more than sixty appeals that year.
23 'Ousting of Miller in Ohio Assailed', *New York Times*, 10 August 1931.
24 *Bombay Chronicle*, 13 March 1930.

personal opinion that the race issue underlines much of the animus against me' (Sabine, 1931: 467).[25] Miller's active engagement with the Urban League, his links to historically Black universities as well as his 'laboratory practice' in race relations, which included (voluntary) trips with students to Wilberforce University, raised concerns among the Board members who repeatedly refused to enrol a Black student, although the Urban League provided full funding for her.[26]

Conclusion

The fact that Miller had a full exoneration from the AAUP report which received nationwide attention had no impact on the decision not to re-engage him at Ohio State. For the next two years, Miller was active on the lecture platform. William H. Cowley, of the *Journal of Higher Education*'s editorial office, who acted as Miller's agent after his dismissal, put on offer lectures on seven subjects (Gandhi of India; The Rise of the East; Dynamic China; Three World Personalities – Lenin, Gandhi and Sun Yat-sen;

---

25 Miller put stress on this aspect also in his letter to the investigating committee of the AAUP: 'My own conviction is that the race prejudice is very largely at the bottom.' Letter from Miller to the Committee of the AAUP, Columbus, 15 June 1931, Special Collections Research Center, George Washington University, AAUP Records, Committee A on Academic Freedom and Tenure, Box 106, Folder 2: Series 6, Subseries 1.

26 As late as 1933, almost two years after Miller's dismissal, Samuel A. Mitchell, a member of the AAUP committee in Miller's case, wrote to Harry W. Tyler, general secretary of the AAUP, that he saw no chance of Miller to be returned to Ohio State despite continuing activities in his support. 'With so few positions available it will depend on the strength of the friendship and loyalty of Professor Miller's friends. He was probably a little too free in his statements regarding racial equality and especially in his mixing of the blacks and whites in his experimental (?) sociology.' Letter from Mitchell to Tyler, 11 March 1933,. Special Collections Research Center, George Washington University, AAUP Records, Committee A on Academic Freedom and Tenure, Box 106, Folder 2: Series 6, Subseries 1.

The American Race Problem; The World Race Problem; The Present Importance of Academic Freedom).[27]

Understandably, the Ohio State affair had a detrimental effect on Miller's sociological career and, irrespective of extensive public support, contributed to the marginalisation of his positions in the discipline. Essentially, Miller's understanding of disciplinary purpose in the 1930s differed much more significantly from the standard (professional) positions within the discipline than had been the case in the 1910s or early 1920s. In the main, it had moved away from giving primacy to sociology's public and pedagogic roles to emphasise research instead, a step that Miller was disinclined to take.

In 1933 Miller was 58 years of age and was appointed to a position at Bryn Mawr College. As required by the statutes of the college, he had to be appointed on the lowest rung as a lecturer with a salary commensurate with that role. His brother-in-law, Paul Cravath, privately, and without the knowledge of the Millers, made an annual subvention to the college to lift his salary.[28] His public activities remained extensive, as did his involvement with Bryn Mawr. Such was his standing that when he gave a commencement address at Cheney University, a local Black college, he was described in the local press as the President of Bryn Mawr, not as a lowly lecturer.[29]

Postscript

We have saved our discussion of the conflict over racial integration at Black Mountain College until now, to be able to draw upon a more fully established understanding of Miller as sociologist and as

27 Letter from Cowley to Tyler, 8 August 1931, Special Collections Research Center, The George Washington University, AAUP Records, Committee A on Academic Freedom and Tenure, Box 106, Folder 2: Series 6, Subseries 1, p. 3.
28 Letter from Park to Cravath, 5 May 1938. Herbert Adolphus Miller Papers, Bryn Mawr College Special Collections.
29 As reported in the article 'Colored Races Are World's Hope, Says Bryn Mawr Prexy', published in *The Afro-American* (Baltimore, MD), 20 June 1934. We have not been able to locate a text of the speech.

advocate for racial equality, including his management of a similar set of issues at Fisk. What we know of the episode comes from Martin Duberman's (1972) discussion, which was based on faculty minutes and interviews with former students and faculty members. By his own account, his book involved his own immersion and imaginative identification with the experience of the college. He writes from his own perspective as a civil rights activist – gay rights, in particular – in the late 1960s. This includes sympathy with those he perceives to be social and political 'radicals' at the college and distrust of those he understands as 'conservative', although, as we observed earlier, the designations are swapped around where pedagogic practice is concerned.[30]

One of the founding members of Black Mountain College, theatre studies academic Bob Wunsch, had sounded out a number of Black colleagues about the matter, some of whom he had known at Rollins before his dismissal. Zora Neale Hurston had written to him, saying, 'even at this distance I can see the dynamite in the proposal to take negro students *now*. Confidentially, some of these Left-wing people get me down. They always want to spring some sensation that gives *them* great publicity, but which does *us* no good. Sometimes *positive* harm' (cited in Duberman, 1972: 181). Significantly, Wunsch had worked with Hurston to stage performances of 'Negro folklore', *From Sun to Sun* (O'Sullivan and Lane, 2014). These were put on off-campus to mixed audiences in January 1933 to great acclaim, but a performance on campus in February was to a White-only audience.[31]

---

30 He set out these sympathies by analogy to the circumstances of his own resignation from Princeton in 1971, 'all of which temperamentally aligned me with Black Mountain's "outsiders" before I knew they existed – a bond further strengthened, once I did discover it, by a shared sympathy for radical politics' (Duberman, 1972: 177).
31 Wunsch remained important to Hurston. He sent a short story of hers to a magazine which led to the publisher Bertram Lippincott to ask if she were writing a novel, which she began – *Jonah's Gourd Vine* – and dedicated to Wunsch (O'Sullivan and Lane, 2014). Significantly, Duberman seems unaware of Hurston's significance as a literary figure and describes her simply as an 'anthropologist'. Wunsch was himself arrested for 'acts against nature' with a marine in his parked car in Asheville in June 1945. The crime involved a mandatory prison sentence, but the judge changed the charge to

The dispute between John Rice, Wunsch and others with President Hamilton Holt of Rollins College had been simmering since January, and by May they were under threat of dismissal. His sympathy for issues of racial justice was longstanding and active.

As might be expected, a majority of the student body at Black Mountain College was in favour of the immediate admission of Black students (by a factor of two to one), but the debate was galvanised by two faculty members. The first was Clark Foreman, a White civil rights activist from Georgia, who had come to Black Mountain College having been part of the Roosevelt administration between 1933 and 1941. He was ousted following a move by Southern conservatives in Congress to have a Black housing project in Detroit redesignated for Whites. He was a founding member of the Southern Conference for Human Welfare (SCHW) in 1938, to which he returned as President after he left the federal administration in 1941. He joined Black Mountain in 1944 and brought an executive meeting of the SCHW to the college for some days, at which the issues of integration at the college were discussed. The other figure was Eric Bentley, a charismatic individual with a talent for provocation. He had a reputation for affairs with female students (several at the same time, in his account to Duberman), albeit that he came out as gay some years later in 1969.

The debate seemed to be over the speed with which integration might proceed and the reaction of the local community. There is no indication that any faculty members were opposed to integration as such. However, both Foreman and Bentley wanted to proceed at full speed and challenge the local community of Asheville, although neither had any indication of the attraction of the college to Black students or faculty. It seems that some tentative moves had taken place the previous year, with a visit of a professor and two students from Fisk. As far as we are aware, Miller was the only faculty member with connections at Fisk, where he was a trustee. We have also seen that he participated with Charles Johnson in the National Interracial Conference in 1928. He had previously been instrumental

> 'trespass' and gave a suspended sentence. Wunsch left the college immediately, overnight, and without seeing anyone, with Duberman (1972: 231) attributing to him a sense of shame and self-disgust.

in resolving the dispute at Fisk that led to the resignation of Lafayette McKenzie and was adept at managing difficult situations towards a progressive outcome. He had also had to deal with the creation of a Columbus Urban League scholarship for a Black student and the refusal of Ohio State University to honour its obligations. Duberman's attribution of Miller's reserve over the proposals from Bentley and Foreman to his conservatism, rather than his experience, would seem to derive from his lack of curiosity about him and his stance (as we have seen, he describes him as a 'former historian', and makes no mention of him bringing the Friends' Refugee Scholar programme to Black Mountain the previous year).

Some indication of the sensitivities involved is evident in what followed the decision before the summer break in 1944 to proceed more slowly than the 'radical' faction had wished. Clark Foreman had already left the college to join the campaign to re-elect Roosevelt and two other members left following an altercation with Theodore Dreier (one of the founders of the college, along with John Rice). Eric Bentley remained; however, as Duberman comments, 'demonstrating a commitment to integration that many of his antagonists had doubted, [he] took up a summer teaching post at Fisk' (1971: 185). The appointment would prove to be fateful. Once again, although there is no direct evidence for Miller's involvement in setting up the appointment (it is not part of Duberman's interview with Bentley, nor is it indicated in minutes or letters), we suspect that he facilitated the visit for Bentley's education.[32]

Two 20-year-old female students close to Bentley had stayed on at the college during the break and decided to visit him. Against advice, they hitch-hiked. On their way back, they were arrested by police outside Chattanooga on charges of prostitution. They were

---

32 Duberman says that the invitation involved a sociologist at Fisk, George Redd (Duberman, 1972: 185). Redd was Professor of Education and it was he who had come to the college with two students the previous year. Redd was involved in the Fisk Social Center (a settlement house set up in 1938) and had organised an Institute for Youth Study in 1940. See Preston Valien with Johnnie R. Clarke and Ruth E. Vaughn, 'History of the Department of Social Sciences, Fisk University, 1911–48', unpublished manuscript, 1950, Fisk University, John Hope and Aurelia E. Franklin Library, Special Collections.

held in custody overnight and, the following morning, subjected to an examination for sexually transmitted disease, with one of them found to have an infection. In court, they were sentenced to 60 days. The college intervened and Dreier managed to get the sentence suspended and kept out of the local papers. Duberman regards the episode as one of sexual freedom against conservative social mores, pointing towards future activism.[33] The ensuing inquest at the college led to one of the students (and her boyfriend) leaving, as well as censuring the faculty adviser to the two students, Fran de Graef, for failing to prevent their hitch-hiking. Bentley did not return.

The risks to the reputation of the college are clear and the actions of the 'radicals' were, at best, ill-judged and, at worst, cavalier. We have suggested that it is likely that Herbert Miller was acting behind the scenes to facilitate understanding. The only evidence of his role in the matter is provided by Faculty minutes, which record his support for the 'conservative' position, and which, we have suggested, was also much more nuanced than Duberman presents and involved individuals like Miller, but also Wunsch and others, with a genuine commitment and record of action towards racial justice. We think it likely that Miller was the source of contact with Fisk University, since no other member of Faculty had his connections, and his appointment included 'outreach' west of the college where Fisk was to be found. However, we can find no archival evidence to confirm this supposition.

The Millers continued at Black Mountain College until September 1947.

33 Duberman's own text betrays the serious implications of what happened. In his later interviews with the young women, they describe that the Chattanooga police had thought that Black Mountain College was a 'red' college, and that the judge had cited the 'Scottsboro Boys' case in sentencing them. One of the women describes how she thought that the test results for sexually transmitted disease was because she might have been infected by the examining doctor and that she had been given medication so that if any subsequent test proved to be negative it could be attributed to the medicine. The episode may show the brutality of Southern justice, applied even to Whites caught up in racial disputes, but Duberman (and his interviewees) are remarkably sanguine about the consequences for others and its normal operation against Blacks in the South.

7

A political sociology of domination

So far, we have discussed the development of Herbert Adolphus Miller's thought in the context of his social and political activism. However, we have been at pains to point out that his arguments did not derive from his activism, but that his activism developed out of his sociological arguments. Nonetheless, it is clear that those arguments were honed as Miller tested them against his experiences. Indeed, we have been able to give a very strong sense of the distinctive substance of his sociological positions in the way he put them to use through his different public engagements. In this chapter, we will set them out in a more formal way in order to demonstrate their distinctive character. Miller developed them in academic articles and in public lectures and articles for magazines, including *The Survey*, *The World Tomorrow* (a Christian magazine with socialist leanings) and in *World Unity* (a magazine of the Baha'i ecumenical faith). The last two magazines also published articles by representatives of the 'Harlem renaissance'. However, two books represent Miller's most complete sociological framing of the questions that engaged him – *Races, Nations and Classes: A Psychology of Domination and Freedom* (1924) and *The Beginnings of To-morrow: An Introduction to the Sociology of the Great Society* (1933). It is to the systematic presentation of Miller's arguments in these two books that we now turn.

Public opinion

Miller exhibits a strong commitment to a sociology rooted in pragmatism, especially the sociology of Charles Horton Cooley.

The latter, more than George Herbert Mead, was the important figure in the development of a pragmatist sociology in the US in the first quarter of the twentieth century.[1] His concept of the 'looking-glass self' (Cooley, 1902) established a social psychological grounding to sociological ideas of the individual and the group. It was directly taken up by other sociologists, including those of the Chicago school like Robert E. Park and William I. Thomas, as well as the generation that followed them. It was broadly similar to Mead's conception of the 'social self', which came to eclipse it as symbolic interactionism came to be a focus of the 'second Chicago school' (Fine, 1995; Huebner, 2014).[2]

Cooley was among those early sociologists taking up the challenge of understanding the relation of sociology to social reform that Mead (1899) had proposed in his articulation of the 'working hypothesis in social reform'. The latter had addressed the emerging 'business' of municipal activities and the nature of local democracy in addressing social problems. He raised issues of the relation between elite interests, local groups and sociological

1 Darnell Rucker (1969) sets out very large claims for the significance of the Chicago school of philosophy established around John Dewey in his relatively brief tenure in Chicago between 1894 and 1904, including their significance – especially that of Mead – for sociology at Chicago. In terms of the development of a sociological 'psychology' of the self and its interactions with others, Cooley provided the more substantial elaboration. As Daniel Huebner (2014) argues, Mead's influence in Chicago sociology comes later reflecting the role of Herbert Blumer in the promotion of 'symbolic interactionism' as a distinctive contribution of Chicago sociology.
2 Although Mead's *Mind, Self and Society* was published posthumously out of lecture notes only in 1934, the ideas it contained were already familiar from early work, as Ellsworth Faris noted in his review, commenting further that 'Mind, self, and society is the reverse order to that which the structure of Mead's thought would seem to make appropriate. Not mind and then society; but society first and then minds arising within that society—such would probably have been the preference of him who spoke these words. For societies exist in which neither minds nor selves are found, and it is only in human societies that a subject is its own object—only in these is there consciousness of self. Man, he held, is not born human; the biological accident becomes a personality through social experience' (Faris, 1936: 810).

knowledge. As we have seen, in large cities like Chicago this also involved charities, social workers, municipal boards and the settlement houses catering to poor and immigrant communities. The issue for Cooley was how sociological knowledge might contribute to the formation of *public opinion* as a check on elite and business interests.

'Public opinion' was understood by Cooley (1909) to be something more than a simple aggregate of individual opinions. Public opinion was generated within distinct social groups and in the relations among them. Sociology's contribution was to understand how public opinion was formed and, in turn, how expert knowledge produced within the social sciences could help to shape public debate. Our discussion of the Pittsburgh and Cleveland Surveys showed how business and elite interests predominated and municipal authorities were captured by them. One of the consequences was the turning of sociological arguments away from direct engagement with public debate towards a professional concern with the production of warranted useful knowledge. It was not until towards the end of the period when Miller was most active that the nature of what was at issue would come to be crystallised in a debate between Walter Lippmann and John Dewey.

In *The Phantom Public* (1925), Lippmann set out the process by which government had become a matter of efficient administration served by experts in which democratic processes had become attenuated. The public, for Lippmann, was increasingly ill-equipped to make the sort of judgements attributed to it within democratic theory. He argued that the public had become a 'phantom category' (that is, something that functioned only in theories of democracy and which had little real substance in everyday practices). For Lippmann, this was a necessary consequence of the complexity of modern societies that increasingly required organised expertise of various kinds. In consequence, 'expert opinion', he argued, would replace 'public opinion', and democracy would necessarily be attenuated. Indeed, as Ellen Lagemann (1989: 6) has argued, that was increasingly the direction taken by the Carnegie Corporation as it developed its research programmes as a means to 'govern indirectly'.

Dewey countered Lippman's arguments in *The Public and its Problems* (1927). He began from what was essentially a sociological argument that the individual is necessarily a social being involved in 'associative life', and that this was as true of what are conventionally regarded as private actions as well as of public actions. For Dewey, individuals form associations, but they are also formed by associations. At the same time, the multiplicity of associations and their interconnected actions have consequences. In all of this, Dewey's idea of a 'public', and of the several nature of 'publics', is crucial. It contains a strong idea of democracy associated with participation and dialogue, but does not deny that there will be functionally differentiated publics, whose articulation will be at issue.

The key to his definition of a public is contained in the idea of action in the world having effects and consequences that are ramified and impact upon others who are not the initiators of the action. Essentially, all action is associative action, but a public is brought into being in consequence of being indirectly and seriously affected by those actions of others. Dewey's analysis of the problem of modern democracy, then, is concerned with the imbalance in the development of publics and the proliferation of problems in areas where the public cannot properly defend itself.

Although Miller does not discuss the ideas of Lippmann and Dewey directly, his own sociological practices are fully engaged with the matters being debated. As we saw in the earlier chapter on Miller's pedagogy, the two texts that he most frequently set his students were Cooley's *Social Organization* (1909), which addressed the idea of public opinion and its formation within social groups, and Graham Wallas's *The Great Society* (1914). The latter was dedicated to Lippmann and described as having its gestation in conversations in a discussion course they both joined at Harvard in the spring of 1910. Wallas's book sets out the challenges posed by the increasing complexity of modern industrial society. Wallas was a familiar writer in the Anglophone world (if neglected now; see Kang, 1979) and his books stressed the role of the non-rational (and irrational) in politics and the problems of managing the complexities of large-scale social organisation brought about by industrialism.

The books are also the context for Miller's own syntheses of his sociological views in *Races, Nations, and Classes* (1924) and *The Beginnings of To-morrow* (1933). In the first, he addresses the problems of domination and oppression in the relations among groups that are absent from Cooley's discussion (or, indeed, endorsed by him as his expression of the cultural superiority of some groups and the inferiority of others). A similar absence is found in Dewey's rather anodyne discussion of publics that avoids issues of their 'racialised' (and gendered) character. Unlike Wallas, Miller addresses the 'great society' as a global problem of a world order and not simply as an issue of national societies. Miller (1933: 4) was interested in the solutions offered by other civilisations and 'the substitution of the Cosmos (the world) for the state'. As such, the great society of tomorrow is a post-imperial society that respects racial equality. The national and the international, for Miller, are continuous and the latter needs to take predominance over the former.

Miller did not believe that the 'internationalisation' of the great society undermined the possibilities of sociological influence in the formation of public opinion (and, thus, a reversion to expert influence in the corridors of power).[3] Whether in addressing the national or international contexts, Miller shared Dewey's understanding that 'the essential need ... is the improvement of the methods and conditions of debate, discussion and persuasion. That is the problem of the public' (Dewey, 1927: 208). 'Majority' rule may be a problem, Dewey allows, but that derives from how majority opinion is formed and the extent to which minority opinion can have the possibility of becoming a majority subsequently, a standard problem of democratic theory and the succession of governments. However, Dewey offered a comparison that skated over the issues that Miller addressed: 'think of the meaning of the "problem of minorities" in certain European states, and compare it with the status of minorities in countries having popular government' (1927: 208). While Dewey was concerned that the public was increasingly a 'phantom', he did not discuss the extensive emergent publics associated with Black civil rights – whether the NAACP, the Urban League or the those associated with the 'new Negro' – just as

---

3 Significantly, Lippman was appointed as secretary to President Wilson's Inquiry on its formation until leaving in spring 1918 to take up an appointment in military intelligence (Gelfand, 1963).

he ignored the self-organisation of the immigrant groups in which Miller was also involved.[4]

Miller's commitment to sociology shared pragmatist concerns about the nature of its contribution to democracy and also the preparation of public opinion. As we have seen, he wrote that 'psychology deals with method while sociology deals with purpose, the one looks backward and the other forward, and if there is any single requirement for education it is that of preparing for the future' (Miller, 1914d: 35). He commented further, 'if sociology cannot command respect in any other way, it should "butt in" and offer its services'. The one thing of which we can be sure is that Miller did butt in. He butted in practically to help create new forms of association, new publics, to represent 'minorities', minority opinion and subject minorities alike. However, he also butted into sociological debates to reformulate concepts and to redirect research towards problems of domination and racial inequality on a national and international scale.

Miller's 'scientific sociology' was thoroughly pragmatic and was also understood by him to be *a process*, not an outcome expressed in 'laws'. It was a process in which engagement with the world was a necessary part and one that produced the need for continual readjustment and reformulation. Science as a set of 'objective truths' produced by disinterested inquiry is vain: 'The complexity of society is infinite and a panacea is inconceivable. Pragmatism insists that the truth about phenomena inheres in the way things work. If we look at the chaotic world about us we shall see that social philosophy has been largely dominated by theories that are *not working*. As we make practical adjustments to truth discovered in action, we may hope to substitute progress for chaos' (Miller, 1924a: xvii).

Domination and freedom

We have already seen that Miller was both a critic of empire as a social and political formation and of 'ethno-nationalism' as a

---

4 John Narayan (2016) suggests that Dewey did subsequently develop an understanding of global publics.

response by subject minorities to their domination. He endorsed what he called '*proportionate* patriotism' and he was always conscious and critical of 'nationalist patriotisms', including those of formerly subject peoples and the operation of what he called an 'oppression psychosis' (Miller, 1921). This reflected his deep interest in issues of ethnic conflict formed by his experience of the First World War and also the break-up of the Mid-European Union over nationalist exclusions of minority rights within the proposed new nations (the reason for his interest in the Soviet Union). He was also concerned about an emerging new threat of war and of rising anti-Semitism in Europe and the threat posed by fascist ethno-nationalism. He was, however, an advocate of 'revolution' against racial political orders, or what we would now regard as movements of decolonisation, even if these did pose 'dangers' of atavism associated with group identities deriving from how they were formed under conditions of domination. But Miller never renounced his commitment to a plural, multicultural political order both locally and globally (with America as a microcosm of problems with a global scale): 'The intensity and diversity of opinion over the campaign for "Americanization" have done much to stimulate thought. The Great War, the disorganization of Europe, the Ku Klux Klan and political restlessness have called attention to the need of a rational program rather than for a rationalized justification of status' (Miller, 1924a: vii).

We have already remarked that in the few places where Miller is discussed in the secondary literature, he is misrepresented. This is, in part, because of a misunderstanding of the wider context – philosophical, as well as political – of the development of Miller's thought. Fred Wacker (1983), for example, as we have seen, argues that while Miller harboured 'nationalist' sympathies up to the end of the First World War, he subsequently allied national consciousness with racial and class-consciousness and saw them all as equally 'pathological'. According to him, Miller's position became a conservative position concerned with threats to stability and order (Wacker, 1983: 26). However, it is clear that Miller did not operate in terms of an idea of 'order' but of 'chaos' and 'progress'. Importantly, the latter is not presented in terms of a teleology of (Western) 'enlightenment', but of a plural, cosmopolitan global order.

We can, perhaps, best describe *Races, Nations and Classes* as offering a complement to Émile Durkheim's *Professional Ethics and Civic Morals* (1957), albeit that Miller develops an analysis of group conflict and international relations that is absent from Durkheim. The latter has also been accused of conservativism. Both authors converge on what Miller calls 'proportionate patriotism', with human values at the pinnacle of the system alongside group solidarities. Significantly, race relations and their construction through domination are absent from Durkheim (Bhambra and Holmwood, 2021), while Miller's conception of human values, we shall suggest, is also more expansive than that of Durkheim.[5]

Miller arrives at this position from a pragmatist sociology, which Durkheim (1983) famously repudiated, albeit directed at the arguments of William James about whose epistemological arguments Miller had also initially expressed his reservations. Moreover, Miller's description of his aim as being a *psychology* of domination and freedom also suggests a failure to accept Durkheim's account of the social as *sui generis*. This is something also taken up by Roscoe Hinkle (1952) in his survey of theories of stratification, in which he characterises Miller's position as 'individualist'.

Yet, like Durkheim, Miller begins with the *group*, a starting point he derives from Cooley. Thus, he writes, 'the individual, according to the theory maintained in this study, brings to the group a predisposition to identify himself with it, and its influence on him arises from his own nature. By nature he is adapted to the group' (Miller, 1924a: 4). This aspect of human sociability is the condition of the survival of the species, where 'each individual unconsciously postulates his own existence in the continuity of his group, because in the struggle for survival there was no other possibility of existence' (Miller, 1924a: 5). Miller argues, 'we are the product of social relationships, or, in other words, of the groups to which we belong. We react in terms of our groups, and must always be understood as

---

5 Although already set out in lectures given between 1890 and 1900, *Professional Ethics and Civic Morals* was published posthumously and could not have been known by Miller. There are no citations otherwise to works by Durkheim.

reflecting them' (Miller, 1924a: 10). There is, then, a 'consciousness of kind' and it is sustained through practices (including rituals) that reinforce membership. Moreover, the individual is seen by others in terms of his or her membership of the group, as sharing its characteristics and identifications.

Miller shared a general interest of the Chicago school with 'disorganisation', or what Durkheim would call 'anomie'. However, this is not his primary focus, which is conflictual relations among groups and the domination of one group over another. He argues that 'when the family ceases to hold the attention of the boy he joins a gang, for whose reality he will fight bloody battles. The adult must be in some group such as a family, club, or neighbourhood; otherwise he will be restless and lost like a rudderless ship' (Miller, 1924a: 6). This informed his criticisms of the standard approach to Americanisation, which sought to break the bonds that tied individuals to their groups, sustained through family, language and religion (including in the case of the Czechs, their freethinking clubs and gymnastic associations). The immigrant was not naturally disorganised, but could be made such and demoralised by a programme of Americanisation which failed to respect multiculturalism and facilitate a plural American culture, presenting instead the culture of one group as the culture to which others must adapt.

But the focus of Miller's book is not the problem of disorganisation, but of conflict, involving the mobilisation of solidarities. All groups, according to Miller, embody emotional identifications and there are processes associated with bringing group identity to the fore. These are processes of 'consciousness-raising' that can help to bring a group into being and, for Miller, they are no different whether the object is religious, national or economic. Thus, 'when the Englishman says that there would be no Irish question, if it were not for the agitators, or the capitalist that labor would be content if it were not for the professional organizer, they are looking at an incident, not at a main cause. Does the agitator represent a potential group into which those whom he is trying to influence will naturally fall when they are aroused to a consciousness of the significance of the group to themselves? If the agitation makes good, this will be unquestionable' (Miller, 1924a: 10). Once the group is formed it will inspire loyalty (solidarity) and an impulse to self-determination (freedom). This will potentially involve conflict between groups, which, if self-determination is denied, will be consolidated as domination of one group over another.

Domination, for Miller, involves a singular consciousness of superiority, and he devotes a chapter to the 'myth of superiority', and racial superiority in particular. This rehearses his earlier criticisms of IQ tests and 'pseudo-science'. For those who are dominated there is also a form of 'double consciousness', an analysis that Miller takes from Du Bois. One aspect is the group consciousness necessary to the struggle for freedom, the other involves the forms of consciousness that represent adaptations to the situation of being dominated. The dominant group advocates gradualism and mobilises stereotypes associated with acquiescence to justify its position at the same time as praising the acting out of deference.

Miller is clear that a global revolution against the different forms of domination is necessary, but there is also a danger that the symbols mobilised by the group to achieve its freedom will contain the seeds of the domination of others, as in various forms of ethno-nationalism or religious identifications. Miller does not denigrate different religious traditions and he argues the necessity of learning from their different ethical precepts. In offering a scientific examination of the problem at hand, Miller eschewed both a scientific fundamentalism and a fundamentalism about Western civilisation as the embodiment of reason. Each has been used to justify domination of others and has presented that domination in racialised terms. Group consciousness, for Miller, is a necessary part of the process of achieving freedom, but it is not the end point of any struggle. Nor could assimilation be the desired outcome, since the pathologies associated with the dominant group also needed to be overcome. These are expressed within Anglo-American values as conventionally understood and expressed within the dominant idea of Americanisation. Miller was interested in values of freedom that would transcend local patriotism and would govern inter-group relationships.[6]

6 There was renewed interest in the Chicago school's approach to race and ethnicity after the 1970s, which is when mention of Miller's role comes to be partially recognised. However, this was after controversy associated with

In common with William I. Thomas, Robert E. Park and other Chicago sociologists, Miller's starting point is Cooley's distinction between primary and secondary groups. The former is associated with the family and kin relationships, while the latter represents wider associations which can have a voluntary character. The typical development of these ideas addresses different cultural forms expressed within secondary groups in different settings – for example, rural and urban settings, peasant society and industrial society – and is a large part of the development of Chicago sociology's ecological approach. The relation between primary and secondary group was also used by Miller to address the problem of Americanisation where immigrant children were asked to repudiate the culture of their families in order to identify with American values; shame is one of the pathologies of domination and it does not serve integration but demoralisation.

However, Miller also develops a novel conceptual distinction between the *vertical* and the *horizontal* group. Membership in the nation involves membership in a vertical group, while membership in a class involves a horizontal group. Both involve claims to solidarity and, since they are frequently cross-cutting, there can be mobilisation against class-conscious lower classes that they are disloyal or unpatriotic. Miller also understood religion to be a vertical group, one that can be mobilised in support of the nation. It is in this context that Miller addresses subject groups and the fact that they frequently exhibit religious and linguistic differences. Attempts can be made to unify the nation by seeking to suppress minority languages and religions, but this is doomed to failure and it only has the effect of raising religious and linguistic difference to the status of a symbol within the definition of the group. The technologies of domination elicit a reaction that serves to reproduce and strengthen the dominated group. Much of the book is dedicated to demonstrating these processes across different

Patrick Moynihan's (1965) description of the African American family as 'dysfunctional' and 'pathological', which, as Orlando Patterson (2019) has recently written, rendered reference to pathologies of oppression as problematic, notwithstanding that these had been identified from Du Bois through to Kenneth Clark.

contexts and involving different groups, from Jews and anti-Semitism, Ireland and India under British rule, Middle Europe, Japan and Korea, to the US with regard to Mexico, Hawaii and the Philippines, as well as race relations within the US. The common aspect is the issue of self-determination in the context of external rule, deriving for the most part from empire (not all the examples are associated with colonialism and empire, but it is a major part of Miller's account).

In Miller's analysis, the vertical group is the one that provides risks of oppression of other so-called minority groups. This is the case for the nation and 'nationalism' and it can also be reinforced by religious and ethnic identification (including disidentification in the form of representation of religious and ethnic minorities as 'other'). This is the context in which Miller argues against 'nationalism' and the 'national state'. It is not in opposition to the representation and self-determination of subject minorities, but in recognition that the sentiments developed in the struggle for freedom from domination may create new forms of oppression. The argument is significant precisely because it is not secured by a claim for a civilisational process deriving from Western global domination.

In a generous, but limited, review of the book in the *American Journal of Sociology*, Park comments that Miller 'sketches in outline what is practically a new division of the social sciences, namely, the sociology of politics' (Park, 1926: 536). He also acknowledges the significance of Miller's distinction between vertical and horizontal groups. He argues that the distinction is an important and novel conception, one which establishes an effective way of addressing social and political conflict. However, Park suggests that Miller's idea of an 'oppression psychosis' is overworked, 'particularly as it involves the tacit assumption that conflict in some form – not necessarily war – is something less than the normal relation of social groups'. Significantly, he refers implicitly to the context of Miller's research on the Carnegie project, but not to the book that appeared under their joint names, despite its conclusions being at issue. So, notwithstanding the complaint about the oppression psychosis, Park reproduces Miller's own understanding of problems in central Europe as if they are neglected in the book, stating, 'the volume outlines the rise of race and national consciousness among the so-called "oppressed minorities" of Europe, most of whom, by the way, are now, since the changes brought about by the war, eagerly engaged in oppressing other racial minorities, some of whom were formerly their oppressor' (Park, 1926: 536).

Indeed, Park indicates that his own approach to the topic proceeds from scientific 'principle', rather than process. He comments, 'as a matter of fact, nationalities, like political parties, exist for the purpose of conflict. There is no other way of maintaining the disinterestedness which we call "idealism" in individuals, nor the discipline which we call "morale" in social groups. The struggle to rise of the peoples who are down is one of the most wholesome exercises in which human beings have ever engaged. It was in such struggles that democracy was conceived, and it is only through similar struggles that it can be maintained' (Park, 1926: 536.).

Of course, Miller is far from denying the significance of conflict, though he demurs from providing it an ontological status. Moreover, his focus is not 'people who are down'. But specifically inter-group relations of *domination*. The context of his arguments is also that of international relations and the political domination over others exercised by European (and American) empire, alongside the unequal treatment of racial minorities at home. Miller is both less sanguine about democracy, as well being committed to racial equality on national and global scales, something elided by Park, who broadly endorsed the civilising nature of empire (Lyman, 1992; Magubane, 2014).

We have already seen that Anthony Smith (1983) cites Louis Wirth's (1936) typology of nationalism as one of the few discussions of the topic in US sociology in the inter-war period. Wirth cites mainly German authors – Friedrich von Wieser, in particular – and makes no reference to Miller at all, despite covering much the same ground. Thus, he distinguishes four types. The first is 'hegemonic nationalism', which he associates with movements of national unification in the name of an integrated state and national sovereignty. Imperialism is associated with this type, although Wirth provides no more than a passing remark, with German fascism described more extensively as falling within this category (fascism also incorporated an imperial ambition). The second type was 'particularist nationalism', which he associated with 'secessionist' demands for political sovereignty arising in eastern and central Europe. The third type was 'marginal nationalism', involving the claims of minority populations occupying frontier regions between two states. Finally, for Wirth, there was a 'nationalism of the minorities' within nation-states, as for example, Germans, White Ruthenians, Ukrainians and Jews within Poland.

Wirth puzzles over 'why there is no question of minorities in the United States', writing that, 'while there are undoubtedly problems that are fundamentally similar to those found in Europe to be found in the United States, such as the Negro problem, especially in the South and in the large cities of the North, the difference between Europe and America is principally that in Europe the minorities live together in large numbers and are not recent immigrants who have been anxious to, and at least partially successful in, shedding their cultural heritage' (1936: 735). The argument is aligned with the Chicago view on the assimilation of immigrants, albeit that the process has been absent in Europe. What is missing in Wirth's analysis is the wider context of the problems in empire and the global aspect of the problem of inter-group relations as addressed by Miller. Wirth writes, 'the tendency of hegemony nationalism to develop ever more aggressive imperialistic claims and aspirations is exemplified by the most recent trends in foreign policy of the fascist dictatorships of Europe' (1936: 729), but he is silent on the 'nationalisms' of European overseas empires.

Unlike Wirth, Miller was conscious of nationalisms as not only fact, but also pathology. If democracy was the answer, which Miller believed to be the case, then it is a pluralist democracy that recognises the self-determination of groups. This includes, as we shall see, the economic sphere and the functional representation of classes through industrial democracy. Despite the fact that the title of Miller's book is *Races, Nations and Classes*, issues of economic class proper are assigned a scant few pages (eight pages out of a total of just under two hundred). In part, this is because Miller regards groups as 'classes' and vice versa, so that the title of the book would be rather better represented as *Races, Nations and Groups*. However, he does argue that capitalism produces economic classes as horizontal groups that extend beyond national borders. This is also associated with a problem in the organisation of employment, where the technical division of labour in pursuit of 'quantity production' produces alienation of the worker, 'divorcing the laborer from his product' (Miller, 1924a: 162). This, combined with class endogamy and problems of economic conditions, provides conditions for a revolutionary conflict between capital and labour, which can be mitigated only by progressive social reform addressing both the alienation of work and fair distribution. Thus, Miller argues that 'industrial democracy, which is now becoming an objective, is as logical as the self-determination of nations' (1924a: 166). Industrial democracy and political democracy have a common purpose, which 'will be found to be the human values which in the one case may be worked out through production, and, in the other through the organization and the function of the state. But they are both means and not ends of existence' (Miller, 1924a: 166).

Miller's analysis of horizontal and vertical dimensions of groups – of the internationalism of capitalism and the nationalism of states – provides a novel analysis of the particular significance of anti-Semitism from the late nineteenth century onwards. While anti-Semitism has deep historical roots, the diasporic nature of Jewish communities across empires (whether Russian, German, Austro-Hungarian or Ottoman) and their self-organisation makes them an object of antagonism on the part of emerging nationalist movements of groups seeking self-determination as 'nations'. At the same time, the spurious 'national' claims of transnational capitalist corporations – the US Steel Corporation, for example (Miller, 1924a: 95) – as representing 'American' values in the face of an international proletariat also creates the idea of 'Jewish' *international* business, especially in finance. For Miller, the status of 'Jew' as 'other' is subject to multiple determinations.

It is in this context that Miller explained Zionism. It is an understandable response to oppression and, of course, the demand is consistent with other 'nationalist' claims for self-determination. He writes, 'if there could be the dignity of a political state then all Jews who are now subject to the caprice of any state in which they live, but of which they are not a part, could have the added self-respect of being the representatives of a sovereignty' (Miller, 1924a: 103). Miller, of course, was writing in the context of the British mandate for Palestine, of which he was highly critical as an extension of empire. He did not criticise Jewish migration to Palestine, but he did not believe the solution could be an ethno-national state, but a cosmopolitan solution that represented the rights of Muslims, Christians and Jews.

It will not have escaped notice that many of the groups identified by Miller are those that were the focus of the Carnegie project. It is clear from Miller's book that he intended it as a riposte, since his penultimate chapter is the 'paradox of Americanization', with the conclusion entitled 'proportionate loyalty'. The proponents of assimilation identify American values with the dominant group and its definition of the nation. Miller argued that 'every immigrant has had Mayflower qualities' and, further, that 'society is rich through heterogeneity, not through homogeneity' (Miller, 1924a: 124).

Miller inverted the idea of vertical groups to suggest that, as a consequence of migration, religion and ethnicity have become the basis of horizontal groups as well as vertical groups. Indeed, this was a theoretical expression of Miller's view that immigration provided a plural and cosmopolitan sensibility to the host society, by lifting its eyes to what can be learned from the experiences of others and providing an influence over domestic foreign policy – what we might call making 'internationalism' national as part of a 'proportionate patriotism'. He writes, 'the foreign-born offer us the opportunity of appropriating spiritual values in unfamiliar forms. Unless we become able to do this we shall not be prepared to live in the new era' (Miller, 1924a: 177). This is the basis of 'proportional patriotism', the 'internationalisation' of groups, including classes, who become the basis of more diverse human values that embed local democracies.

Initially, Miller sets this out in a manner reminiscent of the Government's Memorandum on Americanization that influenced the final stages of the Carnegie project, only to represent what the latter perceived to be the risk as the solution. He writes, 'the foreign-born will never forget the land of their origin and their responsibility for it so long as injustice prevails there; the identification of America with the problems of Europe, therefore, is so close that we cannot escape our share in the responsibility however we may wish. There can be no real Americanization of the immigrant unless there is a real league of nations, as the symbol of a real organization which will substitute in Europe a reign of justice for the reign of immorality' (Miller, 1924a: 177).

Cosmos versus state

The idea of a plural cosmopolitanism was something that Miller would develop more fully as a global perspective in *The Beginnings of To-morrow* (1933). The situation that obtained locally as a consequence of immigration also applied globally as a consequence of imperialism: 'there are India, China, Korea. Egypt, Pan-Africa – more than half the human race still in national relationships in which national self-respect is demanding satisfaction' (Miller, 1924a: 183). As Luther Bernard and Jessie Bernard put it in their descriptive survey of sociological contributions to international relations, for Miller, nationalism 'is essentially a revolt against political and cultural imperialism. It flourishes to best advantage under repression, and as a consequence it develops an oppression psychosis. He believes it to be a disease, but thinks it must run its course and, … that its cure will be the disappearance of imperialism' (Bernard and Bernard, 1934: 63–4).

Miller argued that the 'nationalistic epidemic [was] induced by the reaction in Asia to European imperialism … In Europe it is the boomerang sent out by imperialism, returning to strike a deadlier blow at the sender' (Miller, 1933: 9). Further, 'nationalism, which began about a century ago, has swept the world until all imperialism seems doomed. Closely related to nationalism is the growing resentment of the colored races to white control' (Miller, 1933: 21). In these respects, his argument is a precursor of that by Partha Chatterjee (1986) that nationalism is a 'derivative discourse' of the colonial world, and not the expression of local traditions and ethical ways of thinking that could contribute to a global and plural cosmopolitanism that did not raise one culture above another in the scale of human values. Nor was Miller suggesting only that 'nationalism' had become 'internationalised' in the sense argued by Erez Manela (2007) as being the consequence of the 'Wilsonian moment' of an emphasis on self-determination after the First World War.

Miller's deeper concern was the reciprocal one of how the 'national' might become 'internationalised' and do so on the basis of a plural cosmopolitanism, rather than a cosmopolitanism understood in terms of Western civilisation and enlightenment. For Miller, the latter was in deep crisis. After all, it had produced domination over others and economic injustice.

Indeed, his talks and lectures to Black audiences reiterated that the problem of racial oppression in America was part of a global situation where they were one among other oppressed peoples. Far from denying conflict, Miller endorsed revolution as progressive. In a commencement speech in 1934 at Cheyney University he drew attention to the rise of the Nazi movement in Germany and their treatment of Jews. 'The white races of the world are facing a crisis because they have built a culture in which money and power are the leading factors ... the colored races are world's hope.'[7] Unity among oppressed peoples was Miller's constant refrain.

For Miller, the end of empire and the creation of new nation-states was fraught with internal conflicts and ethno-nationalist calls, particularly when the principle of 'self-determination of nations' was construed as the interest of the nation over the rights of minorities. Miller's own approach to issues of domination and minority rights saw the principle of self-determination of nations as problematic. In effect, this principle sidelined the urgency of issues of minority rights and pursued the priority of assimilation in the formation of new nation-states. Much of the abstract meaning that he assigned to nationalism – the group seeks to secure its own individuality – wielded a very effective political framework to address the problem of minorities. Empires were, in a sense, federations organising a plurality of groups under conditions of domination and hierarchical order. The task was to imagine plurality under conditions of freedom and equality and this could not be done under the nation(alist) state, which was, nonetheless, the political form that was emerging after empire.

---

7 As reported in the article 'Colored Races Are World's Hope, Says Bryn Mawr Prexy [President]', *The Afro-American* (Baltimore, MD), 20 June 1934.

Miller maintained a consistent position across his life. He was a thoroughgoing advocate of equality between groups and of democracy. If democracy was the answer, as he argued it to be, then it must be a pluralist democracy that recognised the self-determination of groups. However, the nature of domination was that the dominant group was unlikely simply to concede equality. Revolution against domination was a necessity, but it was one that potentially created its own problems as groups would continue to occupy the same spaces and participate in common political institutions. The answer could not lie in the assimilation of one group to the values of another, since the values of each had been forged in mutual conflict and the insistence on assimilation would simply reproduce the problems that the revolution against domination had sought to resolve, now inverted and imposed on a new 'other'. What was needed was a process of mutual recognition and adjustment, one where the consciousness of the group defined in opposition would necessarily diminish: 'self-determination of nations does not mean race segregation but an opportunity to develop normally; in other words, so that the group may survive without the use of defensive antipathies. Not until groups are normal is assimilation possible' (Miller, 1919b: 205).

At the time, the standard orientation to global problems was based upon a European civilisational analysis, which orders the world in a developmental sequence and claims universal and world historical significance for European values. As a pragmatist, Miller was interested in problem-solving and human development, but he did not believe that European values represented the apex of human possibility. Europe could not claim universal values, precisely because its civilisation was based upon the illegitimate domination of others. Moreover, its capitalist form of economic organisation had also failed to achieve a just distribution of rewards. Europe had much to learn from other civilisations, especially those to the 'East'. There was no 'clash of civilisations', but instead the possibility of a plural, cosmopolitan global order.

Conclusion

We do not claim that Miller's advocacy of a plural cosmopolitanism – a global consciousness – deriving from the world's religions and cultures was unique. It was the dominant understanding of the participants at the First Universal Races Congress that met in London in 1911, which Du Bois attended (Rudwick, 1959). However, Miller was the first to address it within a sociological framework. Moreover, it was a framework that he used in his practical engagements with civil-society organisations. Nico Slate (2011) has written of the complexities of a 'colored cosmopolitanism' that was developing separately within the US and India from the last quarter of the nineteenth century onwards. In the former it involved organisations struggling for racial equality and civil and political rights. In the latter, it was an anti-colonial struggle directed at British rule, one which also addressed how religious and caste divisions had been exacerbated as a feature of that rule. As Slate shows, it was not simply that there were new forms of association pressing for equality and self-determination, they were also in conversation with each other. These were real, not 'phantom' publics and Miller was also engaged with 'colored cosmopolitanisms', including those associated with East Asia. Moreover, he developed his political sociology of domination specifically in the context of these movements. His political sociology of domination was, however, a distinctive and substantial contribution to sociological debates, albeit largely ignored.

Conclusion

We have sought to rehabilitate the sociological thought and career of the 'forgotten' sociologist Herbert Adolphus Miller. In the course of doing so we have demonstrated a public engagement that was exemplary, consistent and continuous throughout his academic career. Moreover, it was a public engagement through which he developed a distinctive set of sociological arguments as well as applying those arguments to reflect upon public issues and develop new initiatives. His was a career devoted both to a sociological understanding of racial and colonial domination and action to counter it. The puzzle is why his contribution has been forgotten.

We have suggested that the idea of a professional social science as disinterested inquiry was taking over from the idea of sociology as a contribution to public opinion across the period in which Miller was most active. In the standard representation of the history of the discipline, this shift involved the refinement and consolidation of a body of sociological knowledge that represented a collective effort of schools or 'theory groups' (Mullins, 1973), albeit galvanised by leading figures. In this context, Miller represented something that was being left behind. His was a sociological practice that was developed through education. In this respect, he falls into a category that Stephen Turner (2007) has described as being that of a 'public intellectual' sustained by a teaching position at a provincial university and applying sociological arguments to public debates.

There is much that is accurate in this description. However, Miller was also involved in major research projects with the Cleveland Survey and the Carnegie Corporation's research into

Methods of Americanization, both of which involved scholars who would go on to be assigned to the other side of the emerging divide. For example, Robert E. Park and William I. Thomas were both involved in the Carnegie project and would be associated with the emerging professionalism of the discipline. For those involved in telling the story of Chicago sociology as a 'collaborative circle' (Farrell, 2001), such as Jean-Michel Chapoulie (2020), figures like Park and Thomas provided conceptual innovations on which a collective effort was built, leaving behind those who could not work in the new way. From this perspective, Miller was little more than a gadfly buzzing around in the Chicago milieu. He was marginal to the development of sociology and, unlike other public intellectuals, he had placed himself outside mainstream (White) public opinion by his deep commitment to racial equality.

We have shown that neither characterisation would be accurate. Miller's sociology of race relations was conceptually more advanced than that of the Chicago school by virtue of him placing it in the context of a theory of domination and freedom, a context provided by his political interests. The closest equivalent is to be found in the work of W. E. B. Du Bois. We are not suggesting that Miller was a figure of equivalent stature to Du Bois, but that within a segregated academy, Miller was one of the few White sociologists to transcend that racial divide and to develop his sociological theories and practices on that basis. He was outside mainstream public opinion precisely because of his commitment to racial justice and opposition to empire and colonialism.

Miller's reputation has also suffered because of the way in which the Second World War and the postwar expansion of sociology in Europe and North America has served to create a break with what went before. This is the context in which sociologies before that war were sorted and fashioned to fit with the expansion of the discipline and its theory groups, especially in the 1950s and after. This might be considered to be the high point of the professionalisation of sociology, alongside perceptions of amelioration institutionalised within Western welfare states. Explicit reflection on the political purposes of sociology could perhaps be put 'on hold' within a liberal public sphere understood to entail a gradual expansion of civil and political rights.

This perception quickly came to an end with the impact of anti-colonial struggles and the division of the world into capitalist and communist blocs (and, of course, for a time, non-aligned countries). The Vietnam War and the civil rights movement of the 1960s and 1970s had a profound impact on US sociology. These were movements that re-energised the academy around issues of racial segregation, gender inequality and anti-colonial movements. They began a process of disrupting standard histories of the discipline, which created the space for a more critical understanding of the role of race and gender in the construction of the discipline in terms of both its institutional and conceptual structures.

Whereas, under the motif of professionalism, the history of the discipline has frequently been presented in terms of convergence (even if that was not on a single paradigm), the discipline now seems to be characterised by dissonance, or what Andrew Abbott (2001) has called 'chaos'. We think that this is a positive and productive situation and one in which Miller can be a guide. We have been at pains to avoid anachronism in our account of Miller and to present him in his context and in relation to the intellectual currents of the time. Nonetheless, he did stand against those currents and in ways that speak directly to our times.

In a presidential address to the American Sociological Association Michael Burawoy (2005) called for 'public sociology', echoing an earlier address by Herbert Gans (1989). Burawoy's call was for a sociology that utilised empirical evidence and theoretical arguments to illuminate pressing public issues and to address future possibilities. In this context, it would be wrong to suggest that Miller was a public sociologist *avant la lettre*. He was among those sociologists to define public sociology in the early years of the discipline. He was explicitly committed to sociology as part of the education of public opinion. Moreover, he developed that view in terms of sociological knowledge as a *process*, not a set of fixed *principles*. It was a knowledge that was formed and re-formed in the engagements with the world, including social movements. However, as we have seen, this also involved critical engagement with those movements, especially, in Miller's case, for racial equality and over the dangers intrinsic to ethno-nationalist responses to colonialism.

Conclusion

As we set out in the Introduction, during his lifetime Miller confronted the evident failure of nearly all of the political projects with which he was associated – the rise of anti-Semitism, fascism and other ethno-nationalist conflicts leading to the Second World War; the end of Czechoslovakian independence with the Sudetenland invaded by Nazi Germany in 1938 and Slovakia seceding to form a client state of Germany; the end of Japanese occupation of Korea after the Second World War devolving into a new war and division of the Korean peninsula; and Indian independence and the violence of partition, as well as obdurate racial inequality in the US. Yet he was resilient in the face of any setback. The task of sociology was to discern the 'beginnings of tomorrow' and to provide the sociological knowledge that would facilitate a just global order brought into being. His was a global sociology, not only a public sociology. In our present situation, the Second World War looks less like a dividing line in a short twentieth century. We seem now still to be living the unresolved problems of a Western imperial order that was breaking down in the First World War, but whose legacy is not behind us. Miller's context, in important ways, remains our context. Truly, Herbert Adolphus Miller was a sociologist for a global age.

Bibliography

Archives

Bryn Mawr, College Archives.
Columbia University Libraries New York, Rare Book and Manuscript Library. Carnegie Corporation of New York Records. Americanization Studies, 1918–1945.
Fisk University, John Hope and Aurelia E. Franklin Library, John Hope and Aurelia E. Franklin Library, Special Collections.
George Washington University, American Association of University Professors records.
Oberlin College Archives, Herbert A. Miller Papers, 1911–1979.
Temple University, Samuel Paley Library, Conwellana-Templana Collection, personal papers of Herbert Adolphus Miller.
Masaryk Institute and Archives of the Czech Academy of Sciences, Prague.
Tulane University, Amistad Research Center.
University of Chicago Library, Hanna Holborn Gray Special Collections Research Center, Burgess, Ernest. Papers.
UMass Amherst, Robert S. Cox Special Collections & University Archives Research Center, W. E. B. Du Bois Papers, 1803–1999.

Works by Herbert Adolphus Miller

Miller, Herbert A. 1905. 'The Race Problem and Psychophysics'. PhD thesis, Harvard University Archives.
Miller, Herbert A. 1906. 'Some Psychological Considerations in the Race Problem', *Bibliotheca Sacra* 63 (April): 352–363.
Miller, Herbert A. 1914a. 'Nationalism in Bohemia and Poland', *North American Review* 200(709), 879–886.
Miller, Herbert A. 1914b. 'The Psychological Limits of Eugenics', *Popular Science Monthly* 84: 390–396.

Miller, Herbert A. 1914c. 'The Rising National Individualism', *American Journal of Sociology* 19(5): 592–605.
Miller, Herbert A. 1914d. 'What are the Best Contributions Sociologists Can Make at the Present toward the Conditions of Life in the United States, Particularly the Central Portion of the Country?', in *Publications of the American Sociological Society* VIII: 35. Chicago: University of Chicago Press.
Miller, Herbert A. 1914e. 'Is It Possible for American Sociologists to Agree Upon a Constructive Program?', in *Publications of the American Sociological Society* VIII: 165–166. Chicago: University of Chicago Press.
Miller, Herbert A. 1915. 'A Prophecy of Slav Domination', *New York Times Sunday Magazine*, 23 May: 10.
Miller, Herbert A. 1916. *The School and the Immigrant*. Cleveland, OH: Survey Committee of the Cleveland Foundation.
Miller, Herbert A. 1917. 'With the Peasants of Moravia', *Oberlin Literary Magazine*, June.
Miller, Herbert A. 1918a. 'The Lost Division', *The Survey*, 15 June: 307–309.
Miller, Herbert A. 1918b. 'Bulwark of Freedom: Beginning a Discussion of the Cohesive Forces at Work among the Subject Nationalities of Central Europe I: Emergent Democracies', *The Survey*, 5 October: 5–10.
Miller, Herbert A. 1918c. 'Bulwark of Freedom II: The Rebirth of a Nation: The Czechoslovaks', *The Survey*, 2 November: 117–120.
Miller, Herbert A. 1919a. 'Treatment of Immigrant Heritages', *Proceedings of the National Conference of Social Work*: 730–738.
Miller, Herbert A. 1919b. 'The American Spirit and the Organization of Mid-Europe', *Publications of the American Sociological Society* XIII: 180–187. Chicago: University of Chicago Press.
Miller, Herbert A. 1920. 'Discussion: Democracy and Race Problems', in *Papers and Proceedings, 14th Annual Meeting, American Sociological Association*: 203–205. Chicago: University of Chicago Press.
Miller, Herbert A. 1921a. 'The Oppression Psychosis and the Immigrant', *Annals of the American Academy of Political and Social Science* 93(1): 139–144.
Miller, Herbert A. 1921b. 'The Group as an Instinct', *American Journal of Sociology* 27(3): 334–343.
Miller, Herbert A. 1921c. 'The Case of Korea', *The Survey*, 1 October: 10–11.
Miller, Herbert A. 1921d. 'In the Cradle of Wars', *The Survey*, 15 January: 563.
Miller, Herbert A. 1922. 'The Myth of Racial Superiority', *The World Tomorrow* 5(3): 67–70.

Miller, Herbert A. 1924a. *Races, Nations and Classes: The Psychology of Domination and Freedom*. Philadelphia: J.B. Lippincott & Co.

Miller, Herbert A. 1924b. 'Founders' Day Address', *Fisk University News*, December: 10–13.

Miller, Herbert A. 1925. 'The Quest for the Real: Commencement Address', Ohio State University.

Miller, Herbert A. 1926. *The Book on Czechoslovakia*. Unpublished manuscript. Temple University, Pennsylvania, PA: Conwellana-Templana Collection.

Miller, Herbert A. 1927. 'Changing Concepts of Race', *Papers and Proceedings of the American Sociological Society* 21: 106–112.

Miller, Herbert A. 1929. 'One Man's War', *Everyday Week Magazine*, 9–10 November: 3–5.

Miller, Herbert A. 1931a. 'Racial Inter-marriage', *The Crisis* 40(10): 337.

Miller, Herbert A. 1931b. 'The Negro and the Immigrant', in Kimball Young (ed.) *Social Attitudes*, pp. 328–346. New York: Henry Holt.

Miller, Herbert A. 1933. *The Beginnings of To-morrow: An Introduction to the Sociology of the Great Society*. Boston, MA: D. C. Heath & Co.

Miller, Herbert A. 1940. 'What Woodrow Wilson and America Meant to Czecho-Slovakia', in Robert J. Kerner (ed.) *Czecho-Slovakia: Twenty Years of Independence*, pp. 71–84. Berkeley: University of California Press.

Miller, Herbert A. 2018. 'Address', in Floyd W. Tomkins (ed.) *First Korean Congress: Philadelphia, 1919*, pp. 20–21. Forgotten Books.

Other works

Abbott, Andrew 1999. *Department and Discipline: Chicago Sociology at One Hundred*. Chicago: University of Chicago Press.

Abbott, Andrew 2001. *Chaos of Disciplines*. Chicago: University of Chicago Press.

Abbott, Andrew and Rainer Egloff 2008. 'The Polish Peasant in Oberlin and Chicago: The Intellectual Trajectory of W. I. Thomas', *American Sociologist* 39(4): 217–258.

Abbott, Grace 1917. *The Immigrant in the Community*. New York: Century Co.

Adorno, Theodor, Frenkel-Brunswik, Else, Levinson, Daniel and Nevitt Sanford (1950). *The Authoritarian Personality*. New York: Harper.

Allen, David 2023. *Every Citizen a Statesman: The Dream of a Democratic Foreign Policy in the American Century*. Cambridge, MA: Harvard University Press.

Anghie, Anthony 2006. 'The Evolution of International Law: Colonial and Postcolonial Realities', *Third World Quarterly* 27(5): 739–753.

Ates, Alex 2022. 'A Quaker History of Black Mountain College', *Journal of Black Mountain College Studies*, 13, online.
Athens, Lonnie 2020. 'The Renunciation of Robert E. Park: Myths About His Sociological Work', *American Sociologist* 51(1): 76–91.
Ayers, Leonard P. 1917. *The Cleveland School Survey: Summary Volume*. Cleveland, OH: Survey Committee of the Cleveland Foundation.
Baldwin, Davarian L. 2003. 'Chicago's New Negroes: Consumer Culture and Intellectual Life Reconsidered', *American Studies* 44(1/2): 121–152.
Bannister, Robert C. 1987. *The American Quest for Objectivity, 1880–1940*. Chapel Hill: University of North Carolina Press.
Bernard, Luther. L. and Jessie Bernard 1934. *Sociology and the Study of International Relations*. St Louis, MO: Washington University Studies.
Bernard, Luther L. 1944. *War and Its Causes*. New York: Henry Holt & Co.
Bhambra, Gurminder K. 2014. 'A Sociological Dilemma: Race, Segregation, and US Sociology', *Current Sociology* 62(4): 472–492.
Bhambra, Gurminder K. and John Holmwood 2021. *Colonialism and Modern Social Theory*. Cambridge: Polity.
Blackman, Shane 2023. 'Black Ethnographic Activists: Exploring Robert Park, Scientific Racism, The Chicago School, and FBI Files Through the Black Sociological Experience of Charles S. Johnson and E. Franklin Frazier', *Symbolic Interaction* 46(3): 287–310.
Blumer, Herbert 1939. *Critiques of Research in the Social Sciences: An Appraisal of Thomas and Znaniecki's The Polish Peasant in Europe and America*. New Brunswick, NJ: Transaction.
Breslau, Daniel 2007. 'Theorizing a New Science', in Craig Calhoun (ed.) *Sociology in America: A History*, pp. 39–62. Chicago: University of Chicago Press.
Brewer, John D. 2000. *Ethnography*. Buckingham: Open University Press.
Brožek, Aleš 2011. ´Did the United States Influence the Czechoslovak National Flag?´ *Proceedings of the 24th International Congress of Vexillology*, Washington, DC, 1–5 August: 73–82.
Bulmer, Martin 1981. 'Charles S. Johnson, Robert E. Park and the Research Methods of the Chicago Commission on Race Relations, 1919–22: An Early Experiment in Applied Social Research', *Ethnic and Racial Studies* 4(3): 289–306.
Bulmer, Martin 1983. 'The Society for Social Research: An Institutional Underpinning to the Chicago School of Sociology in the 1920s', *Urban Life* 11(4): 421–439.
Bulmer, Martin 1996. 'The Social Survey Movement and Early Twentieth Century Sociological Methodology', in Maurine W. Greenwald and Margo Anderson (eds) *Pittsburgh Surveyed: Social Science and Social*

Reform in the Early Twentieth Century, pp. 15–34. Pittsburgh, PA: University of Pittsburgh Press.

Bulmer, Martin 2017. 'W. E. B. Du Bois and Robert Park', *British Journal of Sociology* 68(1): 23–30.

Burawoy, Michael 2005. 'For Public Sociology', *American Sociological Review* 70(1): 4–28.

Burns, Allen T. 1920. *American Americanization*. New York: Educational Department of the Municipal Court.

Burns, Allen T. 1921. 'Immigration, the Matrix of American Democracy', *Annals of the American Academy of Political and Social Science* 93(1): 144–149.

Buxton, William and Stephen Turner 1992. 'From Education to Expertise: Sociology as a "Profession"', in Terence C. Halliday and Morris Janowitz (eds) *Sociology and Its Publics*, pp. 373–407. Chicago: University of Chicago Press.

Camic, Charles 1995. 'Three Departments in Search of a Discipline: Localism and Interdisciplinary Interaction in American Sociology, 1890–1940', *Social Research* 62(4): 1003–1033.

Chambers, Clarke A. 1971. *Paul U. Kellogg and the Survey: Voices for Social Welfare and Social Justice*. Minneapolis: University of Minnesota Press.

Chapoulie, Jean-Michel 2020. *Chicago Sociology*. New York: Columbia University Press.

Chatterjee, Partha 1986. *Nationalist Thought and the Colonial World*. London: Zed.

Chicago Commission on Race Relations (1922). *The Negro in Chicago: A Study of Race Relations and a Race Riot in 1919*. Chicago: University of Chicago Press.

Coben, Stanley 1975. 'The Assault on Victorianism in the Twentieth Century', *American Quarterly* 27(5): 604–625.

Cohen, Adam S. 2016a. 'Harvard's Eugenics Era', *Harvard Magazine* 118(4): 48–52.

Cohen, Adam S. 2016b. *Imbeciles: The Supreme Court, American Eugenics, and the Sterilization of Carrie Buck*. New York: Penguin.

Cohen, Steven R. 1991. 'The Pittsburgh Survey and the Social Survey Movement: A Road Not Taken', in Martin Bulmer, Kevin Bales and Kathryn K. Sklar (eds) *The Social Survey in Historical Perspective*, pp. 245–268. Cambridge: Cambridge University Press.

Commission on the Church and Race Relations of the Federal Council of the Churches and the Commission on Inter-racial Cooperation 1925. *Toward interracial cooperation; what was said and done at the first National Interracial Conference*. Available at https://babel.hathitrust.org/cgi/pt?id=ia.ark:/13960/s2wcb5rt93k&seq=3.

Commons, John R. 1907. *Races and Immigrants in America*. New York: Macmillan.
Connelly, John 1999. 'Nazis and Slavs: From Racial Theory to Racist Practice', *Central European History* 32(1): 1–33.
Contee, Clarence G. 1972. 'Du Bois, the NAACP, and the Pan-African Congress of 1919', *Journal of Negro History* 57(1): 13–28.
Cooley, Charles H. 1902. *Human Nature and the Social Order*. New York: Charles Scribner's Sons.
Cooley, Charles H. 1909. *Social Organization: A Study of the Larger Mind*. New York: Charles Scribner's Sons.
Crocker, Ruth 2006. *Mrs Russell Sage: Women's Activism and Philanthropy in Gilded Age and Progressive Era America*. Bloomington and Indianapolis: Indiana University Press.
Cox, Oliver Cromwell 1948. *Caste, Class, and Race: A Study in Social Dynamics*. New York: Doubleday.
Crawford Mitchell, Ruth 1980. *Alice Garrigue Masaryk, 1879–1966: Her Life as Recorded in Her Own Words and by Her Friends*. Pittsburgh, PA: University Center for International Studies.
Deegan, Mary. J. 1988. *Jane Addams and the Men of the Chicago School, 1892–1918*. New Brunswick, NJ: Transaction.
Dewey, John 1927. *The Public and Its Problems*. Athens, GA: Swallow Press.
Diaz, Eva 2014. *The Experimenters: Chance and Design at Black Mountain College*. Chicago: University of Chicago Press.
Diner, Stephen J. 1970. 'Chicago Social Workers and Blacks in the Progressive Era', *Social Service Review* 44(4): 393–410.
Duberman, Martin 1972. *Black Mountain: An Exploration in Community*, Evanston, IL: Northwestern University Press.
Du Bois, W. E. B. 1899. *The Philadelphia Negro*. Philadelphia: University of Pennsylvania Press.
Du Bois, W. E. B. 1906. *The Health and Physique of the Negro American: Report of a Social Study Made under the Direction of Atlanta University, together with the Proceedings of the Eleventh Conference for the Study of the Negro Problems, Held at Atlanta University, on May the 29th, 1906*. Atlanta, GA: Atlanta University Press.
Du Bois, W. E. B. 1910. 'Reconstruction and Its Benefits', *American Historical Review* 15(4): 781–799.
Du Bois, W. E. B. 1921. 'Opinion of W. E. B. Du Bois', *The Crisis* 21(3): 101–105.
Du Bois, W. E. B. 1924a. 'Diuturni Silenti', *Fisk Herald* 33(1): 1–11.
Du Bois, W. E. B. 1924b. 'The Dilemma of the Negro', *American Mercury* 3(10): 179–185.

Du Bois, W. E. B. 1924c. 'Opinion of W. E. B. Du Bois – "Fisk"', *The Crisis* 28(6): 251–252.
Du Bois, W. E. B. 1925a. 'Fisk', *The Crisis* 30(1): 40–41.
Du Bois, W. E. B. 1925b. 'Opinion of W. E. B. Du Bois – "Fisk"', *The Crisis* 29(6): 247–251.
Du Bois, W. E. B. 1935. *Black Reconstruction: An Essay Toward a History of the Part which Black Folk Played in the Attempt to Reconstruct Democracy in America, 1860–1880*. Philadelphia, PA: Albert Saifer.
Du Bois, W. E. B. 1995 [1940]. 'Propaganda and World War', in David L. Lewis (ed) *W. E. B. Du Bois: A Reader*, pp. 388–408. New York: Henry Holt & Co.
Durkheim, Émile 1957. *Professional Ethics And Civic Morals*. London: Routledge & Kegan Paul.
Durkheim, Émile 1983. *Pragmatism and Sociology*. Cambridge: Cambridge University Press, 1983
Faris, Ellsworth 1936. 'Review of *Mind Self and Society* by George H. Mead', *American Journal of Sociology* 41(6): 809–813.
Faris, Robert E. L. 1967. *Chicago Sociology: 1920–1932*. San Francisco, CA: Chandler Publishing Co.
Fallace, Thomas D. 2011. *Dewey and the Dilemma of Race: An Intellectual History, 1895–1922*. New York: Teachers College Press.
Farrell, Michael P. 2001. *Collaborative Circles: Friendship Dynamics and Creative Work*. Chicago: University of Chicago Press.
Fields, David P. 2019. *Foreign Friends: Syngman Rhee, American Exceptionalism, and the Division of Korea*. Lexington: University Press of Kentucky.
Fields, Karen E. 2012. 'Individuality and the Intellectuals: An Imaginary Conversation between Émile Durkheim and W. E. B. Du Bois', in Karen E. Fields and Barbara J. Fields, *Racecraft: The Soul of Inequality in American Life*, pp. 225–261. London: Verso.
Fine, Gary A. 1995. 'Introduction: A Second Chicago School? The Development of a Postwar American Sociology', in Gary A. Fine (ed.) *A Second Chicago School? The Development of a Postwar American Sociology*, pp. 1–16. Chicago: University of Chicago Press.
Fink, Carole 2004. *Defending the Rights of Others: The great Powers, the Jews, and International Minority Protection, 1878–1938*. Cambridge: Cambridge University Press.
Foulkes, Julia 2017. 'On James Baldwin and The New School: What It Means to be a Progressive University', *Public Seminar: A Global Intellectual Commons*. Available at https://publicseminar.org/2017/12/on-james-baldwin-and-the-new-school/.
Fretwell, Erica 2020. *Sensory Experiments: Psychophysics, Race, and the Aesthetics of Feeling*. Durham, NC: Duke University Press.

Friends and Relatives of Allen T. Burns (1954). *In Memoriam Allen T. Burns, 1876–1953.* Cleveland, OH: privately printed.

Funk, Rainer 2019. *Life Itself is an Art: The Life and Work of Erich Fromm.* New York: Continuum.

Furner, Mary O. 1975. *Advocacy & Objectivity: A Crisis in the Professionalization of American Social Science, 1865–1905.* Lexington: University of Kentucky Press.

Furner, Mary O. 2000. 'Seeing Pittsburgh: The Social Survey, the Survey Workers, and the Historians', *Journal of Policy History* 12(3): 405–412.

Galloway, Fred J. 1994. 'Inferential Sturdiness and the 1917 Army Alpha: A New Look at the Robustness of Educational Quality Indices as Determinants of Interstate Black-White Score Differentials', *Journal of Negro Education* 63(2): 251–266.

Gans, Herbert J. 1989. 'Sociology in America: The Discipline and the Public American Sociological Association, 1988 Presidential Address', *American Sociological Review* 54(1): 1–16.

Gelfand, Lawrence E. 1963. *The Inquiry: American Preparations for Peace, 1917–19.* New Haven, CT: Yale University Press.

Gillette, John M. 1914. 'What are the Best Contributions Sociologists Can Make at the Present toward the Conditions of Life in the United States, Particularly the Central Portion of the Country?', *Publications of the American Sociological Society* 8: 29–31. Chicago: University of Chicago Press.

Go, Julian 2020. 'Race, Empire, and Epistemic Exclusion: Or the Structures of Sociological Thought', *Sociological Theory* 38(2): 79–100.

Gordon, Milton M. 1975. 'Review: The American Immigrant Revisited', *Social Forces* 54(2): 470–474.

Greble, Emily 2021. *Muslims and the Making of Modern Europe.* Oxford: Oxford University Press.

Green, Dan S. and Edwin D. Driver 1976. 'W.E.B. Du Bois: A Case in the Sociology of Sociological Negation', *Phylon* 37(4): 308–333.

Gross, N. (2008). *Richard Rorty: The Making of an American Philosopher.* Chicago: University of Chicago Press.

Hansen, Peo and Stefan Jonsson 2014. *Eurafrica: The Untold History of European Integration and Colonialism.* London: Bloomsbury Academic.

Hansen, Randall and Desmond King 2013. *Sterilized by the State: Eugenics, Race, and the Population Scare in Twentieth-Century North America.* Cambridge: Cambridge University Press.

Hartmann, Edward G. 1948. *The Movement to Americanize the Immigrant.* New York: Columbia University Press.

Hempson III, Donald A. 2013. 'New to the Game: Czechs, Economic Unions, and the Diplomacy of Contested Zones', *International History Review* 35(2): 256–273.

Hinkle, Roscoe C. 1952. 'Theories of Social Stratification in Recent American Sociology'. PhD dissertation, University of Wisconsin-Madison.
Hinkle, Roscoe C. 1980. *Founding Theory of American Sociology, 1881–1915*. Boston, MA: Routledge.
Hisakazu, Inagaki 2016. 'Kagawa's Cosmic Purpose and Modernization in Japan', *Zygon: Journal of Religion and* Science 51(1): 145–160.
Huebner, Daniel R. 2014. *Becoming Mead: The Social Process of Academic Knowledge*. Chicago: University of Chicago Press.
House, Floyd N. 1936. *The Development of Sociology*. New York: McGraw Hill.
Hughes, E. C. 1979. 'Epilogue: Park and the Department of Sociology', in W. Raushenbush, *Robert E. Park: Biography of a Sociologist*. Durham, NC: Duke University Press, pp. 178–192.
Jani, Pranav 2013. 'Bihar, California, and the US Midwest: The Early Radicalization of Jayaprakash Narayan', *Postcolonial Studies* 16(2): 155–168.
Jackson, Walter A. 1990. *Gunnar Myrdal and America's Conscience: Social Engineering and Racial Liberalism, 1938–1987*. Chapel Hill: University of North Carolina Press.
Jeszenszky, Géza 1988. 'The Idea of a Danubian Federation in American Thought during World War I', *Acta Historica Academiae Scientiarum Hungaricae* 34(2/3): 271–278.
Jogarajan, Sunita 2018. *Double Taxation and the League of Nations*. Cambridge: Cambridge University Press.
Johnson, Charles S. 1931. *The Negro in American Civilization: A Study of Negro Life and Race Relations in the Light of Social Research*. London: Constable & Co.
Johnson, Charles S. 1987. *Bitter Canaan: The Story of the Negro Republic*. New York: Transaction.
Jones, Angela 2011. *African American Civil Rights: Early Activism and the Niagara Movement*. Santa Barbara, CA: Praeger.
Jones, Plummer A., Jr 2013. 'Cleveland's Multicultural Librarian: Eleanor (Edwards) Ledbetter, 1870–1954', *Library Quarterly: Information, Community, Policy* 83(3): 249–270.
Kallen, Horace M. 1998 [1924]. *Culture and Democracy in the United States*. New Brunswick, NJ: Transaction Publishers.
Kang, Sugwon 1979. 'Graham Wallas and Liberal Democracy', *Review of Politics* 41(4): 536–560.
Kellogg, Paul U. 1918. 'The "Wilson Policies"', *The Survey*, 19 October: 250–251.
Kim, Richard S. 2011. *The Quest for Statehood: Korean Immigrant Nationalism and U.S. Sovereignty, 1905–1945*. Oxford: Oxford University Press.

King, Desmond S. 2000. *Making Americans: Immigration, Race and the Origins of the Diverse Democracy*. Cambridge, MA: Harvard University Press.

Kivisto, Peter 2017. 'The Legacy of Robert Ezra Park', in Peter Kivisto (ed.) *The Anthem Companion to Robert Park*, pp. 1–16. London: Anthem Press.

King, Katrina Q. 2022. 'The Global Color Line and White Supremacy: W. E. B. Du Bois as a Grand Theorist of Race', in Aldon Morris (ed.) *The Oxford Handbook of W.E.B. Du Bois*, online edition (accessed 15 April 2023). Oxford: Oxford Academic.

Kovtun, George J. 1988. *Masaryk and America: Testimony of a Relationship*. Washington, DC: Library of Congress.

Kuhn, Thomas S. 1962. *The Structure of Scientific Revolutions*. Chicago: University of Chicago Press.

Lagemann, Ellen C. 1989. *The Politics of Knowledge: The Carnegie Corporation, Philanthropy and Public Policy*. Chicago: University of Chicago Press.

Lamon Lester C. 1974. 'The Black Community in Nashville and the Fisk University Student Strike of 1924–1925', *Journal of Southern History* 40(2): 225–244.

Law, Alex and Erik Lybeck 2015. 'Sociological Amnesia: An Introduction', in Alex Law and Erik Lybeck (eds) *Sociological Amnesia: Cross-currents in Disciplinary History*, pp. 1–15. Farnham: Ashgate.

Lewis, David L. 1993. *W. E. B. Du Bois: Biography of a Race, 1868–1919*. New York: Henry Holt.

Lippmann, Walter 1925. *The Phantom Public*. New York: Harcourt, Brace & Co.

Liss, Julia E. 1998. 'Diasporic Identities: The Science and Politics of Race in the Work of Franz Boas and W. E. B. Du Bois, 1894–1919', *Cultural Anthropology* 13(2): 127–166.

Locke, Alain (ed) 1925. *The New Negro: An Interpretation*. New York: A. & C. Boni.

Lovejoy, Arthur O. and Austin S. Edwards 1933. 'Academic Freedom and Tenure: Rollins College Report', *Bulletin of the American Association of University Professors* 19(7): 416–439.

Lyman, Stanford M. 1992. *Militarism, Imperialism and Racial Accommodation: An Analysis and Interpretation of the Early Writings of Robert E. Park*. Fayetteville: University of Arkansas Press.

Macartney, Carlile A. 1934. *National States and National Minorities*. London: Oxford University Press and H. Milford.

Magubane, Zine 2014. 'Science, Reform, and the "Science of Reform": Booker T Washington, Robert Park, and the Making of a "Science of Society"', *Current Sociology* 62(4): 568–583.

Masaryk, Thomas G. 1927. *The Making of a State: Memories and Observations 1914–1918*. London: Allen & Unwin.
May, Arthur J. 1957. 'H. A. Miller and the Mid-European Union of 1918', *American Slavic and East European Review* 16(4): 473–488.
Matthews, Fred H. 1977. *Quest for an American Sociology: Robert E. Park and the Chicago School*. Montreal: McGill-Queen's University Press.
McLaughlin, Neil 1998. 'How to Become a Forgotten Intellectual: Intellectual Movements and the Rise and Fall of Erich Fromm', *Sociological Forum* 13(2): 215–246.
McLaughlin, Neil 1998. *Erich Fromm and Global Public Sociology*. Bristol: Bristol University Press.
Manela, Erez 2007. *The Wilsonian Moment: Self-determination and the International Origins of Anticolonial Nationalism*. Oxford: Oxford University Press.
Maul, Daniel 2012. *Human Rights, Development and Decolonization: The International Labour Organization, 1940–1970*. Basingstoke: Palgrave Macmillan.
Mead, George H. 1899. 'The Working Hypothesis in Social Reform', *American Journal of Sociology* 5(3): 367–371.
Mead, George H. 1934. *Mind, Self, and Society from the Standpoint of a Social Behaviorist*. Chicago: University of Chicago Press.
Meier, August and Elliott Rudwick 1969. 'The Boycott Movement against Jim Crow Streetcars in the South, 1900–1906', *Journal of American History* 55(4): 756–775.
Miggins, Edward M. 1986. 'The Search for the One Best System: The Cleveland Public Schools and Educational Reform, 1836–1920', in David D. Van Tassel and John Grabowski, *Cleveland: A Tradition of Reform*, pp. 135–155. Kent, OH: Kent State University Press.
Miggins, Edward M. 2014. '"No crystal stair": The Cleveland Public Schools and the Struggle for Equality, 1900–1930', *Journal of Urban History* 40(4): 671–698.
Miller, David. H. 1928. *The Drafting of the Covenant*, Vol. 2. New York: Putnam.
Mills, C. Wright 1943. 'The Professional Ideology of Social Pathologists', *American Journal of Sociology* 49(2): 165–180.
Mills, C. Wright 1959. *The Sociological Imagination*. New York: Oxford University Press.
Minawi, Mostafa 2016. *The Ottoman Scramble for Africa: Empire and Diplomacy in the Sahara and the Hijaz*. Stanford, CA: Stanford University Press.
Morey, Maribel 2021. *White Philanthropy: Carnegie Corporation's An American Dilemma and the Making of a White World Order*. Chapel Hill: University of North Carolina Press.

Morris, Aldon D. 2015. *A Scholar Denied: W. E. B. Du Bois and the Birth of Modern Sociology*. Oakland: University of California Press.

Moynihan, D. P. 1965. *The Negro Family: The Case for National Action*. Washington, DC: Office of Policy Planning and Research, US Department of Labor.

Mullins, Nicholas C. 1973. *Theories and Theory Groups in Contemporary American Sociology*. New York: Harper & Row.

Myrdal, Gunnar 1944. *An American Dilemma: The Negro Problem and Modern Democracy*. New York: Harper & Bros.

Narayan, John 2016. *John Dewey: The Global Public and Its Problems*. Manchester: Manchester University Press.

Odum, Howard. T. 1913. 'Negro Children in the Public Schools of Philadelphia', *Annals of the American Academy of Political and Social Science* 49(1): 186–208.

O'Sullivan, Maurice J. Jr. and Jack C. Lane (2014) 'Zora Neale Hurston's Challenge to Rollins', Winter 2014. Available at https://winterparkmag.com/2015/06/05/zora-neale-hurstons-challenge-rollins/.

Parris, Guichard and Lester Brooks 1971. *Blacks in the City: A History of the National Urban League*. Boston, MA: Little, Brown.

Parsons, Talcott 1937. *The Structure of Social Action*. New York: McGraw Hill.

Park, Robert E. 1918. 'Education in Its Relation to Conflict and Fusion of Cultures, with Special Reference to the Problems of the Immigrant, the Negro, and Missions', *Publications of the American Sociological Society* 13: 38–63.

Park, Robert E. and Herbert A. Miller 1921. *Old World Traits Transplanted*. New York: Harper & Bros.

Park, Robert E. 1922. *The Immigrant Press*. New York: Harper & Bros.

Park, Robert E. and Ernest W. Burgess 1925. *The City*. Chicago: University of Chicago Press.

Park, Robert E. 1926. 'Review of Races, Nations, and Classes: The Psychology of Domination and Freedom by Herbert Adolphus Miller', *American Journal of Sociology* 31(4): 535–537.

Park, Robert E. 1950. *Race and Culture*. Glencoe, IL: The Free Press.

Patterson, Orlando 2019. 'The Denial of Slavery in Contemporary American Sociology', *Theory and Society* 48(6): 903–914.

Pattie, Frank A., Jr 1939. 'William McDougall: 1871–1938', *American Journal of Psychology* 52(1): 303–307.

Pedersen, Susan 2006. The Meaning of the Mandates System: An Argument', *Geschichte und Gesellschaft* 32(4): 560–582.

Pedersen, Susan 2015. *The Guardians: The League of Nations and the Crisis of Empire*. Oxford: Oxford University Press.

Persons, Stow 1987. *Ethnic Studies at Chicago, 1905–45*. Urbana and Chicago: University of Illinois Press.
Platt, Anthony J. 1991. *E. Franklin Frazier Reconsidered*. New Brunswick, NJ: Rutgers University Press.
Platt, Jennifer 1991. 'Anglo-American Contacts in the Development of Research Methods before 1945', in Martin Bulmer, Kevin Bales and Kathryn K. Sklar (eds) *The Social Survey in Historical Perspective*, pp. 340–58. Cambridge: Cambridge University Press.
Platt, Jennifer 1996. *A History of Sociological Research Methods in America, 1920–60*. Cambridge: Cambridge University Press.
Raushenbush, Winifred 1979. *Robert E. Park: Biography of a Sociologist*. Durham, NC: Duke University Press.
Report 1931. 'The 1930 Enquiry Commission to Liberia', *Journal of the Royal African Society* 30(120): 277–290.
Reuter, Edward B. 1918. *The Mulatto in the United States, Including a Study of the Role of Mixed-Blood Races throughout the World*. Boston, MA: R. G. Badger.
Reynolds, Katherine Ch. 1998. *Visions and Vanities: John Andrew Rice of Black Mountain College*. Baton Rouge: Louisiana State University Press.
Roberts, Priscilla 2005. 'Paul D. Cravath, The First World War, and the Anglophile Internationalist Tradition', *Australian Journal of Politics and History* 51(2): 194–215.
Ross, Dorothy, 1979. 'The Development of the Social Sciences', in Alexandra Oleson and John Voss (eds) *The Organization of Knowledge in Modern America, 1860–1920*, pp. 107–38. Baltimore, MD: Johns Hopkins University Press.
Rucker, Darnell 1969. *The Chicago Pragmatists*. Minneapolis: University of Minnesota Press.
Rudwick, Elliot M. (1959) 'W. E. B. Du Bois and the Universal Races Congress of 1911', *Phylon*, 20(4):. 372–378.
Sabine, George 1931. 'Academic Freedom and Tenure at the Ohio State University: Report on the Dismissal of Professor Herbert A. Miller', *Bulletin of the American Association of University Professors* (1915–1955) 17(6): 443–473.
Shapiro, Stanley 1971. 'The Twilight of Reform: Advanced Progressives after the Armistice', *Historian* 33(3): 349–364.
Schneiderhahn, Eric 2011. 'Pragmatism and Empirical Sociology: The Case of Jane Addams and Hull House, 1889–1895', *Theory and Society* 40(6): 589–617.
Skinner, Quentin 1969. 'Meaning and Understanding in the History of Ideas', *History and Theory* 8(1): 3–53.

Slate, Nico 2011. *Colored Cosmopolitanism: The Shared Struggle for Freedom in the United States and India*. Cambridge, MA: Harvard University Press.

Smith, Anthony D. 1983. *Theories of Nationalism*. New York: Holmes & Meier, 2nd edn.

Smith, Christi. M. 2016. *Reparation and Reconciliation: The Rise and Fall of Integrated Higher Education*. Chapel Hill: University of North Carolina Press.

Smith, Mark C. 1994. *Social Science in the Crucible: The American Debate over Objectivity and Purpose, 1918–1941*. Durham, NC: Duke University Press.

Smith, William. C. 1939. *Americans in the Making*. New York: D. Appleton-Century Co.

Southern, David. W. 1987. *Gunnar Myrdal and Black-White Relations*. Baton Rouge: Louisiana University Press.

Sorrels, Katherine 2016. *Cosmopolitan Outsiders: Imperial Inclusion, National Exclusion, and the Pan-European Idea, 1900–1930*. New York: Palgrave Macmillan.

Stanfield, John H. 1987. 'Introductory Essay: Bitter Canaan's Historical Backdrop', in Charles S. Johnson, *Bitter Canaan: The Story of the Negro Republic*. New York: Transaction.

Strickland, Arvarh E. 1966. *History of the Chicago Urban League*. Urbana: University of Illinois Press.

Sultan, Nazmul 2022a. 'Between the Many and the One: Anticolonial Federalism and Popular Sovereignty', *Political Theory* 50(2): 247–274.

Sultan, Nazmul 2022b. 'Moral Empire and the Global Meaning of Gandhi's Anti-imperialism', *Review of Politics* 84(4): 545–569.

Sun, Yu 2020. 'A Brief History of the American Sociological Archives: Challenges to Development and Preservation'. PhD dissertation, Pennsylvania State University.

Švec, Luboš 2007 'Herbert Adolphus Miller, psychóza útisku a středoevropská otázka [Herbert Adolphus Miller, the Psychosis of Oppression and the Central European Question]', Slovanský přehled [*Review for Central, Eastern and Southeastern European History*] 93(2): 289–320.

Takeuchi, Yoshimi 2004. *Japan and Asia*. Seoul: Somyong.

Taylor, Alrutheus. A. 1924. *The Negro in South Carolina During the Reconstruction*. Washington, DC: Association for the Study of Negro Life and History.

Taylor, Alrutheus A. 1952. *Fisk University, 1866–1951: A Constructive Influence in American Life*. Alrutheus Ambush Taylor manuscript, 359, Amistad Research Center, New Orleans, LA.

Teeters, Negley K. 1951. 'Herbert Adolphus Miller, 1875–1951', *American Sociological Review* 16(4): 563–564.
Teeters, Negley K. 1966. 'Herbert Adolphus Miller and the Dissolution of the Hapsburg Empire', *Hartwick Review* 2(2), 4–15.
Turner, Stephen 2007. 'Charles Ellwood and the Division of Sociology', in Craig Calhoun (ed.) *Sociology in America: A History*, pp. 115–154. Chicago: University of Chicago Press.
Thomas, William I. 1909. *Source Book for Social Origins*. Chicago: University of Chicago Press.
Thomas, William I. 1912. 'Race Psychology: Standpoint and Questionnaire, with Particular Reference to the Immigrant and the Negro', *American Journal of Sociology* 17(6): 725–775.
Thomas, William I. and Florian Znaniecki 1996 [1918–20], ed. Eli Zaretsky. *The Polish Peasant in Europe and America*. Chicago: University of Chicago Press.
Thompson, Elizabeth. F. 2020. *How the West Stole Democracy from the Arabs: The Syrian Arab Congress of 1920 and the Destruction of Its historic Liberal-Islamic Alliance*. New York: Atlantic Monthly Press.
Thompson, Frank V. 1920. *Schooling the Immigrant*. New York: Harper & Bros.
Throntveit, Trygve 2011. 'The Fable of the Fourteen Points: Woodrow Wilson and National Self-Determination', *Diplomatic History* 35(3): 445–481.
Throop, Robert. and Lloyd. G. Ward 2007. '"Biography"-ing Thomas: Some Chapters in the life of William Isaac Thomas'. Toronto: Mead Project. Available at https://brocku.ca/MeadProject/Scrapbooks/Circulation/Biographying.html (accessed 9 June 2021).
Tittle, Diana 1992. *Rebuilding Cleveland: The Cleveland Foundation and its Evolving Urban Strategy*. Columbus: Ohio State University Press.
Turner, Stephen 1996. 'The Pittsburgh Survey and the Survey Movement: An Episode in the History of Expertise', in Maurine W. Greenwald and Margo Anderson (eds) *Pittsburgh Surveyed: Social Science and Social Reform in the Early Twentieth Century*, pp. 35–50. Pittsburgh: University of Pittsburgh Press.
Unterberger, Betty M. 1989. *The United States, Revolutionary Russia, and the Rise of Czechoslovakia*. Chapel Hill: University of North Carolina Press.
Vaughn, Stephen. L. 1980. *Holding Fast the Inner Lines: Democracy, Nationalism, and the Committee on Public Information*. Chapel Hill: University of North Carolina Press.
Volkart, Edmund H. 1951. *Social Behavior and Personality: Contributions of W. I. Thomas to Theory and Social Research*. New York: Social Science Research Council.

Wacker, R. Fred 1983. *Ethnicity, Pluralism and Race: Race Relations Theory in America before Myrdal*. Westport, CT: Greenwood Press.
Waskow, Arthur I. 1966. *From Race Riot to Sit-In, 1919 and the 1960s: A Study in the Connections between Conflict and Violence*. New York: Doubleday.
Wells, D. Collin 1907. 'Social Darwinism', *American Journal of Sociology* 12(5): 695–716.
Wallas, Graham 1914. *The Great Society*. New York: Macmillan Co.
Wilder, C. S. 2013 *Ebony and Ivy: Race, Slavery, and the Troubled History of America's Universities*. New York: Bloomsbury Press
Willoughby-Herard, Tiffany 2015. *Waste of a White Skin: The Carnegie Corporation and the Racial Logic of White Vulnerability*. Oakland: University of California Press.
Wilson, Francille Rusan 2006. *The Segregated Scholars: Black Social Scientists and the Creation of Black Labor Studies, 1890–1950*. Charlottesville: University of Virginia Press.
Wirth, Louis 1936. 'Types of Nationalism', *American Journal of* Sociology 41(6): 723–737.
Wright, Earl II 2010. 'The Tradition of Sociology at Fisk University', *Journal of African American Studies* 14(1): 44–60.
Wright, Earl II 2020. *Jim Crow Sociology: The Black and Southern Roots of American Sociology*. Cincinnati, OH: University of Cincinnati Press.
Zimmerman, A. 2010. *Alabama in Africa: Booker T. Washington, the German Empire and the Globalization of the New South*. Princeton, NJ: Princeton University Press.

Index

Abbott, Andrew 4, 18 n. 4, 23, 31, 85, 88, 88 n. 12, 178
Abbott, Grace 78 n. 12
activism 75, 134, 148, 155–156
  academic 50
  library 77
  political 12, 156
  reformist 10, 31
Addams, Jane 15–16, 55, 118 n. 9
Adorno, Theodor W. 17 n. 1
Advisory Committee on International Relations 105, 110
African Methodist Episcopal Church 104 n. 34
Albers, Anni 61
Albers, Josef 61
alienation 170
Allen, Devere 57 n. 27
amelioration 41, 177
American Association of University Professors 19, 59, 133, 146
American Creed 107
American Economic Association 22
American Historical Review 30
American Journal of Sociology 7, 22, 42, 88, 109, 167
American Missionary Association 38
American Sociological Association 8, 42
American Sociological Review 35, 37 n. 2
American Sociological Society 8, 19, 42, 110
American Statistical Association 22
Americanisation 6, 11–12, 24, 30, 59, 63, 76–78, 81, 82 n. 4, 83, 86 n. 9, 87, 87 n. 10, 90, 92–95, 100–103, 106–107, 109, 112, 121, 140, 162, 164–166
  American 81, 84
  German 84
  Government Memorandum on 92, 171
  methods of 3, 12, 42, 71, 80, 84, 177
  of immigrants 28, 171
  paradox of 171
An American Dilemma 5, 12, 103, 106 n. 37, 107
anomie 164
anti-Semitism 110, 130, 162, 170, 179
Army tests 68, 70, 80
ashram 141, 146

Index

assimilation 3, 6, 12, 26–27, 66, 72, 79–80, 83–84, 100, 109, 112, 121–122, 127, 165, 171, 173–174
  cultural 111
  gradual 29, 106
  of immigrants 6, 127, 169
  two-stage process of 83 n. 6
Atlanta University 20, 36, 69
Authoritarian Personality 17 n. 1
Ayres, Leonard 74–75

Beginnings of To-morrow 13–14, 38, 109, 113, 127, 156, 159, 172, 179
Beloit College 19, 58
Beneš, Edvard 123, 126
Bentley, Eric 61–62, 153–155
Bernard, Jessie 109–110, 110 n. 1, 111 n. 3, 122, 172
Bernard, Luther 7, 109–110, 110 n. 1 and 2, 111 n. 3, 122, 172
Bibliotheca Sacra 69
Black Lives Matter 2
Black Mountain College 9, 13, 19, 58–63, 63 n. 36, 151–152, 152 n. 30, 153–155
Black Reconstruction 30
Blumer, Herbert 21, 23, 87, 157 n. 1
Board of Trustees 18 n. 5, 39, 134, 136–138, 146, 146 n. 16, 148
Boas, Franz 6, 27, 66, 69
Bombay speech 56, 63, 146, 146 n. 16, 147, 149
Bowdoin Prize 38, 70
Brewster Academy 37
British Mandate for Palestine 170
Brumfield, Thomas W. 138
Bryn Mawr College 19, 35, 40 n. 5, 58, 114 n. 4, 151
Bulmer, Martin 21, 25, 71–72, 84 n. 7, 109

Burawoy, Michael 178
Bureau of Education 93, 101
Burgess, Ernest W. 23–24, 46, 86 n. 9
Burns, Allen T. 73–74, 77–78, 80–82, 82 n. 4 and 5, 83, 86, 86 n. 9, 92–93, 99–102
business efficiency 73–75, 77

Camp Sherman 63, 96, 101 n. 30, 124 n. 13
canon 1, 4, 16, 24
capital 170
capitalism 48, 142, 169–170
Carnegie Corporation 3, 12, 80–82, 82 n. 4 and 5, 85, 86 n. 9, 87 n. 10, 89–90, 93, 100–101, 103, 140, 158, 176
caste 29, 38, 106, 106 n. 38, 142, 175
Chang Kai-Shek 143
Chapoulie, Jean-Michel 18 n. 4, 24, 30–31, 33, 88 n. 11, 106 n. 38, 140, 177
Charities and the Commons 71
Charles I of Austria 120
Chatterjee, Partha 172
Chicago Commission on Race Relations 84 n. 7, 91 n. 17, 104 n. 35
Chicago Commons 17, 74, 84 n. 7
Chicago School of sociology vii, 3, 10, 15, 17, 20, 24–25, 28–29, 29 n. 9, 30–31, 66, 72, 72 n. 7, 83, 83 n. 6, 84 n. 7, 85, 106, 140, 157, 157 n. 1, 164, 165 n. 6, 177
  First 4, 23
  Second 23
Chicago School of Civics and Philanthropy 74

Chicago Settlement Movement 15–17, 31, 31 n. 11, 49, 74, 93
Chicago Urban League 33, 84 n. 7, 134
Christianity 115 n. 6, 141, 143–144
Cicero 135
civilisation 37, 65, 112, 116 n. 7, 129, 167, 174
  Western 117, 141, 160, 165, 173
civilising process 26–27, 29, 168
civil rights 39, 62, 86, 133, 152–153, 160, 175, 177
  movement 178
Civil War 26, 28, 38
Clark, Kenneth 166 n. 6
class x, 63, 72, 74, 79, 162, 166, 169–171
  consciousness 121
  exploitation 3
  justice 3
Cleveland Americanization Committee 77
Cleveland Foundation 73–74
Cleveland Public Library 90, 90 n. 15
Cleveland Survey 11–12, 42, 71–75, 78, 84, 158, 176
Coben, Stanley 72 n. 7
Cohen, Adam 67
collaborative circle 31, 31 n. 11, 33, 177
Collinge, L. Elizabeth 138
colonialism 1–2, 29, 29 n. 9, 32, 125, 130, 167, 177–178
color line 32, 106, 109
Columbus Urban League 8, 132, 154
Commission on the Church and Race Relations 104, 104 n. 34
Committee on International Relations 8, 19, 55, 110

Commons, John R. 33, 65,
community 19, 43, 60 n. 32, 61–62, 72 n. 7, 73, 76, 92, 120, 133, 153
  American 59
  Black 134, 138
  democratic 58
  White 134
Community Chests and Councils of America 82 n. 5
conflict 2, 13, 17, 60, 72 n. 7, 110, 112, 114, 117–119, 143, 149, 151, 162–165, 168, 170, 173, 179
  imperial 115
  social and political 14, 167
Confucianism 143
Congo Reform Association 26–27
consciousness 42, 64, 110, 122, 145, 157 n. 1, 164–165
  class 121, 162
  double- 97, 165
  global 8–9, 175
  group 165, 174
  national 121, 162, 167
  of kind 164
  racial 121
Cooley, Charles Horton 14, 23, 45, 46 n. 13, 156–157, 157 n. 1, 158–160, 163, 166
Cosmic Purpose 144 n. 11
cosmopolitanism 13, 54, 112, 144 n. 11
  plural 145, 172, 173, 175
cosmos 127, 160, 172
Coudenhove-Kalergi, Richard 119
Covenant of the League of Nations 116 n. 7, 120, 130, 131 n. 23
Cowley, William H. 150

Cox, Oliver Cromwell 106, 106 n. 38
Crane, Charles 95 n. 24
Cravath Elisabeth (Bessie), *see* Miller, Elisabeth (Bessie)
Cravath, Erastus M. 38–39, 113 n. 4, 132, 137
Cravath, Paul 39, 39 n. 5, 100, 101 n. 30, 113 n. 4, 133, 136–138, 140, 151
Creel, George 100
Crosthwait, Minnie Scott 138
culture 25–26, 65, 77, 86–87, 107, 109, 120, 164, 166, 172–173, 175
  alien 18
  Anglo-American 26, 91, 164
  dominant 66
  immigrant 72
  lower 26
  national 26
  peasant 26, 91
  political 112
  rural 26
  superior 110, 131
  traditional 72
  Western 65
Culver, Helen 22

Daniels, John 81
Danubian Union 126, 126 n. 16
Dartmouth College 35–37, 66
Davis, Jerome 55
Declaration of Common Aims 123–124, 124 n. 14
Declaration of Independence 107
  Czechoslovakian ix–x, 5, 109, 120, 123
  Korean 5, 128
decolonising the university 1
Deegan, Mary Jo 24–25, 31 n. 11
De Graef, Fran 155

democracy 20, 59, 63, 70, 128–130, 157–159, 161, 168–170, 174
  American 58
  industrial 169–170
  pluralist 27, 169, 174
de-racination 106
Dewey, John 14, 19, 23, 32, 59, 65, 118 n. 9, 157 n. 1, 158–160, 161 n. 4
dialogue 36, 43, 48, 63, 159
Díaz, Eva 60
Dillingham Commission 80, 83
discrimination 58
disorganisation 11, 24, 72, 76, 79, 162
  social 24, 72 n. 7, 79
Division on Immigrant Contributions 12, 32, 78, 81, 88, 90
Division on Immigrant Press and Theatre 81, 89
domination vii, 11–14, 16, 32, 34, 36, 38, 57, 63, 66, 79, 81, 107, 109, 119, 127, 129, 130 n. 20, 132, 142, 160–165, 174
  colonial vii, ix, x
  global 10, 33,
  pathologies of 121–122
  psychology of 70 n. 5, 163, 166
  racial 6
Dreier, Theodore 59, 61–62, 154–155
Driver, Edwin 32 n. 12
Duberman, Martin B. 61–62, 63 n. 36, 152, 152 n. 31, 153–154, 154 n. 32, 155, 155 n. 33
Du Bois, W. E. B. 11, 25, 27, 32 n. 12 and 13, 105 n. 36, 110 n. 1, 166 n. 6, 177
  Americanisation 107
  Atlanta University 20, 36, 69
  Chicago race riots 91 n. 17, 134

Du Bois, W. E. B. (*cont.*)
    Chicago School 28, 31
    colour line 32, 106, 109
    diuturni silenti speech 135
    double-consciousness 97, 165
    double-death 97
    Dunning school 30
    Encyclopedia of the Negro 105
    First Universal Races Congress 118, 118 n. 9, 175
    Fisk University 5–6, 39, 113 n. 4, 134
    Fisk University crisis 1924–1925 30, 40, 135–139
    Harvard University 11, 38
    Liberia 105 n. 36
    McKenzie and 134–136, 136 n. 2, 137–139
    Myrdal and 12, 106–107
    new Negro 33, 67
    Niagara Movement 134
    Pan-African Congress 118
    Philadelphia Negro 20, 71
    race problem 27, 66, 105
    race relations 91 n. 17
    racial equality 97, 135
    The Crisis 36, 91 n. 17, 134, 136, 139
    war 97, 97 n. 25, 134
    Washington and 29, 136
Du Bois, Yolande 135
Dummer, Ethel Sturges 88
Dunning School of historiography 30, 30 n. 10
Durkheim, Émile 14, 163, 164

education 10–11, 19, 36–37, 42–44, 50, 55, 57–61, 63, 69–70, 72, 74–75, 78, 81, 134, 145 n. 12, 161, 176, 178
    Bureau of Education 93, 101
    citizenship and 43, 104
    civic 107
    Cleveland educational system 77
    Deweyan principles of 19, 59
    higher 21, 29, 39, 133
    immigrants and 75, 77
    progressive 43, 59
    public 20, 74
    purpose of 11, 69
    race and 135–136
    social reform and 70
    sociological 37
    Western 55 n. 24
    of women 37
economics 44–45, 59
economy 19–20, 44, 48 n. 18, 58, 81 n. 3, 116, 124, 142–143, 148 n. 21, 149, 164, 169–170, 173–174
Egloff, Rainer 88, 88 n. 12
Eliot, Charles W. 67
Ellwood, Charles 22
empire ix, 2, 6, 10, 13, 26, 66–67, 103, 110, 113, 118, 120, 125, 127, 142, 161, 167–169, 171, 173, 177
    Austro-Hungarian 2, 6, 32, 50, 63, 99 n. 26, 112, 115, 120, 126, 170
    Belgian 2
    British 2, 20, 115
    Dutch 2
    European 11, 39 n. 5, 99, 109–110, 113–117, 127, 131, 168–169
    French 2, 115
    German 2, 32, 99 n. 26, 112, 115, 117, 126, 170
    Japanese 2, 113, 127, 130,
    Ottoman 2, 99 n. 26, 114–115, 170
    Russian 3, 117, 170

Index

equality 13, 33, 39, 61, 67, 78, 87, 129, 129 n. 18, 133–134, 136, 142–143, 173–175
  biological 27, 66
  cultural 27, 66
  racial vii, ix, 1, 6, 8, 13, 65, 100 n. 29, 122, 130–132, 135, 140, 144, 150 n. 26, 152, 160–161, 168, 175, 177–178
Espionage Act 100
ethno-nationalism 13, 110, 117, 129–131, 142, 161, 174
eugenics 2, 6, 11, 25, 67–68, 70, 110, 127
European Union 119
expert knowledge 42, 158
exploitation 3, 116, 119, 148 n. 21

Fallace, Thomas 27, 29, 33, 65–66, 106
family 164, 166
Faris, Ellsworth 23, 157 n. 2
Faris, Robert E. L. 4, 23–24
Farrell, Michael 31
Federal Industrial Relations Committee 73
Fields, Karen 97
First International Eugenics Congress 67
First National Conference on Race Betterment 67
First World War ix, x, 2–3, 12–13, 31, 80, 84, 95, 106, 108, 110, 114–115, 117, 119, 121, 131, 133–134, 162, 172, 179
Fisk University 5–6, 13, 16, 29–30, 37–40, 61–62, 66–67, 96, 104, 113 n. 4, 132–140, 154, 154 n. 32, 155
Fisk University News 135, 139
Foreign Policy Association 8, 19–20, 44, 58
Foreman, Clark 154

Fosdick, Raymond B. 81 n. 3
Frankfurt School 17
Frazier, E. Franklin 29, 29 n. 9, 30
Freedmen's Bureau 38
freedom 11, 55, 63, 77, 96–97, 99 n. 27, 120–121, 125, 129 n. 18, 130 n. 20, 132, 147, 155, 161, 163, 165, 167, 173–174, 177
  academic 147, 147 n. 18, 148, 151
  bulwark of 97–98, 100, 121–123, 141
  spirit of 77, 102, 112, 129
Freud, Sigmund 17 n. 1
Fromm, Erich 17, 17 n. 1
fundamentalism 70 n. 5, 165, 174
  biblical 70
  scientific 165, 174
Furner, Mary 72, 72 n. 7

Gandhi, Mohandas Karamchand 13, 57, 118 n. 9, 141–142, 144–145, 145 n. 12, 146, 149–150
Gans, Herbert 178
Garvey, Marcus 105 n. 36
Gates, George Augustus 134
Gay, Edwin F. 81 n. 3
Gelfand, Lawrence 118
gender 1, 20, 31, 72, 75, 160, 178
Germanification 81, 83, 117
Go, Julian 66
Goff, Fred 73–74
Gordon, Milton 86–87
Great Depression 148
Green, Dan 32 n. 12
group 2, 14, 25–27, 39, 43, 50, 54, 56, 63, 65, 69, 70, 76–77, 86–87, 107, 110, 118, 121, 127, 130, 139, 142, 157, 160, 163–166, 169–170, 173–174
  activist 39

group (*cont.*)
    conflict 163
    consciousness 165, 174
    core 31–32
    dominant 165, 171
    egotism 55
    ethnic 95
    horizontal 166–167, 169, 171
    identity 127, 162, 164
    immigrant 76–77, 85, 101, 122, 161
    internationalisation of 13, 171
    liberal 147
    minority 167
    oppressed 13, 140
    primary 166
    racial 25, 59, 65, 68
    racialised 11, 55, 132
    secondary 166
    social 158–159, 167–168
    solidarity 72 n. 7, 163
    subject x, 166
    vertical 166–167, 171

Hagerty, James E. 56, 147, 147 n. 18
Hansen, Peo 119
Harper, William R. 93 n. 19
Harris Abraham L. 2 n. 1
Hartmann, George 83
Hartwick Review 35, 95 n. 23
Harvard University 5–6, 11, 15–16, 20–21, 37–38, 40–41, 43–44, 67, 70, 70 n. 5, 113 n. 4, 159
Haynes, George E. 104
Hempson, Donald 126
heterogeneity 41, 171
Hinduism 142
Hinkle, Roscoe 41, 70, 70 n. 4
Hinkovič, Hinko 125
Holt, Hamilton 153
homogeneity 54, 171

Horvath, Helen 90, 90 n. 15, 91
House, Edward 117, 120
House, Floyd 4, 15, 84
Howard University 29–30, 106, 134
Howe, Frederic C. 124 n. 13
Huebner, Daniel 23, 157 n. 1
Hughes, Everett C. 29 n. 9, 85 n. 8
Hull House 15
Hurston, Zora Neale 152, 152 n. 31
Hutchins, Robert 18

immigrant 3, 6, 11–12, 15, 26–28, 32, 46–47, 49, 50 n. 21, 54, 56, 72, 75–78, 78 n. 12, 81, 83, 85, 90, 90 n. 15, 91–94, 96, 99, 101, 112, 122, 122 n. 10, 125 n. 15, 127–128, 161, 164
    children 11, 30, 74, 166, 169, 171
    communities 24, 77, 81, 102, 158
    heritages 88, 90, 91 n. 17, 93, 102
immigration 2, 6, 11, 25, 28, 33, 36, 40, 46–47, 50, 59, 65–67, 75, 80, 84, 89, 109, 112, 116, 121, 129, 171–172
    policy 67, 83
imperialism 16, 29 n. 9, 95, 113, 122, 142, 144, 168, 172
    American 109
    cultural 122, 172
    European 1, 109, 113, 130–131, 172
    Western 16
independence 118, 123, 126 n. 16, 129 n. 19, 145
    Czechoslovakian vii, ix, x, 5, 9, 12, 119, 123, 179
    Indian vii, 5, 144–145

Index

Korean vii, 5, 12, 112, 128, 130 n. 22
Independence Hall, Philadelphia x, 123, 128, 128 n. 17
Indian Congress Party 144
industrialism 20, 126, 145 n. 12, 159, 166, 169–170
inequality 117, 142, 161, 178–179
inferiority 25, 66, 160
  myth of racial 27
Institute for Social Research 17, 17 n. 1
integrated college 2 n. 1, 17 n. 2, 37–39
inter-group relations 12, 14, 55, 165, 168–169
International Labour Organization 116
international law 116
international relations 2, 8, 11, 19–20, 40, 55, 58, 95, 109, 113 n. 4, 114, 129, 129 n. 19, 163, 168, 172
internationalisation 13, 160, 171
internationalism 55, 121, 129, 143, 170–171
IQ tests 68, 70, 165
Ivy League 11, 19, 36

Jaisonh, Philip 128
James, William 15, 42, 44, 55, 67–68, 70, 163
Jani, Pranav 144
Japanisation 115, 115 n. 6
Jeszenszky, Géza 126 n. 16
Jewish question 58, 117
Jim Crow laws 28, 134
Jinnah, Muhammed Ali 145
Johnson, Charles S. 5, 29, 40, 84 n. 7, 91 n. 17, 104, 104 n. 35 and 36, 110 n. 1, 139–140, 153
Jones, Plummer A. 77, 90 n. 15

Jones, Thomas Elsa 40, 139–140
Jonsson, Stefan 119
Journal of Higher Education 150
justice 3, 74, 124, 129 n. 18
  class 3
  racial 3, 153, 155, 172, 177

Kagawa, Toyohiko 144, 144 n. 11
Kallen, Horace 27, 100 n. 29
Kellogg, Paul 71, 71 n. 6, 74–75, 99, 99 n. 27, 100, 118
Keppel, Frederick 85, 103, 105–106
Kim, Nodie Dora (Kimhaekim Sohn) 128 n. 17
King, Desmond S. 80
Kraus, Hertha 58 n. 28, 59
Kuhn, Thomas S. 21
Ku Klux Klan 2, 7, 67, 162
Kuomintang 143

labor 164, 170
laboratory practice 36, 46, 49, 150
Lagemann, Ellen 103, 158
Lamon, Lester 138–139, 140 n. 7
Lancaster, Ellsworth G. 44
Lathorp, Julia 95 n. 241
Laura Spelman Rockefeller Memorial 105
Law, Alex 16
League for Small and Subject Nationalities 124 n. 13
League of Central European Nations 88
League of Free Nations 99, 118
League of Free Nations Association 20
League of Friends of Korea 109, 128, 129 n. 18
League of Nations 3 n. 2, 99, 104 n. 36, 110, 112–113, 116, 116 n. 7, 117–118, 126 n. 16, 131 n. 23

League to Enforce Peace 118
Ledbetter, Eleanor 77, 90–91, 91 n. 17, 92–93, 102
Leiserson, William M. 81
Lenin, Vladimir 150
Leopold II of Belgium 26
liberal orthodoxy 103
Liberty Bell 123, 123 n. 12
Library of Congress 8 n. 3
library reformers 11, 77
Lippincott, Bertram 152 n. 31
Lippman, Walter 14, 68, 158–159, 160 n. 3
looking-glass self 23, 157
Ludlow Massacre 73
Lybeck, Eric 16

Macartney, Carlile A. 3 n. 2
MacDonald, Ramsay 145
Mandate System 116
Manela, Erez 129, 129 n. 19, 172
Mann Act 18 n. 4
Marxism 144
Masaryk, Alice 18 n. 3, 49, 93–95
Masaryk, Olga 125 n. 15
Masaryk, Tomáš Garrigue ix, 18 n. 3, 32 n. 13, 49, 49 n. 20, 93 n. 19, 94, 94 n. 20, 122–123, 141
Mattison, Gorman 60
May, Arthur 5–6, 112, 127
McDoughall, William 70, 70 n. 5
McDowell, Mary E. 15, 18 n. 3, 49, 93–94, 94 n. 20, 95
McKenzie, Lafayette 133–138, 154
McLaughlin, Neil 16–17, 31
Mead, George Herbert 18, 23, 23 n. 7, 42, 73, 157, 157 n. 1 and 2
Merriam, Charles E. 22

Mid-European Union vii, 4–7, 12, 35, 88, 94–95, 95 n. 23, 97, 99, 101, 108–109, 112, 118–120, 123, 125–126, 126 n. 16, 127–128, 139–140, 162
migration 24, 26, 29, 32, 77, 104, 117, 133, 171
Miller, Elisabeth (Bessie) Cravath 8 n. 4, 38, 59 n. 29, 141, 147 n. 18
Miller, Maurice 7
Mills, C. Wright 7, 79
Mind, Self and Society 23 n. 7, 157 n. 2
minorities vii, 6, 50, 62, 99, 114, 117, 120, 122, 125, 130–131, 142, 160–161, 168–169, 173
  ethnic 6, 100, 167
  European 96
  racial 168
  rights of vii, 50, 99, 112, 114, 119, 122, 125, 130, 162, 173
  subject ix, x, 2, 6, 11, 50 n. 21, 95, 100, 112, 119, 142, 161–162, 167
minority rights vii, 3, 12–13, 36, 50, 112, 114, 126–127, 129, 143, 162, 173
Mitchell, Samuel A. 150 n. 26
Morey, Maribel 103, 105
Morris, Aldon 20, 25
Mosher, William E. 50
movements vii, 6, 55, 118, 168, 175, 178
  anti-colonial vii, ix, 2, 8, 109–110, 128, 131, 178
  of decolonisation 162
  nationalist 93, 111, 170
  social 10, 178
Moynihan, Patrick 166 n. 6
Mukerjee, Radhakamal 145
mulatto 66

Index

Mullins, Nicholas 21
Muslim question 117
Myrdal, Alva 106 n. 37
Myrdal, Gunnar 5, 12, 103–106, 106 n. 37 and 38, 107

Narayan, Jayaprakash 144, 146 n. 14
Narayan, John 161 n. 4
National Americanization Committee 101
National Association for the Advancement of Colored People 8, 67, 104 n. 34, 106, 118 n. 9, 133–134, 160
National Federation of Settlements 104 n. 34
National Information Bureau 82 n. 5
National Interracial Conference 153
nationalism x, 2, 6, 9, 11, 50, 92, 95, 110–111, 113, 119, 121–122, 125, 129 n. 19, 167–170, 172–173
   American 107
   internationalisation of 129
   pathologies of 97, 121, 126, 144
   Slavic 2, 32
nationalistic epidemic 113, 172
nationalist individualism 50
nation-states 115, 126, 173
National Urban League 29, 104, 104 n. 34, 106, 132–133
naturalisation 76
Nazism 6, 9, 115, 130–131, 173, 179
Nehru, Jawaharlal 145
Nehru Memorial Museum and Library 144
New School for Social Research 100 n. 29
New York Times 73, 149

North American Civic League for Immigrants 83, 93

Oberlin College 5, 7, 16–17, 17 n. 2, 18, 18 n. 5, 35, 38, 40, 45–47, 49–56, 71, 88 n. 11, 95, 101 n. 30, 112, 127, 128 n. 17, 132–133, 140, 147 n. 18
objectivity 44, 72, 161
observation 43, 46, 48
Odum, Howard 30, 69 n. 3
Ogburn, William F. 23
Ohio Sociological Society 19, 19 n. 6
Ohio Sociologist 141
Ohio State University 6–9, 13, 16, 18, 18 n. 5, 19, 19 n. 6, 20, 36–38, 40, 40 n. 5, 55–57, 59, 67, 70 n. 4, 114 n. 4, 128 n. 17, 132–133, 138, 140–141, 144, 146–147, 147 n. 17 and 18, 148, 148 n. 20, 149–150, 150 n. 26, 151, 154
Old World Traits Transplanted 3–4, 15, 17–18, 26–27, 30–31, 80, 83 n. 6, 85–86, 86 n. 9, 89 n. 12, 91–92, 99 n. 26, 102
Olivet College 17 n. 2, 40, 43–44, 46, 49, 71, 128 n. 17, 132
oppression 2, 11–13, 55, 63, 107, 114, 116, 128, 132, 136–137, 142, 160, 167, 170
   cosmopolitan 162, 174
   freedom from 97, 121
   global 13, 106, 144, 160, 162, 174, 179
   international 117, 129
   order 6, 12, 37, 113, 113 n. 4, 121, 162, 173, 179
   pathology of 166 n. 6

oppression (cont.)
  psychosis 122, 145, 162, 167, 172–173
  racial 12, 37, 130, 162
Ovington, Mary White 118 n. 9

Paderewski, Ignacy Jan 32 n. 13, 123
Pan-African Congress 118, 172
Pan-American Union 119
Pan-Asianism 131
Pan-European Union 119
Paris Peace Conference 110, 118, 131
Park, Marion E. 40 n. 5, 114 n. 4
Park, Robert E. 18, 25, 33, 72, 84 n. 7, 85 n. 8, 88 n. 11, 90, 90 n. 15, 91, 111, 122, 166, 177
  Americanisation 3–4, 87 n. 10, 88–90, 177
  assimilation 6, 12, 29
  Chicago race riots 91 n. 17, 133
  Chicago school 3, 10, 21, 23–24, 83, 121, 157, 166
  civilising process 26, 29 n. 9, 168
  Congo Reform Association 26
  Disorganisation 24
  Fisk University 5, 16, 29, 140
  Immigrant Press and Theatre 81, 87, 89
  immigration 6, 24, 111
  Myrdal and 106 n. 38
  Old World Traits Transplanted 3–4, 15, 17–18, 26, 66, 80, 85, 86 n. 9, 89, 102
  pragmatism 15
  professionalisation 177
  racial prejudice 29
  racial relations 16, 29, 29 n. 9, 91 n. 17
  review of *Races, Nations and Classes* 121, 167–168
  social laboratory 46, 49
  Society for Social Research 21
  Tuskegee Institute 16
  Washington and 26
Parsons, Talcott 21, 41, 111
Patel, Sardar 145
patriotism 3, 55, 83, 95, 97, 107, 121, 125, 162, 174
  local 165
  proportionate 3, 12, 97, 121, 129, 162–163, 171
Patterson, Orlando 166 n. 6
peace 12, 93, 95, 100, 102 n. 32, 114, 117–119, 122–125, 129 n. 19, 130 n. 22
  settlement 117–119
  and war 109–110, 113
pedagogy 11, 20, 33, 36, 43, 49, 57, 61, 63, 63 n. 36, 96, 159
Pedersen, Susan 116
Penn State University 8 n. 3, 19, 58
Persons, Stow 24, 32, 84 n. 7, 106 n. 38
Philadelphia Hall x, 63, 123, 128
Philadelphia Negro 20, 30, 71
philanthropy 10, 22, 39, 73, 75, 105, 133, 138
Pittsburgh Civic Commission 74
Pittsburgh Survey 71, 73–75, 158
plantation household 26
pluralism 1, 9, 13, 27, 143
  cultural 12, 33, 49, 67, 87, 95
  multicultural vii
populism ix
power 9, 32, 99, 112–114, 116–117, 124 n. 14, 126, 126 n. 16, 127, 129, 129 n. 19, 130, 143, 160, 173
  imperial 2, 103, 114–115, 122

pragmatism 1, 3, 11, 15, 28, 31–33, 36, 42–44, 54, 63, 65, 71, 71 n. 6, 73, 76–77, 96, 120, 141–142, 149, 156–157, 161, 163, 174
Pritchett, Henry S. 87 n. 10, 101, 103
problem-solving 63, 149, 174
Professional Ethics and Civic Morals 14, 163, 163 n. 5
professionalisation 3, 10–11, 17, 20, 22, 40–41, 71–72, 85, 108–109, 133, 177–178
progress 43, 63, 69, 91 n. 17, 122, 161–162
progressive politics 11, 15, 31, 33, 65–66, 108, 120
progressivism 3, 8, 11, 19, 43, 59, 77, 81 n. 3, 84, 100, 154, 170
protestantism 26, 54, 61 n. 32, 115 n. 6, 129 n. 18
provincialism 54
pseudo-science 165
psychology 38, 41, 43–45, 59, 67–68, 70 n. 5, 157 n. 1
  of domination 70 n. 5
  race 91 n. 17
  social 23, 109
publicity 11, 36, 71 n. 6, 73, 116, 123, 152
public opinion 82, 84, 91 n. 17, 111 n. 3, 115 n. 6, 156, 158–161, 176–178
public policy 2, 24, 83, 85

race 1–2, 13, 16, 25, 27, 29, 37–38, 59, 61–69, 77, 79, 83, 106, 109, 127, 129, 136, 167, 172–173, 178
  ethnicity and 10, 32–33, 106, 165 n. 6
  immigration and 11, 28, 33, 36, 40, 65–67, 109

psychology 91 n. 17
relations viii, 2, 5–6, 10–12, 16, 28–29, 29 n. 9, 30, 32, 36–37, 40, 65, 67, 84 n. 7, 91 n. 17, 103–106, 109, 134, 146, 150, 163, 167, 177
riots 84, 84 n. 7, 88, 91 n. 17, 133–134
sociology of 24, 29 n. 9
Races, Nations and Classes ix, 4, 13–14, 32 n. 12, 55, 79, 108, 127, 140, 156, 159, 163, 169
racial mixing 18, 25, 36, 43, 66–67, 69, 150 n. 26
racial prejudice 29, 67, 106, 150 n. 25
Raushenbush, Winifred 4, 84 n. 7, 87–88, 88 n. 11, 89–90, 92, 99, 102
Redd, George 154 n. 32
reform 3, 10–11, 26–27, 29, 31, 42–43, 64, 72, 74–75, 78, 139, 142
  progressive 77
  social 8, 20, 41–42, 70–71, 73, 75, 77, 97 n. 25, 108, 133, 140, 144, 157, 170
religion 55, 59, 63, 70, 99 n. 27, 112, 117, 127, 142–143, 149, 164, 166, 171, 175
Reuter, Edward 66
revolution 6, 11, 55, 94 n. 21, 122, 132, 143, 162, 165, 173–174
  Bolshevik 7
  nationalist 113
  scientific 21
Rhee, Syngman 32 n. 13, 128
Rice, John A. 19, 59–60, 153–154
Rightmire, George W. 149
Riley, Matilda White 8
Robbins, Raymond 48, 48 n. 18
Roberts, Priscilla 39 n. 5, 113 n. 4

Rockefeller Foundation 22, 73, 85, 105
Rollins College 19, 59, 152–153
Roosevelt, Franklin D. 81 n. 3, 153–154
Roosevelt, Theodore 115 n. 6
Root, Elihu 103
Ross, Dorothy 41
Royce, Josiah 15
Rucker, Darnell 157 n. 1
Russell Sage Foundation 74, 85
Russification 117

Sabath, Adolph 95 n. 24
Sage, Margaret Olivia 22
Salt March 13, 57, 146, 149
Schwendiger, Herman 20
Schwendiger, Julia 20
science 3, 21, 28, 31, 33, 42, 55, 69, 108, 127, 131, 141, 161
scientific racism 2
Scramble for Africa 114
Seal, Brajendra Nath 118, 145
Second World War 9, 21–22, 58, 106, 110, 117, 122, 177, 179
Sedition Act 100
segregation 1, 2 n. 1, 28–29, 37, 69 n. 3, 76, 106, 127, 134–135, 178
self-determination x, 2, 13, 119–120, 129, 142, 164–165, 167, 170, 172, 175
  of groups 169
  national 114, 117, 131
  of nations 120, 127, 170, 173
  principles of 118–119, 173
  right of 129, 129 n. 19
Seminar for Refugee Scholars 9, 58–59, 63, 63 n. 36, 154
settlement movement 15–17, 31, 31 n. 11, 36, 43, 45, 49, 74, 78, 93, 154 n. 32
Shaw, Augustus F. 138–139

Skinner, Quentin 25
Small, Albion 23, 41, 45, 55
Smith, Anthony 111, 168
Smith, Christy 2 n. 1, 38
Smith, William C. 83 n. 6
social control 70, 72 n. 7
Social Darwinism 37 n. 2
Socialist Party of America 7, 48 n. 18, 148
Social Science Research Council 10, 22, 85, 105, 109, 111 n. 3
social self 157
Society for Social Research 21
sociology
  Black 5, 24, 28
  Chicago 3–4, 11, 15–17, 19, 21, 23, 28, 31, 40–42, 66, 72 n. 7, 75, 80, 83, 84 n. 7, 106 n. 38, 121, 140, 157 n. 1, 177
  cosmopolitan 55, 132, 140
  experimental 150 n. 26
  global 55, 132, 140, 179
  political 175
  pragmatist vii, 71, 163
  public viii, 3, 178–179
  scientific 161
  US vii, viii, 9, 28, 30, 70, 168, 178
  White 28, 32, 108, 177
solidarity 72, 164, 166
Sorrels, Katherine 119
Source Book for Social Origins 26, 66
Southern, David 103
Southern Conference for Human Welfare 153
sovereignty 116 n. 7, 129 n. 19, 169–170
  national 168
  plural vii, 13, 97, 121
Spelman, Laura 22
Spence, Adam 137
Spence, Mary 137, 139–140

Spencer, Herbert 41
steamer classes 76
Steer, Margery Wells 47–49
Stone, Julius 146
stratification 70, 163
Streator, George 137, 137 n. 6, 138
structural functionalism 21
Sudetenland 179
Sultan, Nazmul 118, 144–145
Sun Yat-Sen 143, 150
superiority 11, 25, 55, 63, 65, 132, 165
  cultural 106, 160
  myth of 165
  racial 165
survey movement 7, 72–74, 84 n. 7
symbolic interactionism 21, 23, 157
Syrian Congress 118

Taylor, Alrutheus A. 30 n. 10, 39–40, 137–139
Taylor, Graham 15, 82 n. 5, 84 n. 7, 104 n. 35
Taylor, Graham Romeyn 84 n. 7
Teeters, Negley 7, 35, 37, 94 n. 23, 95 n. 23
Temple University 7, 18–19, 35, 58, 94 n. 23
The Crisis 8, 36, 67, 91 n. 17, 119 n. 9, 134, 136–137, 139, 140 n. 7
The Negro in Chicago 84 n. 7,
The New Map of Europe 50, 99
The New Republic 68
The Phantom Public 158
The Polish Peasant in Europe and America 4, 20, 26, 31, 50 n. 21, 85, 88, 91–92, 102
The Public and its Problems 158
The School and the Immigrant 75–78

The Sociological Imagination 7
The Survey 7, 71, 71 n. 6, 75, 96–97, 99, 99 n. 27, 100, 109, 120, 122, 124, 156
theory groups 21, 23, 176–177
Third World 72
Thomas, Norman 48, 48 n. 18, 148
Thomas, William I. 72, 85, 88 n. 12, 90, 93, 106 n. 37
  Americanisation 87, 87 n. 10, 88–89, 99, 102–103, 112, 121, 177
  assimilation 6, 12, 111
  Chicago school 4, 6, 10, 23–24, 66, 83, 157, 166
  disorganisation 24, 79, 91
  immigrant communities 6, 24, 91 n. 17
  immigration 6, 49, 86, 89, 111–112
  Mann Act 18 n. 4
  Oberlin College 18, 45
  Old World Traits Transplanted 4, 15, 18, 26, 31, 80, 85, 86 n. 9, 87, 91, 102
  Polish Peasant in Europe and America 4, 20, 26, 31, 50 n. 21, 85, 88, 91–92
  professionalisation 177
  Source Book for Social Origins 26, 66
Thomas, Dorothy Swaine 106 n. 37
Throntveit, Trygve 120
Turner, Stephen 22, 75, 176
Tuskegee Institute 16, 134
Tyler, Harry W. 150 n. 26

un-national state 3, 3 n. 2, 13, 142
Universal Races Congress 118, 144 n. 11, 175

University of Chicago 2 n. 1, 4, 17–18, 18 n. 4, 20, 23, 29–30, 41, 45, 49, 72 n. 7, 74, 93 n. 19
University of Chicago Settlement House 15
University of Hawaii 30
University of Michigan 23, 45
University of New Hampshire 36
University of North Carolina 30
Urban League 8, 150, 160
US Government Committee of Information 99
US Steel Corporation 170

Versailles Peace System 131
Vietnam War 178
Von Wieser, Friedrich 168

Wacker, Fred 6–7, 24, 84 n. 7, 106 n. 38, 121, 162
Wallas, Graham 14, 46 n. 13, 159–160
Washington, Booker T. 26, 29, 134, 136
Washington, Margaret Murray 136
Waskow, Arthur 134
Weidler, Walter C. 147

Weiss, Hilde 17 n. 1
Wells, David Collin 37, 37 n. 2, 65
White academy 1, 65–66, 177
White, Georgia Laura 137
Williams, Talcott 81 n. 3
Wilberforce University 16, 88 n. 11, 132, 150
Willoughby-Herald, Tiffany 103
Wilson, Woodrow ix, 100, 110, 112, 117–120, 123, 129 n. 19, 131, 131 n. 23, 160 n. 3, 172
Wirth, Louis 23–24, 111, 168–169
Wood, Levi Hollingsworth 133
World Tomorrow 7, 156
World Unity 7–8, 156
Wright II, Earl 20, 37, 140
Wunsch, Robert 152, 152 n. 31, 153, 155

Yerkes, Robert W. 68, 68 n. 1, 70, 80
YMCA 96
Young, Kimball 18, 89 n. 12

Zabriskie, George 62
Zionism 27, 125, 170
Znaniecki, Florian 4, 20, 26, 85, 92, 102, 111

www.ingramcontent.com/pod-product-compliance
Ingram Content Group UK Ltd.
Pitfield, Milton Keynes, MK11 3LW, UK
UKHW022353030225
454636UK00008B/104